THE PROCEEDINGS OF THE 8th INTERNATIONAL HUMANITIES CONFERENCE

ALL & EVERYTHING 2003

Joseph Azize
Len Brown
Keith Buzzell
Wim van Dulleman
Will Mesa
Dimitri Peretzi
Bert Sharp

Published by All & Everything Conferences
2011

Second Edition Published 2011
Published by All & Everything Conferences (on behalf of the Planning Committee)
© Copyright 2011 by Seymour B. Ginsburg and Ian C. MacFarlane

First Edition Privately Published 2003
Published by the Conveners of the International Humanities Conference: All and Everything 2003
© 2003 Seymour B. Ginsburg, Dr. H. J. Sharp, and Marlena O'Hagen-Buzzell

The contents of this publication may not be reproduced or copied in whole or part in any book, magazine, periodical, pamphlet, circular, information storage or data retrieval system, or in any other form without the written permission of the Planning Committee.

Any profit from the sale of these Proceedings will be devoted to the funds for the organization of future Conferences of a similar nature.

Published by All & Everything Conferences

Website: www.aandeconference.org
Email: info@aandeconference.org

Second Edition Print

ISBN-10: 1-905578-24-5
ISBN-13: 978-1-905578-24-5

Also Published as
Second Edition eBook
ISBN-10: 1-905578-25-3
ISBN-13: 978-1-905578-25-2

Cover Photo © Copyright 2003 by Bonnie Phillips

Table of Contents

Foreword 4
Conference Invitation 6
Conference Programme 9
Planning Committee 10
Advisory Board 11
Speakers 13
Beyond the Fourth Way 15
Notes and Other Material Relating to Dr. Philip Groves 20
On the Third Line of Work 26
On the Third Line of Work - Questions & Answers 32
Seminar 1 - Chapters 14 & 15 of Beelzebub's Tales to His Grandson 40
Towards a Historical Study of Gurdjieff and His Legacy 56
A Macroscopic View of the Two Fundamental Cosmic Laws 68
A Macroscopic View of the Two Fundamental Cosmic Laws - Questions & Answers 82
A Forum of Those Who Knew Gurdjieff 84
Papers Written to the Forum "Those Who Knew Gurdjieff" 95
    Paul Beekman Taylor 95
    Dushka Howarth 98
    Kathleen Riordan Speeth 102
    Nicolas de Stjernvall 104
The Great Theme: An Analysis of One of Gurdjieff's Hymns 111
The Unfolding of a Symbol of Law 114
The Unfolding of a Symbol of Law - Questions and Answers 124
His Endlessness and Mr. Gurdjieff 130
His Endlessness and Mr. Gurdjieff - Questions and Answers 139
Seminar 2 - Chapter 16 of Beelzebub's Tales to His Grandson 148
Where Do We Go From Here? 160
Appendix 1 - Obituary of Nicolas Tereshchenko 179
Appendix 2 - Writings by Nicolas Tereshchenko 182
Appendix 3 - Obituary of Joy Lonsdale 184
Appendix 4 - List of Attendees 185
Index 187

Foreword

Marlena O'Hagan Buzzell

The International Humanities Conference - All & Everything convened in Bognor Regis, England, in April 2003.

Last year Paul Taylor shared with the conferees his reflections and recollections of his life with Gurdjieff. This meaningful event together with Professor Thring's recollections at the A&E Conference 2001 emphasized for many of us the importance of the fact that there are fewer and fewer people who knew Gurdjieff and who would share their insights into the man and his teaching. The wish to seize this opportunity evolved and many contacts were made. Professor Taylor proposed the two questions, "What has Gurdjieff given to You? What has he asked of you?" The Forum of 'Those Who Knew Gurdjieff' began to unfold.

We are grateful to Adam Nott and Professor Matt Thring for their active participation at the Conference and to Professor Paul Beekman Taylor for his efforts in contacting those who knew Gurdjieff and for his remembrances. On behalf of the planning committee I wish also to thank Dushka Howarth, Kathleen Riordan Speeth, and Nicholas de Stjernvall for their generous contribution to the conference and these Proceedings.

This year we had a number of new presenters, several of whom have published articles in Stopider, and whose presentations provoked lively discussions.

The unprecedented number of conferees this year (52) presented some interesting challenges logistically for the planning committee and the facilitators of the afternoon sessions. I'm happy to report that the recordings of these sessions were quite good and were more easily transcribed than in the past. The readers of these Proceedings should enjoy an even more comprehensible text!

Among those events which we cannot properly reflect in the Proceedings were an audio recording brought by Wim van Dulleman of Gurdjieff's orchestral works by a Dutch symphonic orchestra. These included compositions that had not been played since their composition in 1923. Also impossible to reflect was a piano recital of the Music of Gurdjieff by Wim with a Movement demonstration by Christian Macketanz.

We would like to acknowledge Dr. H. J. "Bert" Sharp as one of the core founders of The A&E International Humanities Conference, editor of the Conference Proceedings through 1998, a prolific presenter at the conference, and an indefatigable contributor to Planning Committee activities. Bert and Frank Brzeski have been our 'on-the-ground organizers' at Bognor Regis since its inception. Bert's good humor, positive spirit and organizational skills have greatly contributed to the success and essence of the A&E Conference. Bert is stepping out as a member due to his health. He will be greatly missed.

Nicolas Tereshchenko, our dear friend and true 'Companion of the Book', died last September. Nik was also a core founder of the A&E Conference. He was a true scholar of Gurdjieff's teaching, writing extensively in both English and French. His ability to speak fluently in English, French and Russian made him a most valuable comrade in our explorations of *Beelzebub's Tales to His Grandson*. Nik's scholarly review *of Beelzebub's Tales to His Grandson* IN RUSSIAN, Triangle Editions, Inc., 2000 was published in the Proceedings of the A&E International Humanities Conference 2001. Tributes to Nicolas Tereshchenko and extended accounts of his contributions are included in this text.

Joy Lonsdale died in 2002. Mrs. Lonsdale had studied Gurdjieff and associated writings since 1989. For a period in the years following, she participated in Work Groups in Canberra and Sydney. She spent much of her time writing an interpretation of the 'descent' chapters in *Beelzebub's Tales* and a Dictionary on the allegorical use of words, in studying Hermeticism and Alchemy. She was a member of the Rosicrucian Order AMORC. Although she was unable to attend in 2000, Joy submitted a paper to the A&E Conference entitled, "An Inquiring Look at 'The Arousing of Thought' Chapter" which was read by Sy Ginsburg. The Q&A session was facilitated by Nicolas Tereshchenko.

This year Sy Ginsburg presented, "A Commentary on the Work of Joy Lonsdale as presented in her book, *Gurdjieff and the Arch-Preposterous: An Hermetic Descent into the Mind*."

Kerry Lonsdale, her daughter, sent an obituary which is published herein.

In Nicolas Tereshchenko's words - "Live Long and Prosper!"

Conference Invitation

You are invited to...
THE 8TH INTERNATIONAL HUMANITIES CONFERENCE
ALL & EVERYTHING 2003

WEDNESDAY EVENING APRIL 2 TO SUNDAY APRIL 6, 2003
The Royal Norfolk Hotel
The Esplanade, Bognor Regis, P021 2LH, United Kingdom
Telephone: (0)1243 826222 | Fax: (0)1243 826325
Email: reservations@corushotels.com

Visit the All and Everything Conference site on the web at: http://www.aandeconference.org

The All & Everything Conference has become established as an independent forum on the Work of G. I. Gurdjieff, attracting international scholars, artists, scientists, group leaders, students, and speakers from around the world.

Originally conceived as a congenial meeting of the 'Companions of the Book', the conference has developed into a major forum for the presentation and discussion of recent writings and music associated with 'The Work'. It provides an open, congenial & serious atmosphere for the sharing of researches and investigations of G. I. Gurdjieff's legacy. The conference seeks to keep the study of the teachings of Gurdjieff relevant to global scientific, spiritual and sociological developments. The gathering is open, by invitation, to serious students of *All & Everything* and is not under the auspices or sponsorship of any 'Gurdjieff Group' or umbrella organization.

The conference is not intended to be a 'Group Work Event' and thus will not include Work on Movements or on exercises that are related to personal or group Work. The conference will include academic papers, individual view papers, group seminars on specific chapters and on themes common throughout *All & Everything*, and cultural events. The program is scheduled so as to encourage time for dialogue and the developing of personal relationships outside the structured meetings.

The conference is non-profit and is organized by a Planning Committee drawn from a diversity of international students of the Gurdjieff community. The aspiration of the Planning Committee is that the conference should achieve a balance in the presentation of material relating to the practical stimulation and development of the three centers - moving, feeling and intellectual.

Academic and individual view papers are recommended for presentation by a Reading Panel. The Proceedings of the conference are published and provide a permanent record of recent thought on Gurdjieff's legacy.

ALL & EVERYTHING 2003

WEDNESDAY EVENING, APRIL 2, TO SUNDAY APRIL 6, 2003

REGISTRATION

To register, please complete aid return the coupon below.
Registration Fee: £50 (US$75) per person Please remit in £ or US$.
Optional advance purchase discount price of £20 (US$30) including postage for your copy of a transcript of the Proceedings of ALL & EVERYTHING 2003.

ACCOMMODATION

Delegates are asked to make their hotel reservations directly with:

The Royal Norfolk Hotel, The Esplanade, Bognor Regis, P021 2LH, U.K.
Tel: (44) (0) 1243-826222; Fax: (44) (0) 1243-826325;
Email: reservations@corushotels.com

Please request the group rate which is £48 per person, per night. This rate includes dinner, breakfast, morning coffee, afternoon tea, taxes, gratuity and service charge. Single delegates are accommodated in single rooms. Couples are accommodated in double rooms. Please specify that you are a delegate to the International Humanities Conference: All & Everything 2003. Located on the southern coast of the UK, on the sea front, the hotel provides breakfast and dinner in a congenial dining atmosphere. There is a pub immediately adjacent to the meeting hall and a spacious lounge for informal getting togethers between and after the days' events. The hotel is a few minutes walk from the train station which easily links it to London and Gatwick. Book early to avoid disappointment.

PLANNING COMMITTEE LIASON

If you would like an invitation sent to another, require travel information, require an overflow hotel booking, or have other requests, please contact:
Seymour B. Ginsburg

SPECIAL & CULTURAL EVENTS
ALL & EVERYTHING 2003
(subject to revisions as the program moves toward finalization)

THURSDAY EVENING

AUDIO: Recordings of Gurdjieff's orchestral works by a Dutch symphonic orchestra. These include compositions that had never before been played since the compositions were written in 1923.

VIDEO: The performance of a Movements Group.

FRIDAY AFTERNOON
FORUM OF THOSE WHO KNEW GURDJIEFF

As the years have passed since Mr. Gurdjieff left the scene in 1949, there remain fewer and fewer people who actually knew him. This year the conference has arranged a special forum of people who knew Gurdjieff and who have volunteered to share their insights into the man and his teaching. This special forum of those who knew Gurdjieff will address the questions:

WHAT HAS GURDJIEFF GIVEN TO YOU?
WHAT HAS HE ASKED OF YOU?

The Forum Panel will include: Adam Nott, Professor Paul Beekman Taylor, Professor M.W. Thring, and such additional persons as are available.

FRIDAY EVENING
An analysis of one of Gurdjieff's hymns: THE RELIGIOUS CEREMONY

The analysis shows that the hymn can be regarded as a musical example of the Law of Seven, and even more interesting, it shows certain inner aspects of the steps and of the type and quality of the intervals.

SATURDAY EVENING (following the banquet)
A PIANO RECITAL OF THE MUSIC OF GURDJIEFF BY WIM VAN DULLEMAN

Wim van Dulleman, a Dutch concert pianist, entered the Work in 1968. He became a member of the Institute Gurdjieff in France, and played piano for the movements classes of Solange Claustres for 13 years. He has recorded on CD, The Music of G. I. Gurdjieff and Gurdjieff's Music for the Movements. In 2002, he organized the Gurdjieff Movements Foundation in the Netherlands, and the World Forum for Gurdjieff Movements on the Internet. Wim offers selections from Gurdjieff's music.

Conference Programme

DRAFT PROGRAM subject to revisions as the program moves toward finalization

WEDNESDAY, APRIL 2
20:45 Informal Getting to Know You Session

THURSDAY, APRIL 3
08:00 Silent unguided sitting
09:30 The presentation of papers, discussion, questions and answers:
"Beyond the Fourth Way" & "Comments on Dr. Philip Groves" by H. J. Sharp
"On the Third Line of Work" by Dimitri Peretzi
12:30 Lunch break.
14:30 Seminar on Ch. 14 & 15 of *Beelzebub's Tales to His Grandson*
20:45 Recordings of Gurdjieff's Orchestral Works & a Video of a Movements Group

FRIDAY, APRIL 4
08:00 Silent unguided sitting
09:30 The presentation of papers, discussion, questions and answers:
"Toward an Historical Study of Gurdjieff and his Legacy" by Joseph Azize
"The Two Fundamental Cosmic Laws in Relation to the Trajectory of One's Search" by Will Mesa
12:30 Lunch break.
14:30 Special Forum: "Those Who Knew Gurdjieff" addressing the questions: What has Gurdjieff given to you? What has he asked of you?
Adam Nott, Prof. Paul B. Taylor, Prof. M.W. Thring & others as available
20:45 "An Analysis of One of Gurdjieff's Hymns" by Wim van Dulleman

SATURDAY, APRIL 5
08:00 Silent unguided sitting
09:30 The presentation of papers, discussion, questions and answers:
"A Self-unfolding Symbol" by Keith A. Buzzell, D.O.
"His Endlessness and Mr. Gurdjieff" by Len Brown
12:30 Lunch break
14:30 Seminar on Ch. 16, and on The Merciless Heropass
19:30 Conference Banquet followed by a piano recital of Gurdjieff's music

SUNDAY, MARCH 17
09:30 Final session: Conference Impressions & Where Do We Go from Here?

Planning Committee

Harry J. Bennett - USA
Patricia Bennett - USA
Frank Brzeski - UK
Marlena O'Hagan Buzzell - USA
Ana H. Fragomeni - Brazil
Seymour B. Ginsburg - USA
Conti Canseco Meehan - USA
H. J. Sharp - UK

Advisory Board

Professor Masashi Asai holds the chair of English Literature and Cultural Studies at Kyoto Tachibana Women's University and has made a significant contribution to studies of D. H. Lawrence (who visited the Prieuré in February 1924). As an undergraduate in Kyoto, he contacted a working group (which he now leads) instituted by Gurdjieffians from California. His unprecedented contributions to the dissemination of Gurdjieff's ideas in Japan include the translation *of Beelzebub's Tales to His Grandson, Life is Real Only Then, When "I am", In Search of the Miraculous* and James Moore's, *Gurdjieff, The Anatomy of a Myth*.

J. Walter Driscoll is an independent scholar focused on Gurdjieff studies since the 1960's. He met and corresponded with Wilhelm Nyland and his groups in Warwick, NJ and Seattle from 1970 until Nyland's death in 1975. Following postgraduate training in 1978, he embarked on his major work *Gurdjieff an Annotated Bibliography* (Garland Publishing, 1985) in collaboration with The Gurdjieff Foundation of California. He is now engaged on a second edition for which he solicits material and is associate editor of the "Gurdjieff Homepage" at www.Gurdjieff.org. He assisted George Baker with *Gurdjieff in America: An Overview* (American Alternative Religions, 1995).

Wim Van Dulleman is a Dutch musician and musicologist who have placed his gifts at the service of the Work. Shortly after completing his studies under the composer W. Wijdeveld and becoming a professional concert pianist he had a crucial meeting (in 1968) with J. G. Bennett. For 13 years he was the Class pianist for the eminent French Movements teacher Solange Claustres. He has propagated the Gurdjieff/de Hartmann musical 'oeuvre' in 'workshops', articles, courses, lectures, and concerts - sometimes independently and sometimes in collaboration with Mme Claustres and the French pianist Alain Kremski.

Dr. Massimo Introvigne is managing director of CESNUR, the Centre for Studies on New Religions in Torino, Italy. CESNUR's library hosts one of the most significant collections of Fourth Way Books in Southern Europe. He teaches at Queen of The Apostles University in Rome and is the author of twenty books in the field of sociology of religion and contemporary esotericism. He has lectured often and sympathetically on Fourth Way-related subjects.

Professor Wallace Martin teaches modern literature and critical theory at the University of Toledo. His writings include '*The New Age' Under Orage*.

Dr. H. J. Sharp took a first degree is Physiology and an M. Sc. in Metallurgy by private study while working in industry. He later earned his Ph.D. in Material Science. Subsequently, he has become involved in psychological transformation of himself and others, a much more difficult endeavour. In this he has been helped by many including Ronald and Murial Oldham and Lewis Creed, when he was able to visit the Dicker, John Castanios Flores, who led a large Work group in

Mexico and came to Littlehampton to end his days, and by Nicholas Tereshchenko and Sy Ginsburg. There have been many others speaking through the written page and in other ways and perhaps most of all, in a special way, his dear wife and daughter.

Professor Paul Beekman Taylor (who for the past 30 years held the chair of Medieval English languages and literature at the University of Geneva) grew up at the Prieuré and was thus from earliest childhood immersed in a Gurdjieffian milieu. Later adopted by Jean Toomer, he lived in New York City and Doylestown, Pennsylvania, and after the war sustained contact with Gurdjieff in New York and Paris. He has published ten books and over a hundred articles. Published in 1998, *Shadows of Heaven: Toomer and Gurdjieff* (Samuel Weiser, Inc.) draws on his and his mother's experiences with both men. His most recent book *is Gurdjieff and Orage: Brothers in Elysium* (Samuel Weiser, Inc. 2001).

Professor Jon Woodson is a Professor of English on the faculty of Howard University in Washington, D.C. He is the author of *To Make a New Race: Gurdjieff, Toomer, and the Harlem Renaissance* (University of Mississippi Press, 1999). Since commencing work on his doctoral dissertation on the poet Melvin B. Tolson in 1973, he has researched and published in the area of Fourth Way concepts as they have been employed in modern literature.

Sophia Wellbeloved was a member of the Gurdjieff Society in London from 1962 to 1975, she received her doctorate from the Theology Department of King's College, London for a thesis on Gurdjieff's *Beelzebub's Tales To His Grandson*, and has *published Gurdjieff, Astrology & Beelzebub's Tales* (Solar Bound, 2003) and *Gurdjieff: The Key Concepts* (Routledge, 2003).

Speakers

Joseph Azize
Joseph Azize is a historian of the ancient Near East, specializing in ancient Phoenicia. He was a contributing editor to Stopinder: A Gurdjieff Journal of Our Time. He has published articles in the Gurdjieff International Review, The Gurdjieff Journal and Stopinder.

Len Brown
Len is from Vancouver, BC, Canada.

Keith A. Buzzell, D.O.
Dr. Buzzell is a 1960 graduate of the Philadelphia College of Osteopathic Medicine. He met Irmis Popoff (N.Y. Foundation) in 1971 and formed groups under her supervision into the 1980s. Buzzell met Annie Lou Staveley, founder of the Two Rivers Farm in Oregon, in 1988 and maintained a Work relationship with her up to her death. He continues group Work in Bridgton, ME.

Wim van Dulleman
Wim is a Dutch musician and musicologist who have placed his gifts at the service of the Work. Shortly after completing his studies under the composer W. Wijdeveki and becoming a professional concert pianist, he had a crucial meeting (in 1968) with J. G. Bennett. For 13 years he was the Class pianist for the eminent French Movements teacher Solange Claustres. He has propagated the Gurdjieff/de Hartmann musical "oeuvre" in 'workshops', articles, courses, lectures, and concerts - sometimes independently and sometimes in collaboration with Mme Claustres and the French pianist Akin Kremski.

Seymour B. (Sy) Ginsburg, J.D.
Sy Ginsburg was born in Chicago in 1934 and currently resides in Florida. He was introduced to the Gurdjieff Work by Sri Madhava Ashish, an eminent theosophical scholar and Hindu monk, who became his mentor over a 19 year period. Ginsburg was a member of the Gurdjieff Society of Florida and later a co-founder of the Gurdjieff Institute of Florida. Currently, he is a Director of The Theosophical Society in Miami & South Florida and facilitator of the Gurdjieff Study Group at The Theosophical Society.

Will Mesa
Will Mesa received his Ph.D. in electrical engineering from the University of Florida. He spent three years with a group led by Henri Tracol in Paris, and six years with the groups of Nathalie Etievan in Venezuela, followed by four years with the New York Chan Meditation Center. He pursues a lifelong interest in the investigation of certain aspects of the Omnipresent-Okidanokh.

All & Everything Conference 2003

Dimitri Peretzi

Mr. Peretzi is the president of the Gurdjieff Foundation of Greece. With reference to his personal contacts with eminent students of Gurdjieff, Lord Pentland, Madame de Salzmann, Dr. Welch and others, he has authored a number of books and articles that study the problem of consciousness, relating views from the esoteric traditions to those of the contemporary philosophy of mind. Mr. Peretzi did graduate work in Philosophy, at Yale, where he received his Master of Architecture. Having settled in Athens since 1974, he established his own Construction and Prefabrication Company.

H. J. Sharp, Ph.D.

Dr. Sharp took a first degree in Physiology and a M.Sc. in Metallurgy by private study while working in industry. He later earned his PhD. in Material Science. Subsequently he has become involved in psychological transformation of himself and others, a much more difficult endeavour. In this he has been helped by many, including Ronald and Murial Oldham and Lewis Creed, when he was able to visit the Dicker, John Castanios Flores, who led a large Work group in Mexico and came to Littlehampton to end his days, and Nicolas Tereshchenko and Sy Ginsburg. There have been many others speaking through the written page and in other ways and perhaps most of all, in a special way, his dear wife and daughter.

Professor Paul Beekman Taylor

For the past 30 years Professor Taylor held the chair of Medieval English languages and literature at the University of Geneva. He grew up at the Prieuré and was thus from earliest childhood immersed in a Gurdjieffian milieu. Later adopted by Jean Toomer, he lived in New York City and Doylestown, Pennsylvania, and after the war sustained contact with Gurdjieff in New York and Paris. He has published ten books and over a hundred articles. Published in 1998, *Shadows of Heaven: Toomer and Gurdjieff* (Samuel Weiser, Inc.) draws on his, and his mother's experiences with both men. His most recent book is *Gurdjieff and Orage: Brothers in Elysium* (Samuel Weiser, Inc. 2001).

Beyond the Fourth Way

Nicolas Tereshchenko

When in the early 1960s a member of my group in Sydney (N.S.W., Australia) found in a second-hand bookshop an anonymous typewritten document, 138 pages long and titled *Beyond the Fourth Way*, we tried to find out who the author was, and finally met a man who gave us the information that follows.

According to our then informant, in 1950, the year after Mister Gurdjieff's death, a certain "Philip W. Groves" appeared in Sydney (N.S.W., Australia) and organised groups to which he taught a way of self-development he attributed to Mister Gurdjieff whose "private" pupil he claimed to have been. In fact, he said that Mister Gurdjieff had a number of pupils who never were members of any group, and that, in addition to what was given in the groups, he taught them certain things and gave them exercises which were never taught nor given, or even mentioned, in the groups. Apparently, when J. G. BENNETT came to Sydney to organise his "Subud" Latihans, he stayed with "Groves" who at once transferred all his followers to Bennett, left Sydney and disappeared.

When I obtained this information, I tried to trace this man GROVES, but unsuccessfully: no one seemed to know anything about him from the moment he left his groups and Sydney. It was suggested by our informant that he had "gone native", that is, joined one of the then still surviving aboriginal tribes, as apparently he had been "initiated as a man of high degree" in one of the tribes as a youth, and that after leaving Sydney he lived with that tribe and died there, in the heart of Australia, away from all "civilisation". As I had met by then two other persons who had been thus "initiated" by the aborigines, this story appeared possible.

And I continued to believe it until a visit to Australia when I had the surprise of discovering quite by accident that Dr. Philip Groves is not dead, but is living in Balgowlah (a suburb of North Sydney) and continues to teach groups. I had the pleasure of meeting him in December 1995. He is a very interesting and learned individual, with no less than three doctorates (in Biochemistry, Bioneurology and Divinity!) and a Diploma in Psychotherapy. He is also an eminent Egyptologist. He told me that in fact he never met Mister Gurdjieff, but learned all that he knows of the Fourth Way first from J. G. Bennett, when Bennett stayed with him in 1957 while in Sydney introducing Subud to Australia, and then from the various books of P. D. Ouspensky and others. Actually his principal Teacher was a Sufi Master from East Pakistan (now known as Bangladesh). But he did confirm that in his youth he had been accepted as an "honorary member" into an aboriginal tribe. So most of what the person who claimed to have been one of Groves' pupils gave me was utter misinformation in no ways conform to facts.

All & Everything Conference 2003

There is also a further mystery about the "anonymous" text I know as *Beyond the Fourth Way 1*. When I mentioned to Dr. Groves that its typescript had been found in a second-hand bookshop, he was surprised as, so far as he knew, there were only six copies of the text made, and he could not imagine who of the five other holders of it would have sold it to a used books dealer. Moreover, Groves did not seem to remember the list of Mister Gurdjieff's teachings the text in my possession claims were offered to special pupils. He brought his own copy so that I could show him what I was referring to, and I made the astonishing discovery that his "original" text is not only not identical to the one I have, but actually is radically different! Excluding the part dealing with the teachings of an aboriginal tribe (which Groves said is a part of another set of his lessons to his pupils), only less than 5% of the two texts is the same (precisely 16 out of 138 pages), and that virtually word for word, but the bulk of each text is quite different in content and practical (from the Fourth Way Work point of view) quality. Dr. Groves asked me to send him a copy of the text I have, which I did, and he has since published it (that is, the text I sent him) under his own name, but with some omissions, in particular the list of the psycho-spiritual exercises is not given in the published version. Dr. Groves died in March 1999 - may he R. I. P.

Mr. C. Stanley Nott denied that Mister Gurdjieff ever had private pupils unknown to anyone in the groups, but he identified some of the items listed below with what Mister Gurdjieff communicated to small groups of selected pupils. There were though about a dozen items he professed not to know anything about. He also gave me the following list of exercises and/or teachings he received directly from Mister Gurdjieff:

Chemistry - Sociology - Physiology & Psychology of Man.
The Bible.
Good-Being, Evil-Being & Non-Being.
Time.
Incarnation & Reincarnation.
Spiritualism.
Art Science.
Objective Reason.
Conscience.
Laws of Associations.
Pondering.
Purposive thought.
Playing Roles.
Parable.
Evolution & Involution.
Mysticism, Occultism, etc..
Psycho-analysis.
Transmutation of Substances.
Cosmic Chemistry - Sun, Earth, Moon - Sun Absolute - S1 S11.
Centres of Gravity.
Cosmic Laws.

Radiations & Innovations.
Knowing, Being & Doing.
Language: Glossary of System.
Faith. Hope. Love.
Objective Criticism of Man.
Kundabuffer.
Harmonious Development.
Know Thyself: Being.

When I asked the late Madame Jeanne de Salzmann about Mister Gurdjieff's "private pupils", she confirmed that he did have some who could be so described, but would not comment on the list (which follows) of the subjects Mister Gurdjieff is alleged to have taught to such special pupils, over and above what was given in groups.

According to the anonymous author of *Beyond the Fourth Way* (who writes as if he had been present at the time), each one of the techniques listed below was accompanied by explanations that fit it into the general scheme of life. Also he quotes Mister Gurdjieff as saying: "Choose what you want by all means, but choose wisely. What you choose indicates what you are and what you hope to become. Ask yourself sincerely what is it that you want, then you will find whether the technique you choose will help you or not".

Here is the list as given in the *Beyond the Fourth Way* typescript found in a bookshop:

1. Self-Remembering.
2. Non-Identification.
3. Self-Observation.
4. Thob-Thinking.
5. Self-Projection to distant places.
6. Constellatory Thinking.
7. Educing data and power from the Racial Memory.
8. Shedding psychological "skins".
9. Telepathy.
10. Clairvoyance.
11. Projection of Telekinetic Energy.
12. Posture, Consciousness and Thought.
13. Abstracting instructions from Ancient Symbols.
14. Autistic Motivation of the Enneagram in the Psyche.
15. Resolving Paradoxical Situations by the Third Force.
16. Detailed study of the Will.
17. Locating the focus of Real Consciousness within oneself.
18. The use of Hope.
19. On Using the Phylum.
20. The use of Telegics.

21. Progress through Eu-Tempo-Tropism.
22. Mnemonic Re-Capitulation, Re-Permutation and Re-Orientation.
23. Educating the various Aesthetic Faculties.
24. On the Integrative Power of Root Language.
25. Bio-Dynamics of Religion.
26. Functions of Esoteric Philosophy.
27. Capitalising upon one's Genetic Endowment.
28. On Forming a Higher Body.
29. Exercising the Mystical Senses.
30. Modes of Spiritual Healing.

The anonymous author of the above list ads: "This is by no means a complete list of the techniques either directly taught by Gurdjieff to small groups and various individuals, or techniques that he indicated as being useful and whose source he indicated. There is so much knowledge connected with

An Academy.
Existence. Life. Being. Non-Being. Scale of Being.
Tables of Hydrogens.
Effort & Relaxation.
Standard of Values - Degrees of Being.
Reason O Consciousness.
The Norms of Man.
Two Forms of Understanding.
Life, Love, Suffering; Pain.
War & Death & Birth.
Mechanical or Conscious Behaviourism, etc..
Interaction of Movements, Centres.
Positive, Negative, Neutralising.
Sociological Influence.
Psychological Exercises.
Potential. Actual. Ideal.
Sleeping; Waking.
Self & Cosmic Consciousness.
Chief Feature.
Horse, Carriage, Driver; Passenger.
Mutton & Wool.
Succession & Simultaneity.
Meaning & Aim of Existence.
Conditional Immortality.
Definitions of Man.
Micro; Meso; Deftero; Macro; Proto; Megalocosmos.
Purgatory.

Man.
Sex.
Consciousness.
World; Universe: Nature. God.
3 FOODS: Air, Perceptions, Impressions)
Body; Three.
Hypnotism.
Three Centres.
The Method.
Religion & Religious.
Knowledge; Belief.
The Law of the Octave.
Law of Three and Seven.
Essence; Personality.
Will. Individuality. Consciousness.
Self-Observation or Self-Remembering.
Intentional Suffering.
Conscious Labour.
I and It.
The Three Yogas; and The Fourth.
Force. Matter. Energy.
Electricity.

each method that a complete lesson must be given to each one that you may require."

If anyone still living knows about any of these, it is his bounden duty, if he truly is one of "Beelzebub's grand-children", to put what he knows in writing and share it with the other workers in Mister Gurdjieff's vineyard.

© Copyright 2003 - Nicolas Tereshchenko - All Rights Reserved

Notes and Other Material Relating to Dr. Philip Groves

Bert Sharp

There has been substantial correspondence between myself, Nicolas Tereshchenko, Joy Lonsdale, and Philip Groves himself from 1995 to 1999. I have now tried to trace the factual story which we have as a result.

Joy Lonsdale visited Dr. Groves in Sydney several times, spending 2 - 3 hours with him at some of these visits. Her letter to me of 14th July, 1997 about her latest visit at the time contains material of some interest:

There is no doubt that Dr. Groves is the author of the two version of *Beyond the Fourth Way*, which we have and which we know as *Beyond 1* and *Beyond 2*. Indeed he is the author of six such versions and Joy saw these during her visit, including the real original, now yellowed with age.

The reason for the differences in each version is very simple. They were all written as lessons and lectures at different times, for different sets of pupils. So he still retained common material in all, but tailored each for the group it was designed for.

Joy also asked him why it appears form Nicolas's memory of their meeting in 1955 that he did not acknowledge being the author of *Beyond 1*. He said this was not a denial of authorship, but a denial of knowing anything about the *Mazdaznian Philosophy*. He obtained the list of exercises from a different source. The fact that the *Mazdaznian Philosophy* is mentioned in the conclusion of *Beyond 1* is because it was not written by Dr. Groves but by John Mumford. John Mumford is an ex-pupil of Dr. Groves.

This brings us to a letter of 26 August 1997 from Dr. Groves to me excerpts from which are given as follows:

By way of self-introduction I would like to briefly indicate that throughout my 77 years I have been driven by the need to know the meaning of things. This led me into a range of advanced studies including biochemistry, histology, neurology, psychology, marine biology and Egyptology.

Later it was my good fortune to befriend Sheikh Muhammad Iqbal, a member of the Nagshbandi order who gave me private instruction for more than a year. This led me to further contact with Sufis in Sri Lanka and Africa. Names like Dr. Samberino and Tomarus. While meaning nothing to the outside world, but for me were fountains of wisdom and training. Studies continued for a number of years in Indian and Tibetan Philosophy, and an eye kept on scientific development in the Western world. Then I met a man who introduced me to the teaching of Ouspensky and Gurdjieff. Although I was unfamiliar with these writers, the content of their books ran almost parallel with some of the teachings I had received from other sources. I was taken to meet a certain Dr. Koffman at whose place there was conducted a reading from *All & Everything*. At that time I was a complete beginner as far as Gurdjieff's Work was concerned. Needless to say I was considerably surprised to read that Nicolas claimed that I had received instruction directly from Gurdjieff. That is completely false.

Now we need to go to Dr. Grove's last letter to me on 7. 2. 1998. This was hand written and so I will now transcribe it, since it contains some very interesting concepts: which I would suggest augment the Gurdjieff Work:

Dear Dr. Sharp,

Sincere apologies for such as protracted delay in replying to your delightful letter sent some months ago. Friends in other parts of the world are complaining about my lack of correspondence, so I am in big trouble.

My computer is out of action, at present, and I trust you can make sense out of my scrawl. I am very grateful to you for pointing out errors in *Beyond the Fourth Way*. The publisher will make corrections at the next printing. Always grateful to receive comments and criticisms.

At page 95 it was mentioned that a list of exercises would be included in an Addendum. I deliberately removed that list when it was found that certain new students were carrying out their own form of wiseacreing by inventing their own versions of the exercises. Incidentally, the book is used in conjunction with the usual Fourth way literature for new students who join the group. The list that was removed appears in Addendum 7 of the version which was translated into French.

The term "thob-thinking" appears on the list. Originally it was employed to describe the intentional initiation of subtle "throbbings" in various parts of the body in response to a striving stimulus applied to one of the centres. A "shock" applied to the feeling centre does set up resonances elsewhere in the body, and it is possible to detect the nature of these "holes or subliminal throbbings. Gurdjieff once described how a certain piece of music aroused definite responses in the thinking centre, quite different responses in the feeling centre, and still different responses in the moving centre. These multiple and widespread responses are known in some schools as thob thinking.

The list of exercises or processes includes drawing forth energies and states from the racial or phyletic memory, and using the phylum as a means of increasing the dimensions of one's being. Carl Jung's concept of the collective unconscious was an interesting step towards the larger principle of seeing the whole of organic life as the background to human life and experience. This principle was described and thoroughly explored by the great Sufi Rumi hundreds of years ago.

He meticulously explored the phyletic resources of his being and brought forth processes and phenomena which spanned the ages. The phyletic background of life is like the all-pervasive spiritual atmosphere which faithfully preserves the symbols, formulations, principles and processes of the ancient past. It is therefore quite unlike the more superficial transmission of information from generation to generation which is accompanied by the accumulation of errors. Gurdjieff refers to this process in *All and Everything*.

"The Greek language, the spirit and essence of which were transmitted to me by heredity, and the language now spoken by contemporary Greeks, are as alike as, according to the expression of Mullah Nassr Eddin, "A nail is like a requiem". (p. 13)

The phyletic spirit preserves the essence of a thing while its outer manifestations often undergo considerable mechanical changes. Gurdjieff's idea that we can help some of our ancestors is based on the principle that the phyletic stream of life is a tightly organised structure which inwardly links together all beings in a mighty superstructure. If we gain some enlightenment and freedom it is our cosmic duty to share it with those who preceded us, but never gained those things. Much wisdom is transmitted through the phyletic stream, but there are also many anchors and retarding factors. If we Work on ourselves we also work for the liberation of other human souls from dark and difficult states.

Another item on the list of exercises is the integrative power of root language. Two of the schools in which I received early training insisted on the study of root-words in various languages. It was taught that root-words often embodied the thinking- feeling- knowing states of the people who generated the words. Some of these words were to be pondered and allowed to sink into one's subconscious depths; here they were supposed to arouse corresponding psychic states in one's phyletic stream of life. Languages like ancient Egyptian, Sanskrit, Ugdnit, ancient Persian and Akkadian were studied for this purpose.

Gurdjieff displayed a deep interest in aspects of philology and wrote some interesting things in *Meetings with Remarkable Men*. His *All & Everything* is a masterpiece of word units combined in special ways to produce psychological effects. The Nahshbandi Sufis are interested in combining word-roots in special ways to help promote new mental states.

During a recent telephone conversation with Nicolas Tereshchenko I mentioned that you would receive some comments on the list of exercises, and he may be interested in what we have touched upon.

Mrs Londsdale tells me that she has completed her book and has already found a publisher in the U.S.A. I'm looking forward to reading her full work. So far I have only examined a few pages of her manuscript.

Notes and Other Material Relating to Dr. Philip Groves

Well dear Dr. Sharp, I know that you are having a busy time preparing for the coming Gurdjieff congress. I do hope that it turns out to be a happy and fulfilling occasion, and that you get some good help from your companions. Shall be present with all of you in spirit.

With every good wish for happiness, success and ascendance,
Affectionately,
Philip (Groves)

This I think brings us to the list of topics or exercises missing from Dr. Groves now published book although referred to in the text. Nicolas notes it as being included in *Beyond 1* as Addendum 7. This is correct and the text following in *Beyond 1* details a discussion on each of these aspects. But the Conclusion attached to *Beyond 1* we now know was not written by Dr. Groves but most likely by John Mumford. Its title is *The Origins of Gurdjieff's System*. It refers in particular to three particular publications and it is here that the connection with *Mazdaznian Philosophy* comes in. The three publications are:

The Golden Star; by J. Michaud.
A System of Caucasian Yoga; by Count Stefan Colonna Walewski.
Health and Breath Culture According to Mazdaznian Philosophy; by Rev. Dr. Otoman Zar-Adusht-Hanish.

In 1999 details about Hanish, believable or not, were available on the web site www.mazdnan.org. No indication in detail of who his teachers were is given in this. The connection of possible interest to us here is in reference to page 135 of *Beelzebub's Tales* where an extraordinary statement is made:

"- that is to say, you would not be able to restrain yourself from such laughter, if in some way or another, they were suddenly clearly to sense and understand, without any doubt whatever, that not only does nothing like 'light', 'darkness', 'heat', and so on, come to their, planet from their Sun itself, but that their supposed 'source of heat and light' is itself almost always freezing cold like the 'hairless-dog' of our highly esteemed Mullah Nassr Eddin."

"In reality, the surface of their 'Source-of-Heat', like that of all ordinary Suns or our Great Universe, is perhaps more covered with ice than the surface of what they call their 'North Pole'."

One wonders if there is some hidden meaning to the passage or if it is simply included in order to test the credulity of the reader.

If however we go to *Health and Breath Culture According to Mazdaznan Philosophy*, the contents consist of instructions in twelve lessons of a whole series of special exercises with an introduction and comments on each exercise. We need to consider Exercise 6, and I quote:

"We now come to an exercise where all our pupils bow their knees. There is a time in every man's life, whether Jew or gentile, heathen or Christian, when he shall bow his knees in reverence. The principle object of this exercise is to distribute the magnetic circles for aiding in the awakening of the spinal cord, thus expanding the realms of thought, enabling you to reason more logically and be able to perceive through the sense of feeling the inner physical mechanism of your being, guiding you by virtue of the activity of the brain cells to the enfoldment of a perfect consciousness and realisation that you are one with God and nature.

"Kneel at the back of a chair, bowing both knees at the same time. Don't fall upon the knees; do it as gracefully as you perform all previous exercises. Have the chair about three feet from you so you can take hold of the upright bars at the back of the chair, one in each hand. Hands as well as body are to be perfectly relaxed and spinal column firm.

"After the prelude breaths, inhale fully and deeply, at the same time tightening the grasp upon the chair bars. Inhale as long as you can conveniently without the use of effort, and without causing any unpleasant feelings to any part of the body. Retain the breath as long as you can with ease, still holding tightly to the chair, and as you exhale gradually release your hold upon the bars. Exercise in this position for three minutes at a time, and not more than three times a day. You may take this exercise in the evening.

"You need not feel alarmed over the peculiar sensation at the navel and distributing itself over the spinal region in an upward movement to the top of the head as well as downwards to the lower extremities of the body. That peculiar warmth is caused by the generation of electric force in the nervous system, and that cool, fanning sensation felt about the body is the magnetic circles emanating from the inmost soul.

"This position will bring tranquillity and calmness over the mind and open up realms of untold joy. Yet what it will do for you remains for you to experience. But you must not overdo it because of the great benefits you are deriving from this exercise and others. You must think the more the better. It is a very powerful exercise. As soon as you begin to feel the chair move before you, and your knees show the tendency to get above the floor, release the hands at once from the chair and stop the exercise for that day. It will not do to over-exercise if you are to develop all your brain functions equally. The curing qualities of this exercise must be experienced instead of explained. Gradually you will be led higher and higher into realms of consciousness, and wisdom will unfold unto you daily. Things you were unable to comprehend before will begin to appear very simple. In fact there will be nothing you cannot comprehend, and then you will comprehend that even the light which you thought comes from the Sun is but the light of your own planet. You will understand that your senses in their deluded condition of yet undeveloped brain functions have miscomprehended the works divine, and that the Sun is neither a fire ball, nor has it any more light than necessary for the sustenance of it own planetary conditions. You will understand that our planet is a light unto itself, and that 'I am the light of the World'."

Notes and Other Material Relating to Dr. Philip Groves

So we are being told of the importance of relationships; we live in a universe of relationships, a much more sensible commentary. How did it go wrong? Did Gurdjieff get it wrong, or did his collaborators in producing the drafts of *All & Everything* get it wrong?

Published material of Philip Groves as at March 1997

All believed to be by Triam Press, PO Box 21, Castlecrag, NSW 2069, Australia.

1955 - *The Garden of the Mind*:
Previously titled "Lectures": Life, Death & Eternity; Spiritual Dimensions of Biology; Existence, Appearance & Reality; The Garden of the Mind; The More Abundant Life; The Concept of Self Transformation; Power, Truth & Spheres of Life; A Study of Dreams.

1995 - *Mega Nature*:
Nature & Mega Nature; Cycles of Being & Transformation; Soil-Plant-Animal Connections; Phytochemistry & Herbal Resources; Aromas, Molecules & Information; The Oceanic Factor; The Biological Manipulation of Solar Energy; Macro Ecology & Micro Ecology; The Sense Of Place; The Biology of the Spirit; Some Material Hazards; Tapping Natural resources.

1996 - *Beyond the Fourth Way*

1996 - *Spiritual Psychology*:
Vol 1. Introduction to Spiritual Psychology; Regeneration & Human Potential; Die Before you Die; Centres & Self Remembering.
Vol2. The Dynamic Sequence; The Energy of Hydrogens & Transformation; Symbols as Instruments of Instruction; Self Observation of Our States.
Vol 3. Metamorphosis & Metanoia; A Second Education; Ancient Wisdom; A Historical Perspective.

1997 - *The Philosophy of Natural Healing*:
Foundations of the Philosophy; The Vibrant Body; Perspectives and Principles; Nature's Hidden Energy; Metabolism, Nutrition, Fasting; Reactivity in the Body; Health & the Flow of Energy; The Employment of Natural Resources; The Diagnosis of Health; The Psychological Image of Man; The Healing Crisis; A Way of Life.

© Copyright 2003 - Bert Sharp - All Rights Reserved

On the Third Line of Work

Dimitri Peretzi

This booklet I hold in my hand is an inset from the latest issue of "Lipstick", a monthly magazine for girls. It is something like a "Cosmopolitan" for teenagers, I suppose. It is published in several cities in the world, Athens included. In this little booklet a girl can find advice for the kind of make up suited to her personality, for the color of lipstick and nail polish best suited to her type. To know what her type is, she is urged to take a small test which is included in the text.

The point is that this is a test based on the enneagram, on enneagram typology.

For many who have studied Gurdjieff's ideas, the question is as pertinent today as it ever was: Why did he do things the way he did them, what was his exact aim in disseminating his teaching in the manner he did? Who are supposed to be the recipients of its benefits?

It is indeed an incontestable fact that the number of people who are actively participating in the Gurdjieff Work is marginal, when compared to the scope and potential of the knowledge contained in his teaching. There is certainly much to ponder about, for example, when we see that today there exist more than thirty five thousand (35,000) enneagram-related websites, most of them dealing with 'personality types' and 'methods for business strategies', when fewer than thirty are related to Gurdjieff's original presentation of the enneagram, as a tool for observation and Work on one's self.

Is this the inevitable way things are supposed to go?

Are we witnessing the degenerative trajectory that all great spiritual endeavors of man are destined to follow?

The real question of course is not whether there is a large number of people that use Gurdjieff's ideas in strange ways, but whether the practice of the teaching itself, of the "Work", still has the liberating potency to awaken, and the momentum needed to continue to benefit members of the groups well into the future.

For most of those who are in the groups whose lineage goes back to Gurdjieff himself my personal experience is that the answer is a strong "yes". And the enneagram, as well as Gurdjieff's psychological ideas, his "sacred dances", his music, his writings, all these are part of the legacy that has made this possible. When we realize the interrelatedness of this heritage with the Work as it is practiced today, we have to assume that there are people interested in the authenticity of this heritage and in assuming their personal responsibility to safeguard it.

Indeed, how are we to deal with the Gurdjieff legacy, with the enneagram for example, especially when we see that, for the wider public, this very "universal symbol" Gurdjieff gave to his immediate pupils of the Russia years, seems to have sunk into the marshes of New Age superficiality? Are we to concentrate on the practice of the Work in a manner oblivious to the kind of questions that are posed by publications such as the one I showed you, believing that no initiative will ever be able to change the way things seem to be going? Are we to assume that Gurdjieff's personal efforts were the only thing needed to effectuate the Work, and to effectuate the Fourth Way shock that needs to be delivered in this day and age? Are we to be of the conviction that no initiative should ever be taken, that all practitioners of his teaching are "free loafers" who can only hope to take some personal advantage of the solo efforts of the master, and that after him everything will be run "like a Pianola"?

If you think that the questions I pose are exaggerated, I should mention my surprise when I was once told emphatically by a lady of the old guard in Paris, that all the years she was in the Work, more than forty until that time, she had never, not once, taken any initiative. I cannot forget the proud look she had on her face as she said that.

At the same time, Gurdjieff has warned us against "Hasnamussian wiseacreing" with enough intensity to assure that any initiative taken, if not out rightly rejected, will at least be carefully scrutinized by the devotees as to the purity of its intentions and the reality of its results.

One way or the other though, the question cannot go away: if we take no initiative, how are we to manage the Gurdjieff heritage?

There was a meeting somewhere in Europe in the early seventies, which was called by Mme. de Salzmann. I do not know whether Mrs. Staveley was present or not, but I do know that Mr. Bennett was, as well as a number of representatives from groups other than those of the de Salzmann circles. I do not know the exact purpose this meeting had. What I do know is that one of the questions discussed there, was "How are we to manage the Gurdjieff heritage". Lord Pentland, whom I had met with in New York a few days after that meeting and who was the one to tell me all I know about it, mentioned that Bennett was of the opinion that groups should undertake a massive effort to promote the Work to the wider public and, to achieve this goal, they should use massive media advertising, such as prime time television spots, whole page ads in the New York Times, and the like.

Times of course have changed since Bennett's proposal. If there was "something" in the seventies that explained him having had this point of view, this "something" exists no more. The way things are, if the enneagram is included today in an ad for the Work, there will be people who will think that the advertising is about some New Age group, or even worse, about some brand of Lip stick.

No matter how things are however, we cannot shy away from the responsibility to find a way, how to manage the Gurdjieff heritage.

Those who have contributed in making public something as strong as the enneagram cannot behave as if they do not understand the power of what they have done. If in the course of time we realize that the way the people who read about the enneagram in the texts of Ouspensky etc. are misusing it, then the least responsibility we have is to audibly state our good intended critique for the inadequate way the enneagram is put to use. Otherwise, whether we like it or not, we become accomplices to the debasement of the enneagram.

How to become audible, how to become visible, this is the tricky part. There has to be a sensible way for that, a middle ground that lies somewhere between, on the one hand of the nirvana of not taking any initiative at all and expecting everything to proceed "like a Pianola", and on the other hand of going ballistic, believing that the Work should be promoted through mass television advertising.

To explore and define this middle ground, to do something about such problems, this I believe is the domain of the Third Line of Work.

"Mr. Gurdjieff was an unknown person, a mystery," noted Mme. de Hartmann in her memoirs. "Nobody knew about his teaching, nobody knew its origin... but whoever came into contact with him wished to follow him." Gurdjieff's powerful ideas coupled with an intensely compelling personality, assured that, during his life, his teaching received by his pupils the attention needed, for its practice to survive intact after his death, as he surely intended it to and wished for.

What I mean to say is that we were given, both the practical tools, and the theoretical frame of ideas to face successfully the problems created in this case by the inevitable action of degenerative forces. For the Work to proceed effectively and the Fourth Way to achieve its goals in this phase of its reappearance on the planet, all the three lines of Work have to be present: the personal line of Work, which includes self observation and self remembering; the line of Work with the group, which includes the group Work around a given exercise common for all, given by the group leader; and the Third Line, the Work that is dedicated to the Work itself. It is the Third Line of Work that I wish to explore a little further today. I am using the enneagram and the public trajectory it has followed since its appearance, as an example, to illustrate my point. A similar thread of thoughts could be spun, using as examples the public trajectory of the Gurdjieff movements, which today are taught in various places in India, Europe and America, or of ideas like "self observation", a "practice" that has become very popular with various forms of psychotherapeutic practices.

Gurdjieff gave his Russian pupils the teaching of the enneagram as part of the personal contact they had with him as part of the type C influences that define the teacher-student relationship.

Beelzebub Restores our Understanding of Teleology and Ontology

On the opposite end of the spectrum of influences, we have influences A, the kind of influence a girl will receive reading the article in Lipstick magazine on the enneagram. It is the kind of degenerated influence that has become part of the general flow of mechanical life.

My point is that if we are to ignore this kind of degenerative influence, then the enneagram will be lost as part of the Fourth Way, irretrievably.

To ignore the enneagram typology, means to become a silent accomplice to, and therefore a part of the debasement such use of the enneagram entails. To expect that people will learn about the real relationship of the enneagram to the Work by word of mouth and to ignore the fact that the typology of the enneagram has spread through the implacable waves of its public presence, means not to understand the fact that it was Gurdjieff himself who started the process, by putting the enneagram into the awareness of the public. But nothing serious or important has been done so far, and the fact is that the enneagram is fast on its way to become synonymous with New Age superstitious blabber.

Not ignoring it without going ballistic, without acting hysterical about keeping it under control, means providing people with a fair chance, with an alternative. It means to make public the material that is needed for the understanding that, the level which typology is connected to the enneagram with, is not the only level the enneagram can be studied at.

This way of action, in effect, the action needed to create valid alternatives to influences A, that is what the Third Line of Work is about. It is about sacred art standing as an alternative to "roses and mimosas", about sacred literature standing as alternative to cultural garbage. There have to be alternatives to the typology of the enneagram. The action to create such alternatives is the essence of creating influences B.

To take action in such a direction, one has to be in touch, on the one hand with the reality of the progress of Work in himself and on the other hand being in contact with the reality of the world, with the reality of the relationships that arise between the Work and the World.

The publication of *In Search of the Miraculous* was Third Line of Work; so were the public demonstrations of the sacred dances; so was the film "Meetings with Remarkable Men", the one that Mme. de Salzmann did with Peter Brook; so are the lectures some people give, or their authorship of inside books about the Work and the memoirs that have being published, the ones that include first hand accounts of meetings with Mr. Gurdjieff or with the Work.

A thing very interesting to notice is that the action taken along the Third Line of Work, unavoidably, appears to be very similar to advertising.

To give public demonstrations of the sacred dances, this was certainly advertising. In effect, this is how most of the people in Gurdjieff's time learned about him and about the Fourth Way, including Mme. de Salzmann. The public lectures that Gurdjieff or Ouspensky gave, that was also advertising. Their explicitly stated aim was to attract new group members. What can be more effective "Work done for the Work", than to seek out the right people, to work for establishing the right conditions for the Work to flourish? It is not at all easy to define the boundaries between the Third Line of Work and outright advertising. In fact, it is my personal belief that the idea for making the film "Meetings with Remarkable Men" came about as an indirect result of Mr. Bennett's proposal at that meeting, when he advocated all out advertising. The timetable of the way events unfolded, certainly fits this thought.

What about advertising? How are we to think of the boundaries between advertising and the Third Line of Work? What should be the measure of being visible in the "correct" way, of not jeopardizing the essence of the Work while being in contact with the realities of the world? And, last but not least, how are we to deal with money? It is a well known fact that any contact with the world invokes money, even money used in strange and unconventional ways. As Gurdjieff aptly put it, without such use of money, "one cannot even breathe".

The obvious answer is that relationships like these are regulated by the needs of the Work, the needs of the group.

But what are these needs? How are we to define them? Who is to define them? How are we to keep the integrity of the Work intact in the face of "financial needs", in the face of "the need to avoid the lowering of the quality that ensues from making the legacy public", not to mention "the need for respect within the hierarchy", or the "heed to remain united"? Lord Pentland once said that every time the group did something, it was the people that were good organizers, the ones that seemed to be taking over the Work.

In actuality, every activity that aims at the survival of one or another aspect of the Work, or of any endeavor for that matter, can easily end up serving its own self interests. Things done in the name of "financial needs", of "correct organizing", of "respect for the hierarchy", can easily contribute to the general degeneration of the Work.

In matters like these there can be no easy formulas. Anyone might have his opinion, and this opinion is to be respected to the extent that he has taken the initiative to shoulder the corresponding responsibilities.

What I would like to point out, nevertheless, is that the Third Line of Work seems to provide the clues needed to give the appropriate answers to such questions.

When people in the Work see the way the enneagram is treated by the typology psychologists, when we see how the movements are treated by some "schools" in India that are trying to spread in Europe and the US, when we realize how cheap the notion of self observation has become in the hands of some psychiatrists, and in what convoluted way "remembering the self" is practiced within some New Age groups, then we might rightly feel the need to ask:

Beelzebub Restores our Understanding of Teleology and Ontology

"Who let the dog out?"

Well, the truth is that, by agreeing to the publication of *All and Everything*, of *Meetings with Remarkable Men*, of Ouspensky's version of the System in his *Fragments of an Unknown Teaching*, it was Mr. Gurdjieff himself; he was the one who let the dog out.

So, the dog was let out for a purpose, and this purpose is itself a part of the Work. It cannot be otherwise.

If we go beyond the fantasy of the "pianola", if we realize that things do demand our initiative because their mechanical deployment is not enough for them to proceed, and that the Work can be judged to be successful if and only if it can produce people who are capable of undertaking such initiative, then we realize that the work of keeping in check the problems that the loose dog is creating, so to speak, will provide the realistic answer to all the questions that have to do with solving the problems that arise from managing Gurdjieff's legacy.

Work for Work's sake, the Third Line of Work, consists of creating the appropriate kind of influences B to counterbalance the degenerative effect of the advance of influences A. The mathematics here are as simple as they are blunt. Even are not successful in doing this, the world will have "chicked" us. But it is the same mathematics that gives the measure of what is to be done and of the kind of energy that needs to be put.

Such "formulas" define an axis for our contact with reality. They do not give easy answers to the problem of degeneration, but they provide a direction, showing what is to be done. To my understanding, they provide a way of thinking, what kind of parameters one could take into account when deciding how his circle's Work is to proceed.

The emotional pressures we can be under when we feel that things are moving on in an unwanted, degenerative course, can be a guide. Like the adversity of the stream's current flow downwards gives the direction to the salmon by revealing to him the forces against which he should strive, those pressures can reveal the external goal a group should work for, and thus indirectly, it can provide answers to questions such as, what is the number of members the group should have, what level of effort and sacrifice should its members sustain, what kind of demands the group leader is morally justified to have.

All this is valid of course, provided that at least some members of the group never forget the simultaneous Work on the First and Second lines, so that they can wake up the others, the ones who do.

© Copyright 2003 - Dimitri Peretzi - All Rights Reserved

On the Third Line of Work - Questions & Answers

Participant 1: I believe that the question, "How to protect the Work," has only theoretical value. In a practical or legal way, the copyright of the Work is gone, the ideas are public. If I work with the enneagram any which way I please, whether I belong to the Gurdjieff tradition or not, nobody can stop me, really. There is no legal base any more. Some years after the death of a person, his writings become public domain. And that is where the enneagram is.

Dimitri Peretzi: I see your point. But I think that if one seeks to protect, so to speak, the enneagram through keeping the copyright in a legal way, I believe the game to be lost. The question is, what is the extent to which someone can effectuate the safe keeping of the Gurdjieff heritage by his actions. People in the Work should be in position to do so. If the Work is successful then there should be people who know "how to do" and who know "what to do". Otherwise the Work cannot be considered to be successful.

Participant 2: In our early Work with Mrs. Popoff our first group leader, great and continuing emphasis was placed on service. We got the clear impression from Mrs. Popoff that a major aspect of this Work so far as the third line was unremitting service. Could you comment on that in the context of how you approach the question?

Dimitri Peretzi: Thank you very much for the tip. It's a tip I personally need, I think. I am in no position to judge Mrs. Popoff's point of view. So the only way I can use what you say is as a tip.

Participant 1: Is there a possibility that you work to change yourself; that you formalize contacts to the external world by making promotions, the way Gurdjieff did, perhaps in other ways too? I myself entered the enneagram according to an introduction by Helen Palmer. This not your way, I know, but this is how I got acquainted with the enneagram.

Dimitri Peretzi: It is not a matter of it "not being my way". I think that the success of the enneagram within these circles is due to the power it has as a symbol. Recently I have encountered the use of the enneagram, called in this instance a "hologram", applied in business strategies. This is in the context of the MBA curriculum of the University of Kingston, here in the UK.

Participant 1: Some of the big corporations in this country are managed with the use of the enneagram. Philips in the Netherlands is managed with the use of the enneagram.

Dimitri Peretzi: I appreciate what you say. I am sure that there are ways in which the enneagram is also used for the management of some of the operations over in Iraq, for the war there. This is nothing that I can control about that and I definitely do not intend to. What I am saying is that it is good to make sure that there is a fair alternative; you have to make sure that there is a fair chance for someone to understand that there is something deeper in the enneagram than just the management of business.

Participant 3: I think that Dimitri is making a point there. I remember being in George Cornelius' place in America, some years ago, listening to a tape that was recorded when Lord Pentland was staying there. Somebody said that he had engraved the enneagram on the soles of his shoes so that it made an imprint on the snow, as he walked. Lord Pentland said "why not". At that time the spread of the enneagram did not have as many negative sides as it has today, and in that context I can understand Lord Pentland's response. Regarding what initiative can be taken against the down bringing of the enneagram, we might consider giving more emphasis on other aspects of the enneagram, such as the essence types as opposed to the personality types.

Dimitri Peretzi: I agree with you. This could be one of the possible ways, I suppose. Another point to be made concerns the study of the enneagram. Usually the people who use the enneagram outside the Work do not really care for the enneagram itself. They don't care to understand what it's all about.

Participant 1: But if you do not understand the enneagram, then you cannot really use it.

Dimitri Peretzi: Well, the Pythagorean Theorem has been used very successfully as a mathematical tool without it being linked to Pythagoras' ideas. Likewise, the enneagram can work as a symbol and it can produce interesting results, without its user being connected with the ideas that led initially to the investigation of its structure. Indeed, what I have found out is that the people who are not using the enneagram in the context of the Work are not interested in studying it in depth; they're mostly interested in using it to promote this or that idea.

Participant 4: There is nothing that I can do about what other people are doing. So I don't think that we have to be concerned with others here. As for the degeneration of the teaching, there is also nothing we can do. It is inherent in the law. There is evolution and there is involution, everywhere. And we are not going to stop the involution, because we cannot stop the law.

Dimitri Peretzi: I agree with you, I understand what you mean. But my point is that there is no way that you can disregard what the other people are doing. For example, our gathering here, in this space, conforms to the laws that this city holds about gatherings. It is always like that. The things we do conform to some regulation or other, to some reason or other. When we clean the floor, for example, why are we doing it? Why do we tend to have our meetings in clean rooms? We always have others in mind, one way or another.

Participant 4: I didn't finish. What you say is just what I wanted to say. The next thing is, will there be a group of people who goes against the down flow of the involution? That there be a group of people who goes against the down flow of the involution? That is the question. I do not know the answer to that. Will there be a group that goes against the natural involution?

Because the involution is there, you cannot do anything about it. It has affected Christianity, everything.

Dimitri Peretzi: The way I see this issue is comparable to somebody being angry. Maybe there's nothing he can do to stop being angry; but it is possible that he knows that he is angry, and this may be changing something. In the same way, involution may be a law, it may be something doing on all the time, but there is one thing to be conscious of it and another not to be. There is something to be done there. So the question is, how can we be conscious of such forces? And if the Work has any value, then it should be affecting that ability.

Participant 2: I'll raise the question again. In this context it seems to me that it is possible to have a perspective on "work for the Work" which has absolutely nothing to do with everything that has been discussed here, to this point.

Dimitri Peretzi: Can you separate Mother Teresa's actions from advertising? How and why did her movement grow? You could say that her actions do not constitute advertising, that they represent "acts of God that are manifested through her", but in effect they did act as advertising for her movement. Why should we be afraid of the word "advertising"? The idea here is that there is promotion by example. This is what I am trying to say. When we expect someone to come to a meeting we clean the floor, we take care of our meeting room, we sense that the person who will walk in for the first time will know the difference and we care about the image we shall project. Even cleaning the floor is advertising, in a way. This is an aspect we cannot separate from our actions. Everything we do has its own way of "shining". This is not a matter of *acting for* advertising or *not acting for* advertising, it is a matter of being conscious of the kind of influence one has on another person.

Participant 2: If this Third Line is "work for the Work", then the question of advertising or any kind of externalization of effort and so forth, does that have anything to do with "work for the Work", that's what I'm raising as a question. Are we talking, perhaps, about something totally different?

Dimitri Peretzi: When you use money, you cannot dissociate yourself from things like "the war", "the price of oil", etc. If we follow this trajectory of thought we shall realize that we're immersed into society. We could somehow abstract the Work and say, "Well, no, Work is something else", but then Work has to be in society, within society. Where does the Work touch society? Does it touch it in the course of the First or the Second Line, as for example in the course of the meetings of a Work group, the contents of which nobody is supposed to know of except its members? The only possible area that the Work can touch society is the Third Line, and indeed, it does touch it there.

Participant 5: There are forces the aim of which is to turn "influences C" into "influences A". These forces are law - one should respect, so to speak, their results.

Beelzebub Restores our Understanding of Teleology and Ontology - Questions & Answers

Dimitri Peretzi: I agree with you. Similarly, there are natural laws, gravity for example, which force water to flow downward. At the same time salmon, the fish, uses these forces and the water's downward flow to navigate itself upward, upstream, in the opposite direction. This is my point. The forces of degeneration are there, they are lad and you cannot beat them if you try to stop them, but they can also be viewed as an indication of the direction one's actions can follow, in an inverse way. They can be used as a compass. I believe that this can be of very practical value. A group leader, for example, has the responsibility at points to demand sacrifice, and in insisting so he even has to accept the fact that his actions might be seen under a very unfavorable light. What is the basis by which he has the moral authority to do so? Because "he knows best"? Because "he's a good man"? Because "he was told so"? The only way such actions can be judged is vis-à-vis achieving a goal. And how is the goal to be shaped? Who is going to set the goal? Navigating against degenerative forces can be a criterion, the way to set goals.

Participant 1: This is a very dangerous discussion. Who's going to be the judge? On behalf of what? My question is... (1st side of tape ended here.)

Dimitri Peretzi: The need to have clear answers, easy answers, is a need that I understand. But having easy answers can also be dangerous. Sometimes it can be much more productive, I believe, to live with a difficult question. By speaking thus I do not intent to impose myself on anybody. What I want to do is pose some difficult questions. Such questions can be left dangling like that, torturing our souls, so to speak. At the same time, there are people who do not care about this kind of torture. They torture my soul and I am stating some of the problems that I have been through. The answer I gave in my talk was (reading from the manuscript), "in matters like these there can be no easy formulas. Anyone might have his opinion and opinion is to be respected to the extend that he has taken the initiative to shoulder the corresponding responsibilities".

Participant 1: Not positioning yourself clearly on this question can be a choice on its own, perhaps the best.

Dimitri Peretzi: Absolutely. I agree with you.

Participant 3: It was mentioned here, involution and evolution, and it might appear that there is an unnecessary conflict here. The question is not whether to fight the involutionary aspect of the use of the enneagram. Another thought would be that when you see it been misused to use it as a reminding factor, to promote some more essential aspect of the enneagram, the enneagrammatic study of the essence types for example. I do not know that you have all read anything on it. I am sure that this conflict can be viewed in a completely different way. And instead of looking at it as a conflict of evolution and involution, one can use it to be reminded that there is a need for something better, for refinement.

Dimitri Peretzi: I agree with what you said. In fact, that is what the aim of the book I wrote on the enneagram is, and that is what our work with the theatre is about. The way our project with the theatre is turning out, it seems that it will be a twenty year endeavor to develop a repertory of nine myths, each one taken from one of the great traditions of our world, each one staged in ways that it describes the way of development for one of the nine essence types.

Participant 6: What I understand you to be saying about your work with the theatre is that in the broader sense this is third line of Work, "working for the Work" as Participant 2 was suggesting and I think that to the extent that any of us are able, this is part of the Work, to work in that direction. The enneagram itself, the way I understand it, is a universal symbol expressing the two great laws of world creation and world maintenance, therefore encompassing everything. Mrs. Popoff for example, I've seen it in one of her books, she applies the enneagram to maybe twenty different situations, to things like baking bread for example. So even in the case of something like 'lipstick", even if the person using the enneagram in such a way doesn't understand anything about the great laws, it is still putting something out there that maybe is conformable to those laws without even knowing it. It is the same with the enneagram of types. In that sense it is inserting something closer to truth in the broad population, very few of whom will pick it up, and this maybe lawful.

Dimitri Peretzi: Yes, of course it is lawful. And it is also lawful to create "influences B". These are influences that are consciously created by people who are invoked in some kind of Work. So we can say that the Third Line of Work is about creating 'influences B". These influences are needed, I believe, as alternatives. It is not a matter of saying that the enneagram should not be used in topics such as "lipstick". It is a matter of creating an alternative, of finding a way to say that "there is more to the enneagram than what such use implies". There are people who feel aversion to the enneagram and reject it out rightly because it is has come to be identified so widely with New Age blabber.

Participant 7: I'm not sure that I can put this point eloquently. First of all, I think this is a very important and interesting question, the one being discussed right now; I also think we should keep in mind the other Lines of Work, as you mentioned. The enneagram is just an icon for what could happen with other parts of the Work. Having said that, I think we could think about how we would deal differently with those things that haven't degenerated quite so much at this point. We could even imagine what might happen to those other things, as, it seems to me, we have a pretty good example from what is happening with the enneagram. We could question how we could possibly put forth things that are of a more intentional conscious level with respect to the enneagram in such a way that they were available for people to compare them with the other things that are inevitably available. I think not enough is been done on that side. So it's probably up to us, people like the people in this room, to do something about that using the available technology.

Dimitri Peretzi: I do not disagree with what you say. But I would disagree to a possible conclusion that might be drawn from that, that we should forget about the enneagram. Somebody might conclude from what you said that, "the enneagram is gone, it is lost for good, so let us forget about it and concentrate on the things that are not yet lost". I think this would be a mistake. The enneagram cannot be detached and separated from the system. Other than that, I am sure that we

Beelzebub Restores our Understanding of Teleology and Ontology - Questions & Answers

all agree to the need of using the available technology to protect the Gurdjieff heritage, to the extent that we can do so.

Participant 1: When you're trying to protect it, it sounds like taking possession of it. The only thing that you are in fact doing is protecting the original way of the transmission of Gurdjieff; you're not clear enough to say that the times of Gurdjieff have changed and that perhaps we should be communicating differently. Gurdjieff could not communicate on the computer because he didn't have one.

Dimitri Peretzi: Are you defending some specific idea?

Participant 1: I am defending the values of the enneagram.

Dimitri Peretzi: I am also defending values that I choose to defend. So everything is fine. You can defend the values you wish to defend and I shall defend my own values.

Participant 1: There's nothing wrong, they may not be contradictory.

Participant 8: Could you clarify for me, when your group does these plays in Greece and you go to that effort, do you understand that effort to be putting an influence into what we come to call "mechanical life", for the purposes of bringing to the people an impulse that will show them the way to the Work? Is this how you see "work for the Work" and do you see the idea of the creation of influences which don't seek to bring people into the Work but seek to bring beneficial everyday becoming behaviours into mechanical life, do you see that as being something that is contrary to your understanding of "work for the Work'?

Dimitri Peretzi: For me to answer this, I feel the need to become technical and talk a little about statistics. There have been instances where I have given a talk and addressed myself to the public saying, "I am going to talk about Gurdjieff and I am doing this to attract people to his ideas." There are other instances where I will give a talk, maybe without mentioning the name of Gurdjieff and send an e-mail (or a note) to such and such an address. With the performance of the theatre group we make no announcement of this sort, nothing. We do not want our theatre project to be openly connected to the Work. Now, it is interesting to notice that after all these years, most of the people that eventually became interested in the Work and joined the groups have been people that made their acquaintance with the theatre group, after they saw their performances. It has happened that many months or even years after they have seen a performance, they find to their surprise that what we do is connected to the Gurdjieff Work, and often they seek us out. Of course, when you realize that something like three thousand people see every play and out of them maybe four or five make contact with us every year, then you know that all the other people must have been influenced, as well. Of course all this depends on the way we work on the myths and present them to the public. I do not have a better answer to the question you posed.

Participant 4: Going back to the enneagram, I think that there's one thing that we have missed here, one of the fundamental principles of the teaching, the principle of relativity. This states that everything should be considered in relation to its place on the evolutionary scale. The reason I mention this is because, according to this principle of relativity, there are different visions of the enneagram. For instance, I was looking at your enneagram, going through your book, and I don't see it the way you see it. I see it in a totally different way. And even the people who see the enneagram in the popularized version, this has a value in the evolutionary scale. So we should not conclude that the things people are doing with the enneagram have no value.

Dimitri Peretzi: Sorry, I do not understand how we have left out the principle of relativity here.

Participant 4: In the sense that there are different levels to see everything.

Dimitri Peretzi: But we did say that typology and the use of the enneagram in typology have something to say, other kind of enneagram uses have something to say, but the idea is for an alternative to exist as well. So this, I suppose from what you say, you mean it to be the principle of relativity in practice, and I think it is. I do not disagree with you.

Participant 9: I have nothing really to reject about your talk, I think it was excellent, the way you put the problem in front of our eyes. That was very good for me, it was really well presented. I do not have any solution for the problems you mentioned. The only thing I can do is talk about the way we have proceeded with these problems. We deal with the music and with the movements, and we will explain later what we have done and why we did it. When you do not know, you have to experiment. That is one thing for sure. There is no blueprint available that one can follow. So we have been confronted with exactly the same problem that you described. For the movements, I have had many discussions with one of the true experts, one who was close to Gurdjieff. I was saying, "Well look, if you are not going to respond to the need there is, many things are either going to be tremendously distorted or they are going to be lost forever. If you are not going to react, what is it that will happen?" The answer is that many things are simply going to disappear. The curtain will be drawn. That's one way things are going with the movements. The other extreme is people who are looking for kicks and try to do something with movements. But movements are made for Inner Work; they are not made for kicks. So one has to find a middle way. We are still experimenting with this, and we are still adjusting our strategy, how to deal with this problem, with the world and with media. For us the middle way is that we do not want solid institutions and we do not want to throw (such knowledge) out to the street. So for us it is very important to have personal contact. Everything we do should give the possibility that there is personal contact. In personal contact it is possible to define things in a much more precise way than just by media. This is one type of solution that we are trying to find in this middle way. But again, we do not have a definite answer yet, we are still searching, how to deal with the difficult problem that you have put so well in front of us.

Beelzebub Restores our Understanding of Teleology and Ontology - Questions & Answers

Dimitri Peretzi: I thank you very much for saying this and I thank you for bringing up something that I think is essential, that there is a need of taking a risk here. I am sure that some things will be done wrong, but on the other hand I think that without taking any risk nothing will be done.

Seminar 1 - Chapters 14 & 15 of Beelzebub's Tales to His Grandson

Facilitator: Harry Bennett

Facilitator: I have been asked to volunteer to facilitate our first seminar. I would invite anyone who has chosen to put themselves in the back to join us up front if they would like to make that extra effort. As I see it, my role is simply to remind us to be considerate of our time and everyone's needs to express themselves and I invite everyone to share something. It need be nothing more than a question that has resulted from your reading, it need not be an answer, or anything more than that, but I hope you will take what opportunity arises to participate. Some individuals have prepared more formal responses. When we have finished the seminar some of those will be available in written form on the back of the counter to be looked over. Having said that I invite anyone who would like or share an impression to begin.

Participant 1: Could I just ask one question. Why have you chosen these particular chapters? I would just like to know how the conference decided upon these particular chapters for study. Have you been working through the book from the beginning?

Facilitator: It's not been methodical since the beginning of the conference. Seminars on the *Tales* have developed over time. Initially there were not blocks of time specifically dedicated to the study of the *Tales*. Then, when we started to incorporate the *Tales*, specific chapters were chosen by the planning committee. More recently we began to work our way forward from the beginning of the book. Over the course of meetings this is where we have come to.

Participant 1: How long ago were the chapters now under discussion chosen?

Facilitator: They were chosen shortly after last year's conference.

Suggestibility

Participant 1: I have a question I would like to put out. How does anyone understand that the most terrible being-particularity of our psyche is suggestibility? Does anyone else understand why it is suggestibility vs. other particularities?

Participant 2: I am going to say something; it is not answer; just to underline the question. Once a group had organized an exhibit for people in Paris for the January 13th celebration. And this group, who were told to gather, were just doing some haphazard movements and these people

Seminar 1 - Chapters 14 & 15 of Beelzebub's Tales to His Grandson

more and more started getting together with the same rhythm in their feet and little by little the audience began to pick up the same rhythm and at one point everyone stopped and the audience didn't know what they were doing so they stopped, and it was very quiet. And then there was a voice heard that said simply, 'suggestibility.'

Participant 3: I think there is something about suggestibility which is abdicating your own reason and responsibility for thinking. It is a giving up of a power that you could have, giving it to some external authority. So you cease to exist. You become a puppet of something external to yourself. I've just thought about the word suggestibility as being open to other authorities apart from your own reason and determination.

Participant 1: Does that seem to you the most terrible of our abnormal being-particularities?

Participant 3: Because you don't exist in that condition.

Participant 1: But you don't exist in self-pride or self-love, or vanity.

Participant 4: I think in adding to what John said, it is the giving up of my will to something outside of myself and that is more had to our being than pride and vanity.

Participant 3: I think there is more of an element of myself in pride and vanity, egoism and self love. At least I am involved in that to some degree. Whereas with suggestibility I am quite absent. I am an instrument of external forces. I think it is lower than these other things.

Participant 5: Maybe suggestibility has to be there to have self-pride and vanity? Maybe suggestibility is the platform on which the other rests.

Participant 1: Is that your experience or is that a working theory?

Participant 5: Well I am thinking about my own egoism I have to be suggested to see myself a certain way. So I am suggesting it to myself I can't be blown up in my egoism unless I am suggestible to that.

Participant 6: I think that this is half of the consequences of Kundabuffer. He talks about Kundabuffer and says it causes us to see everything upside down and to accept everything that is repeated as true. So there is an easiness to believe in everything repeated. It is the root of all...

Participant 7: But maybe the statement is not meant to be taken as literally true. Perhaps it is meant to stimulate us to ask what suggestibility is and do we then, quite suggestively, take it as true and rationalize why it's the worst? I am stumped. I am not convinced that it is the worst but it raises the question.

Facilitator: Following Sophia's lead I'm going to suggest that if you have something you would like to say that you raise your hand up so that I know you're not being passed by as other people choose to jump in.

Participant 8: Because this chapter is all about time and the catastrophe that time has brought into our world I think that suggestibility, seen within the context of the chapters, means; that which is passively receptive to change. So it is a question of being changed and, as John said, it is at the abdication of reason. These chapters look at the difference between reason, which belongs to the Sun Absolute, and what happens when time is being pushed out of the Sun Absolute and then, how does that upset things and get set off in a chain of events. Suggestibility is another kind of disaster, not like the comet but a small personal disaster, in which you have no direct cause and effect, no perception of what will follow. You don't understand really the context of where you are. You just accept, and change just moves you along the devolutionary time frame. So I see it within the context of the chapters.

Participant 9: I hadn't considered it at the time that I read it but it seems to me that the chapter about Samlios, King Appolis and what happens to the town folk follows on from the idea that suggestibility is one of the worst conditions because that was the condition of King Appolis in acceding to the suggestion of the young kinsman. The result was absolutely terrible. The destruction of the city administration and the effects on the tribe.

Participant 10: I thought about forms of advertising this morning in connection with suggestibility and later I thought that Mr. Gurdjieff said that, "if you have not a critical nature there is no use your being here" as a critique of suggestibility.

Participant 11: This follows on in my mind to a kind of tribal or group instinct. I never forget the first time that I took my son to a nearby bus stop in his school uniform with his bag slung over his shoulder waiting for the school bus to arrive. I was amazed to see that boys had already turned up who were used to using the school bus and that they all had slung their satchels onto the ground. My son did exactly the same with his. So, what they did, he did. So it's something that could have to do with belonging; with being a part of a group. It also happens in the animal kingdom where an animal will eat a banana or something with the skin still on it and then one will peel it and then the behavior will spread. So it occurs to me that this can be the source of terrible things such as mass destruction and so on but it can also be used to improve the situation if it's not too late. So it can be used for good.

Participant 12: I am not clear on the difference between credulity and suggestibility.

Participant 1: We have a dictionary here.

Participant 3: I notice that not everyone can hear what is being said. We do have a problem with this pillar so I would ask everyone to speak up a bit louder. To follow on from the question; credulity has to do with belief systems and what we believe, in an abstract way, about the structure

Seminar 1 - Chapters 14 & 15 of Beelzebub's Tales to His Grandson

of the universe. Suggestibility is more about behavior in the way we have been discussing. Credulity is more a mental thing, an abstraction; I believe this in my mind. Whereas suggestibility works more on a person through their moving or emotional center. Everybody is doing this, so I do this. Everybody feels this way, so I feel this way. To my understanding, which may be wrong, I think credulity has to do with believing. So its more concerned with reason, Suggestibility is more concerned with feelings and behavior.

Facilitator: Do you want to follow on that comment or are you going in another direction?

Participant 13: No. I was just going to say that the word itself I am puzzled by because we use these words in everyday life. Now I really want to know what it means. It seems to me that it means to suggest that something external or internal is suggesting something to me and it needn't be external to me. It could be my ordinary inner thoughts or feelings or whatever it is. It suggests that I do something which may be opposed to my interest. So now I am not sure what suggestibility means.

Participant 14: I see it as being Chameleon like or people pleasing; being concerned with what people are saying.

Suggestibility and Hypnosis

Participant 1: I was just wondering - I was going to ask Keith if you think it has anything to do with hypnotism?

Participant 2: Why ask me?

Participant 3: There is a nice quote in this book by Med Thring on suggestibility. I'm not sure where the quote is from, "I must discover at all costs some manner or means for destroying in people the predilection for suggestibility which causes them to fall easily under the influence of mass hypnosis." So that's the danger really isn't it?

Participant 4: It's just good to mention about hypnosis that that seems to be a very important consideration in suggestibility; the degree to which I may be hypnotized by any particular situation. If I go into a situation where there are other people around then the mere presence of other people can be a hypnotic influence or effect, in which case I am more prone to suggestibility. So the hypnosis part of it seems to me to be a key element in suggestibility as it's just been mentioned.

Participant 5: Credibility, just an academic point, comes from the Greek Credos: Truth. So, credibility and suggestibility almost can be looked at as two opposite points of a spectrum.

Participant 6: I'm not sure that hypnosis is emotional. If suggestibility is emotional then I'm not sure hypnosis is. But I'm pretty sure that suggestibility must have something to do with hypnosis.

Participant 7: I think in this chapter suggestibility has to do with the chapter before, the previous chapter. It says, "Why in Man's Reason Fantasy May Be Perceived as Reality." He is connecting here this chapter with the other. He says: "in general any new understanding is crystallized in the presence of this being only if Smith speaks of somebody or something in a certain way and then if Brown says the same the hearer is quite convinced it's just so and couldn't be otherwise." This is what happens to us. If my mother tells me I'm useless, I begin to believe it. Then if my father tells me the same I believe it even more. This is what happens every day to us. We are suggested to; this is this, this is so, but it is not our own way of thinking and we believe it.

Participant 8: There is the whole matter or question of maturation, of developing from the desires and suggestible state of the child who does what his or her parents tell them to.

Participant 7: Yes, this is exactly what I'm saying. We have been told that war is good by some people, now what happens; people believe it. And now we are fighting each other. So you have to think for yourself for you. The center of gravity must be in the thinking brain not in the emotional or moving brain because it's only then that we become an individuality; an individual. The center of presence is in the feeling brain but the center of gravity must be in the thinking brain and that makes us individuals.

Participant 8: I'm glad you mentioned the subject of war, which is in the previous paragraph, and in fact he calls it the chief particularity, even in a sense more significant than all of these others, including suggestibility. In taking this example you mentioned from real life, I don't want to take us off on a discussion of the Iraq war, but I've been reading this book for a long time and throughout the book there is a huge theme on the stupidity of the reciprocal destruction of each other's existence and yet I have been trying to observe what's going on in myself. I always thought of myself as a pacifist, yet I've had a certain kind of emotion that this guy running Iraq has to be taken out; killed! And I've noticed here in England that at the beginning the population was against this whole thing and now it's changed around. So what is going on here? I don't know what's going on even in myself. You talk about thinking independently and I consider myself an independent thinker and yet I wonder if I am being manipulated?

Participant 7: You are, we are. Because it's too much weight.

Participant 9: It seems to me that the underpinning to why suggestibility is such a terror is that it is not a three-brained activity. It never is. That's the vulnerability. It can be the first brain or the second brain or the third brain or the second and third without the first. It can be any combination but if it is not three-brained we are suggestible. We are open, vulnerable to whatever is out there and it will come out as a warped, topsy-turvy reality. And that is real for us in that moment. But it's not three-brained. And that's why it is the worst of the dilemmas or vulnerabilities because it leaves us nowhere. We don't have a catch point for reality. So as long as we are suggestible we are vulnerable to whatever it is, first brain input, second brain, third brain; it makes no difference. That is why this chapter for me is the "beginnings of perspectives." It is interesting, what perspectives does he present in this chapter? You can list them off: Atlantis, Kundabuffer,

Seminar 1 - Chapters 14 & 15 of Beelzebub's Tales to His Grandson

unbecoming behaviors, suggestibility. What is the whole of the *Tales* about? This is a 'DO'. This chapter, as short as it is, is a 'DO'. If the six descents are one way of seeing the play out of that octave, it is the play out of this little octave here. He sets the DO and in the inner vibrations of those things he brings up is the whole rest of what he is going to unfold in the chapters that follow. The beginnings of perspectives; beginnings; DO. Maybe.

Participant 10: This is just a general point. There is such a lot of story in these two chapters. It's just a huge amount of content in them. As we are here specifically to look at the actual text itself I'm really wondering about extrapolating one word and then spending three quarters of an hour on a discussion about that which could be done between us at any other time. I don't know how people perceive the function of studying the book but I think that it is a chance to really explore the text itself. Of what it means within this particular bit as in fact Keith has been saying. If I stop to talk about suggestibility in myself and my own understanding of the war or something then we are right off track according to my way of thinking. That's all. I mean, I'm willing to hear other people's views of it. I mean, if it just turns into a general kind of internal, "this is my thinking and how I understand it" then I think we miss a really good opportunity for looking at what we've got.

Participant 11: Well I'm going to say one thing before changing the direction towards what Sophia wants to do. We use the term collusion in our group. And if you take the two words apart you get collective illusion. And that is going on all day. It is going on in every group. There is a collective illusion. If you see somebody else, if you were first alone and then somebody comes in there starts a collective illusion and it is a sort of third force that dictates your behavior, you have to react. And how does it matter because all the behavior you do, no matter what you are was there before you were born and will be there after you die. And nothing is yours. It doesn't matter from which class of the population you come, whether you are an academic or whatever. There are collusion's going on all over the place, all over the world. So I think what Sy says is a really good point. You have to observe it in yourself and one day you think, well this man must be taken out of power and another day you think maybe not. I wrote a piece about violence a couple of weeks ago when I was looking that evening at a program on the television about General Custer and what he did at the Little Big Horn with the Indians. And I was here on my stool when they chopped him to pieces and I thought it was wonderful that they did that.

Facilitator: Chris, you said you had something to say?

Participant 12: I said I would support Sophia by what I have to say. What I find structurally interesting in this first group of two chapters is the fact that it is really talking about the change in presence that was necessary and it all seems to me to be around that. These new properties that have appeared and of course in every one of these chapters there's many, many points, so it's difficult to fix on one, but that seems to me pretty central. And, in the next chapter you get this beautiful story of how this change of properties is to be seen with these people who won't pay. But what I find especially interesting is that this young guy from Beelzebub's tribe is characterized as young and inexperienced, naive twice, a simpleton. But he is also said by King Appolis to have a higher reason than him. Now this is very interesting because if you consider the story of the stupid saint it has a certain kind of being quality that this kinsman of Beelzebub has and that isn't enough. You also have to have these properties that King Appolis has. It's called the Arch-cunning. The kind of archetype of the sly man who will find his way through and I really think its very striking that this higher-reason-being finishes up as a bailiff which actually tells you what reason divorced from practicality does for you. It's a kind of incomplete manifestation.

And just about suggestibility, which I don't think we should go back to, but there is one actual suggestion which we all share which is extremely dangerous and that is that we are immortal and going to live forever and that it doesn't matter. Now you may say that you know the opposite but we live, most of the time, as if that were not a suggestion and I think it is a fundamental suggestion of our ... It is addressed in the last sentence of the book' So that's trying to see a kind of structural overview and its not the only one. Sophia mentioned time and linked suggestibility to time.

Facilitator: So is there anyone else, other than myself who would like to say anything else about suggestibility before we move on?

Participant 13: The source, where it comes from, the people we respect are more likely to have an influence on us even when they are wrong. If somebody tells you the truth and you don't respect them you will have a tendency to not accept the truth. If it's a close friend you tend to accept it much easier and be less critical. That's a very dangerous relation. You shouldn't trust or respect anybody.

Facilitator: What I wanted to mention was that what came up for me in the chapter Will had gone back to just previously, and when Toddy first raised the question; the answer for me as to what makes it the worst is that it is described as the one we are responsible for. He separates it from Kundabuffer and claims that it is the result of unbecoming behaviors on our part and that seems to put it into a different category. So is there anyone who...

Participant 14: In terms of a comment on suggestibility... a kind of brief overview of the planet, it seems that suggestibility is the one thing that runs most people's lives most of the time. All the factors that predominate in all daily lives and daily functioning are based on suggestibility and are the dominant factors for just that reason.

Participant 15: Beelzebub promises to explain suggestibility later in his writing and it is possible that he does so in the "Terror of the Situation" in which he says they will be believe any old tale and he leaves until the Ashiata Shiemash chapters to explain it... the terror of the situation.

(Long pause...)

Participant 16: It must be pertinent because the whole television industry runs on it.

The First Descent

Seminar 1 - Chapters 14 & 15 of Beelzebub's Tales to His Grandson

Facilitator: Following on Chris' comment I would be interested in hearing from anyone the degree to which they might see more specifically what characterizes the mistake of the young kinsman? I have thought that it was because he believed that he was right.

Participant 1: I find there is a kind of similarity on the reason why Beelzebub was exiled which was that he interfered with something that was none of his business and what his fellow kinsman did. And this could be even based on suggestibility, I just found out. I don't know what the connection is, but it is.

Participant 2: This is a kind of preliminary thing but this is the first time in the book that the business of a being of our tribe is mentioned and we talk about kinsman here. How do we understand that? And what is Beelzebub's tribe? Perhaps we need to come to some understanding of that before we can understand what is happening in this chapter.

Participant 3: An hour and a half ago Wim told me a very interesting story. Is he here? He said he took a contract to give movements to some executives of some very high company in Holland. So he was faced, all of a sudden with having fifty people that were all executives, very highly opinionated people and very strong etc., and they were all in suits and there was no way he could get them to focus. So he had to stand up on the piano and started shouting "You are shit!" That started to get their attention. Then he gave them an exercise to prove that they were just pieces of meat with a little bit of imagination and they started doing the exercise, and it was proven. But in a hundred and people there was a number of them that could be seen as pockets of understanding in a crowd that was behaving in a silly way. And they got involved with the movement itself, you know they could get up and hook up with the movement and see what it was telling them rather than disseminating energy left and right. I think that these people... I had the feeling as he was telling this story, that they belong to a clan. This is the sense of clan I have related to these stories.

Participant 4: Are we a tribe?

Participant 3: We have to do movements together. (laughter)

Participant 5: In relation to Beelzebub's tribe as it were, the way I would take that, the only thing that came up was beings who aren't under the influence of Kundabuffer for the sake of this story that's what beings of this tribe represent.

Participant 6: Once again there are so many strands that it's always ambiguous to pick out one, and anytime we do this we are limiting, but I'll pick up on this strand. It is really interesting to look at the way Beelzebub's tribe fixed the problem. How they went about it. It reminds me enormously of the way we try to address problems in the Work in the community that I belong to. And that is that if one person does something wrong or makes a mistake everybody is responsible. It is a principle of a real group that take it that there is nobody who is opted out because they made a mistake. So the whole body takes on the burden imposed upon the tribe by that single naive young... and they are willing to take the positions in which they are at risk... in this revolution that is going to come. And the fact that looking at all the facts and deliberating in this way and then unanimously going... I mean to me that is a kind of little icon that Mr. Gurdjieff has given us of the way that serious, mature, inner, tribal coherence operates. I think it's a beautiful model.

Participant 7: I find this image that you just gave very powerful and very strong and it has given me much thought. Just one small question. Couldn't there be this kind of thing referred to earlier? This kind of collective illusion, like collective suggestibility, in cases like this. That's my question. I don't want to...

Participant 6: No, I agree with you and we are often saying to one another "Ah yes, collective hypnosis." Absolutely. Consensual hypnosis, of course.

Participant 8: But I think that the fact that you know, don't you, that the voluntary undertaking and obligation, especially when signed with blood, means to one of our tribe, I think the fact that its blood means that if it is suggestibility it is on a little bit different level. I agree that that's the height of normality. And another thing that really struck me was an indication of how things could be. It really struck me that even though... part of the whole tribe and they decided then and there to elect a small, little governing committee to solve the problem. Beelzebub was not a part of that. I think that is very interesting. He demonstrated to the kinsmen that you could have higher reason but that you're not going to do everything. I think that is a real and direct indication of how things could be.

Participant 9: Related to the same point that was just raised, I was going to raise as a question, Why Beelzebub does not play a more active role in this? He comes down from Mars but then it is the elders of the tribe who stay up all night and come up with the solution. That raises for me more of a question because it contrasts to the other descents. We see how Beelzebub's involvement changes. There is also something here to give a good deal of thought to. He seems almost the passive overseer. Very, very different from the second descent where he goes after Abdil with tongs and this is a very different level of involvement. I think this should raise some questions for us. What is going on here relative to the role of Beelzebub in each of the descents?

Participant 10: Well it's obvious to me that the young kinsmen is naive. To me that means he doesn't have data. To me this like a child who before the age of reason has will, wants to do things but doesn't have the right data to get along in the world, needs to be protected and given instructions from somewhere else. So the kinsman has fine qualities, has high reason.

Participant 11: I agree, and this also goes back to what was said earlier regarding the parallel with Beelzebub himself and his exile. He points out his high reason but is lacking experience. That he became a very good bailiff seems to me to be the result of this experience and the humility he suffered as a result of the errors and having to go back to Mars and admit the failure that he brought on himself and the whole of his tribe. An extraordinary error and problem he had created for King Appolis which he is now powerless to correct. A bailiff is one who is put under the authority of a higher power in court to carry out the decisions made in the court. So he in fact

Seminar 1 - Chapters 14 & 15 of Beelzebub's Tales to His Grandson

becomes a trainee. To conclude that thought, there is clearly a parallel here with Beelzebub himself and his exile.

Participant 12: Historically one of the main actions of the bailiff was to exercise court orders and, judgments for money. So the kinsman, who initially told King Appolis I know how to collect money without using…

Participant 13: So your saying that now he is doing just that only now in a system?

Participant 14: Yeah, he initially said you don't need to use this cunning and threats to get money, then fails, but later actually becomes quite good at operating that very same way. Possibly it's because of his experience. He now understands something about the system and how it works. Or it could just be literary irony, I'm not sure.

Participant 15: I just want to say that I had a talk to Paul Taylor, for those of you who know him, because I did some studying myself and sent him the notes. I was talking about types of story. This story about king Appolis is a wager story. There's a whole set of stories about wagers and bets. Another word for them is hazards from which danger results and the function of these stories is to look at cause and effect. So it's not the idea of time. It's about: how do things work. If I do this, then what will happen? Wagers are about trying to guess what happens. And in all wager stories what you find out is that you can not guess what will happen. Once you set something off in time you can not control it anymore. So I said; well give me another story about wagers and he said "try the Book of Job". So I did. Gurdjieff's story you could see as an inversion of the Book of Job. Because the Book of Job is a kind of bet between Satan and God about how Job will behave. Satan says; "Of course Job loves you because you have never done anything bad to him and God says, "No, however badly I behave towards him he will continue to love me." And so they have this kind of wager. And it is reversed because Satan tries to shift Job, visiting all the terrible plagues and boils and the death of his family. I think its worth looking at what types of story are being told and what are the traditions of that type of story because it helps to open it out instead of just thinking about the story in Work terms and expressing something that Gurdjieff has taught in another form. Why did he put it in this form? It connects with all the other hazard stories, it's a tremendous enrichment.

Another one is the Atlantis story. The Atlantis story is a big catastrophe story and it's at the very beginning of our culture. Plato is the first written introduction of it. It's the very beginnings, as the chapter says, of views which don't promise anything. It's the beginning of views of how catastrophic our world in time is and how one catastrophe follows another. That's what Plato says in the Timaeus, that it's one catastrophe after another, and you see that in the *Tales* and it's echoed in the Bible.

Once time has been created in the Bible, because Adam and Eve come out, then catastrophe follows catastrophe. Not even because of badness or wrong but simply because time brings catastrophe, because time brings decay and death. So I'm lecturing now. I'm sorry. I apologize.

But I just think that the clues are in the text so you look at Atlantis and you could think about the story of Atlantis and what it's done in our culture and what it means. What was it about? And then that will give a clue to what Gurdjieff is talking about. To try to get the clue to what Gurdjieff is about by always referring to something else that he said, in those terms, seems to me incredibly limited.

Ah..., I'm sorry if I'm lecturing but I really do care about this. I would so much like to see more preparation for these seminars instead of having everybody together. It's so difficult to talk about something as complex as this with absolutely no guidelines. We can't cover everything. It's just not practical. It just means that people are worrying away about what they might say. I just think that some slight structure to what we are going to look at might be more effective. But then I am an organizing, bossy person. (laughter)

Participant 16: Thank you for sharing that. (laughter)

Participant 17: It's no longer accurate.

Facilitator: What was that?

Participant 16: It's no longer accurate. He (the young kinsman) has gone on to a higher level for another career. He is no longer the organizer on the Earth because he's gone back to Mars. So his ruling that he first disagreed of; with the King, he becomes wiser through experience and is no longer on our level. He is going through to another scale. That is what I wanted to say.

Participant 19: I am looking at the introduction. "I wish for you specific benefits for your own being." And I'm reading the story and King Appolis has this problem where his rebellious countrymen were taking away money. He is guided by beings. The power possessors of King Appolis' government won't relinquish their power. So these advisor people feed in intelligent men, in our case it would be deputy steward, into the system gradually to replace the egoistic power possessor members of the government. And this subtle, sly infiltration of power restores order. I look on the story as the first line of Work. As to how can it benefit me specifically? I could have a rebellious countryman who is draining my energy... and I have to feed into my organization some intelligent structure because I have 'I's in me that won't surrender. So I have to do it. Sort of...

Participant 20: I just wanted to comment that the story doesn't end there though. Everything goes back to the way it was and so your spinning out does not leave us in a very positive circumstance if when all of this sacrifice has been made by the 'wiser men taking the place of and exposing themselves to all this danger but then they all disappear and the cronies reappear and at the end of the story we have the reestablishment of the government as it was before. There is something very, very, important about that.

Facilitator: What?

Seminar 1 - Chapters 14 & 15 of Beelzebub's Tales to His Grandson

Participant 20: Some things we can do and some things we can't do.

Participant 3: This is where my thought led me. Exactly what Keith says. The minute I realized that what the text is doing is creating (singles from doubles?) and the question is, why is that so? This is what we are left with after the story. That we how we hate them and we don't hate them because they are bad or devils or anything like that...

Participant 20: Who? Where did the devils come from?

Participant 3: Beelzebub's. The people who have tails and hooves.

Participant 6: I think you've been subject to suggestibility.

Participant 3: All I'm saying is that he is talking about a tribe that has hooves and tails and that they take the blame for something they are not entirely responsible for.

Participant 21: I disagree that things were as they were after the governors were replaced because presumably the land had been affected by the placement of these people presumably something has happened.

Participant 20: The whole story is about the consequences of Kundabuffer, it seems to me. The whole question comes in where because King Appolis can't tell who is under the crystallized consequences and the ones who are will cheat and not meet their responsibilities as he says there are "some who are not responsible." For me that's the nexus of the difficulty because King Appolis can't tell who, so he therefore threatens everybody and imposes this and there has to be that re-imposition of the same way of keeping the government going at the end.

Participant 21: But all those governors who are in power stay in power and take the heat why do they have to leave?

Participant 20: That's explained in the book. He had to deflect blame. That's what the tribal people were willing to accept. They were willing to accept the blame and take the risk because their kinsman had committed them to the circumstance and that was the only way out.

Participant 21: I understood all that and read the chapter but I don't understand why those governors that had been there couldn't take the heat. Couldn't stay and dissipate the heat.

Participant 22: It wasn't their responsibility they didn't create the circumstance. I don't know if King Appolis would have let them because it wasn't their responsibility. It was King Appolis' responsibility and they would have been slaughtered.

Participant 21: He comes back and he is scot-free.

All & Everything Conference 2003

Participant 20: He's still got to run the government and that's not scot-free.

Participant 23: I want to say something. It is an interesting theme that higher beings make mistakes. In the text with the moon and so on. Perhaps this is against our suggestibility that we do not believe sacred individuals make mistakes. I find this a very strange thing, that the higher beings make mistakes. I can not sustain it. Ok, thank you.

Participant 20: Higher Beings make bigger mistakes!

Participant 3: Higher risks!

End of Session

Brief Notes for All & Everything Conference Seminar on Chapter 14, 'The Beginnings of Perspectives Promising Nothing Very Cheerful' looked at in relation to story-telling

Looking at the tradition or traditions of stories within which Gurdjieff has decided to frame his narrative enables us, as readers, to place the text outside the confines of his own teaching theory, and read it in relation to the wider context of its own cultural, mythological, scriptural and philosophical origins.

Gurdjieff uses the word beginnings in his title and so we might expect to find some references to origins or beginnings. In terms of myth those which explain/explore the beginnings and origins of, for example, creation, the moon, of man, of the beginnings of agriculture are termed aetiological myths. (from aetiology - the science or philosophy of origins and causes)

The word perspectives can mean either an optical instrument microscope or telescope, or a view as in vista, or a representation of the view, so a means of viewing or a view. Put together this suggests the origins of views which in 'promising nothing very cheerful', we could understand as 'unpromising views', maybe pessimistic views.

Gurdjieff does start this brief chapter with a direct mention of Atlantis. This myth has its written origin in Plato's *Timaeus* and has retained a place in story-telling ever since. It is an early story which has itself been the origin of pessimistic views about humanity, civilizations, catastrophic destruction and uncertain futures, brought about by human as well as natural causes.
Concerning the loss of Atlantis, which is what Beelzebub mentions here, its sinking into the sea is likely to be read by a Gurdjieff reader as a reference to his notion that human conscience has sunk into the subconscious. Especially as the sea is often a symbol for the inner deep. But a wider look at the Atlantis myth, as an idealised 'higher' civilization which fell due to natural catastrophe, shows it to be within the pattern for other Falls presented in the *Tales*. The first disaster came about due to the comet Kondoor's collision with earth, this it self was a cause, which led to the creation of the Moon and Anulios, and to the changes Beelzebub mentions here in the life span

Seminar 1 - Chapters 14 & 15 of Beelzebub's Tales to His Grandson

and quality of vibrations of earth beings. Later in the *Tales*, Beelzebub will return to the Fall of other great centres of culture, in the past Babylon, in the future Paris.

The notions of recurring catastrophes come down through Western European culture from Babylonian astrological thinking of around the third century BC and reflects their ideas about time. They understood that the universe would come to an end recurringly. One end would be by flood, being the result of a line up of planets in the sign of Capricorn, and one end by fire being the result of a line up of planets in the sign of Cancer (these are the solstices, winter and summer).

The flood story is an excellent one to point out how a story can be interpreted to indicate a change of thinking. In the Biblical Fall, Adam and Eve's loss of grace and expulsion is the cause and origin of time (mirrored in the *Tales* by the expulsion of time from the Sun Absolute which resulted in the created universe). The Biblical flood myth ends in God's covenant with Noah that he will never again send a flood. A Christian Interpretation of the story might see this as a challenge to the Babylonian cyclical thinking about time, when there will be flood after flood, and that is how it has often been presented by theologians. However, Hebrew thinking about time was as much cyclical as was the Babylonian, and in fact the Bible records catastrophe after catastrophe: Fall, Deluge, Egyptian captivity, division of Israel into Israel and Judah, conquest by Assyria and Babylon. Gurdjieff's catastrophes, Atlantis included, belong to the Babylonian tradition of thinking about time in relation to cycles and echo Biblical catastrophes.

The notion of the end of time belongs to Millenarianism, in which rather than established ritual adjustments to the cycles of time there is a large scale apocalyptic crisis, brought about by revolt against the established order. After divine intervention, unjust enemies are vanquished; time comes to an end, its slavery replaced by the freedom of eternity. Millenarianism has its own sets of stories (see the Biblical Books of Daniel and Revelation, and early Christianity). The hope of a revolution which will destroy corrupt order and establish a new and better one, has taken many forms including that of Marxist theory.

Revolts and revolutions are interventions to disrupt the cyclical flow of time, both sets of thinking could and did overlap, and both are present in the *Tales* which tells stories of revolt, stresses the remembrance of mortality, our 'end' and expresses a recurring but downward spiral and which seems to suggest a final end. In generalized terms, we could understand the adjustments made to accommodate seasons and other natural cycles as an acceptance of time while Millenarian revolt is rejection of time.

Beelzebub tells Hassein of the cause or origin of changes, that is of temporal events. All the causes of change in the being's presences occurred after the sinking of Atlantis. The changes they made themselves were the cause of further changes made by Great Nature. These changes explain the origins of men on all land masses. This reference to Great Nature suggests the Earth as Mother, determined to feed her children the Moon and Anulios, and connects with stories of the Earth as our Mother, from whom we come, our origin.

Then Beelzebub explains the causes, heredity, conception and other factors which mean that the being's exteriors are all alike. He explains that the differences in colour of skin and formation of hair are caused by the place of birth and upbringing. Again these are themes of origins, how we came to be similar and how different.

The question of war and why it exists is another source of stories; here the cause of the capacity for war is due to a fundamental trait of the general psyche which remains undefined. This occurs along with egoism, self-love and other abnormal functions of the psyches, the most terrible being their 'suggestibility' i.e. passive changeability, being subject to time, to being changed.

Beelzebub starts with the large cosmic disaster caused by the comet and goes on to outline a series of resulting disasters for the planet earth, humanity as a whole, and for the psyches of Individual beings. He ends this chapter by giving the causes of the *Tales*. These are the interest Hassein has shown in earth beings and also the need to 'pass time'. Beelzebub will explain the strange psyche of men via the tales of his six descents, each of which itself had different causes.

There are other kinds of aetiological myths but they are not represented here. The origins of the perspectives within which these tales will be told are myths of catastrophe and multiple Fall, and thus we should not expect anything 'very cheerful' to result. As readers we have already learned how time came to be created. In the subsequent chapters we will learn that time itself causes change, decay, and death. In summation this chapter tells us not to hope, that our prospects are bleak, are as he says 'nothing very cheerful'.

The Turkic oral tradition within which Gurdjieff grew up meant that he had at his disposal a fund of stories commonly known. When a story was told about an event or person, all the 'family' of related facts would also be known, much as when a story is told about someone in our own family, we can understand it in a way that a stranger could not.

As Gurdjieff readers we may already feel part of an exclusive family in that we have some knowledge of his teaching ideas and can recognise expressions of them in the *Tales*, but Gurdjieff drew on our common Western European family of stories and ideas, among them, Babylonian myth, Biblical stories, Greek myth, and Plato's writings. If we can not recognise the references he makes to these origins we shall miss a great deal of the material that is offered to us.

After he read these notes, Malcolm Mitchell sent me some comments which amplify what it is we should be missing and I have included these below:

> If' we cannot recognise the references Gurdjieff makes to these origins we shall miss a great deal of the material that is offered and mistake wider originality, or 'genius', as exclusive to Gurdjieff himself. Reading his material thus blinkeredly, we may well exacerbate fixations on Gurdjieff's own personality and history/mythology, in unconscious acceptance and reinforcement of a new 'Gurdjieffian' tradition - whereas Gurdjieff himself can be seen as consciously *re-presenting* traditional materials to us. He gives this

Seminar 1 - Chapters 14 & 15 of Beelzebub's Tales to His Grandson

'representation' with the ultimate suggestion (clarified implicitly in the final chapter of the *Tales*) to be ourselves 'master' rather than 'slave' of the material within such traditions - Gurdjieff's own included.

Gurdjieff offers tools and materials to use to free ourselves, to grow, to clear out the old to make room for something new, something real. Such specialist tools and materials can inevitably, to some degree, be used for purposes other than those intended for them - as perhaps to build ivory towers or fashion emperor's clothes. Such dangers are naturally part of the price, or 'hazard', of their great essential potential. To appreciate this as a functional dynamic, we must not forget but always try see afresh what Beelzebub/*The Tales* is intended to destroy: and in seeing the workings of this in our own psyche, grasp a key factor in why Beelzebub is thus 'The Devil' to us.

References

For information about ancient astrology I am indebted to:

Campion, Nicholas, *The Great Year, Astrology, Millenarianism and History in the Western Tradition*, London: Arkana, 1994

This is 'an examination of the mythical roots of a series of ideas and beliefs about the nature of time and its relationship to history' (Campion, p. 4)

I recommend the following edition of the *Timaeus*, which has an introduction and appendix on Atlantis by Desmond Lee, who also did the translation:

Plato, *The Timaeus and Critias*, London: Penguin Classics, 1977.

Malcolm Mitchell is the author of *The Hog's Wholey Wash: A Completely Allegorical Manual on Consciousness and Cosmos*, London & Bath, Ashgrove, 2002.

© Copyright 2003 - Sophia Wellbeloved - All Rights Reserved

Towards a Historical Study of Gurdjieff and His Legacy

Joseph Azize

This paper is part of a larger course of enquiry. That investigation deals with the following questions: What were Gurdjieff's chief ideas and practices? How have those in Gurdjieff's tradition, whether his pupils or not, used his ideas and practices? How can a historian place Gurdjieff and his tradition in history? There is an extent to which these questions are inter-related. Any attempt to identify Gurdjieff's ideas must depend upon a critical evaluation of the source materials, and equally, these must be scrutinized in the light of what is established about Gurdjieff's teachings. However, in this paper I deal with two questions only: (1) Is there a reliable starting point for elucidating Gurdjieff's ideas? (2) What place does P. D. Ouspensky hold in the Gurdjieff tradition?

1. Is There a Reliable Starting Point for Elucidating Gurdjieff's Ideas?

What would be a sound starting point for the historian studying Gurdjieff? While Gurdjieff often wrote in ways which would deliberately baffle the reader, I contend that he intended this particular passage from the chapter "My Father" in *Meetings with Remarkable Men* to be read as a sincere, forthright expression of his aspirations and ideas:

> Owing to circumstances of my life not dependent on me, I have not personally seen the grave where the body of my dear father lies, and it is unlikely that I will ever be able, in the future, to visit his grave. I therefore, in concluding this chapter devoted to my father, bid any of my sons, whether by blood or in spirit, to seek out, when he has the possibility, this solitary grave, abandoned by force of circumstances ensuing chiefly from that human scourge called the herd instinct, and there to set up a stone with the inscription:

I AM THOU,
THOU ART I,
HE IS OURS,
WE BOTH ARE HIS.
SO MAY ALL BE
FOR OUR NEIGHBOUR.[1]

---

[1] Gurdjieff (1985) 48-49

To understand why this passage (I shall refer to it as "the epitaph passage") may be taken as a firm point of departure for Gurdjieff studies, one must have an idea of its context. Gurdjieff goes on to say of his father that he was wounded by Turks while protecting his family homestead. He died soon after, and was buried by some old men.[2] Gurdjieff adds that his father's "most fitting memorial" would have been "the texts of the various legends and songs he had written or dictated", but that these have been lost.[3] He then finishes a sketch of his father's individuality, using certain of his father's sayings, and some details of his way of life.[4] Gurdjieff closes the chapter by saying that: "I, for my part, can only say now that with my whole being I would desire to be able to be such as I knew him to be in his old age."[5]

The credibility of the epitaph passage as a sound platform for reconstructing Gurdjieff's ideas rests upon a number of factors, which operate together. First, it is in memory of his father, and we may safely conclude that Gurdjieff loved and respected him. We can be sure of this because we have the testimony of Ouspensky, the only person we know to have seen Gurdjieff and his father together, and leave us a report.[6] For reasons I furnish in the next part, I contend that although Ouspensky's testimony concerning Gurdjieff must be used with care, he is reliable where he provides details which are favourable to Gurdjieff. This vignette is also consistent with the respectful and feeling tone of Gurdjieff's chapter 'My Father" as a whole.

The last piece of corroborating evidence for this passage hails from Olga de Hartmann, who wrote that a certain point of their departure from Russia, they were joined by various members of Gurdjieff's family. However:

> His father did not come. He wished to stay at his home in Alexandropol, where he was, unfortunately, killed later by the Turks on the porch of his house.[7]

This confirms that the direct context given by Gurdjieff for the epitaph passage is literally true, and supports the view that Gurdjieff's epitaph for his father is sincerely meant. If the epitaph passage is a sure point of departure for studying Gurdjieff's ideas, one can then take as fairly equally authentic and reliable, statements similar in content and tone. For example, when in the material published under the title *Life is Real Only Then, When "I Am"*, Gurdjieff speaks of "introducing into practice into the life of people the beneficial truths elucidated for them by me..."[8] This relates to ideas later in that chapter where Gurdjieff describes the aims of his inner world as being:

---

[2] Gurdjieff (1985) 45
[3] Gurdjieff (1985) 45-46
[4] Gurdjieff (1985) 46-48
[5] Gurdjieff (1985) 48
[6] Ouspensky (1949) 340 and 342
[7] De Hartmann (1992) 43. At p. x, Thomas C. Daly states that the material printed in italics (and the passage quoted is italicised in the original) is by Olga de Hartmann.
[8] Gurdjieff (1999) 4

> ...to investigate from all sides, and to understand, the exact significance and purpose of the life of man ... (and to) discover, at all costs, some manner or means for destroying in people the predilection for suggestibility which causes them to fall easily under the influence of 'mass hypnosis'.[9]

The connection between this and the Epitaph passage is apparent in its reference to the condition which makes war possible, called "mass hypnosis" and "herd instinct" respectively. We can take it, then, that Gurdjieff was genuinely distressed by the susceptibility of people to follow others, even into war, and that he set himself a task of trying to finding some means of lessening human suggestibility. The anti-war statements in Beelzebub, particularly in chapter 43, "Beelzebub's Opinion of War" can also be taken as authentic expressions of Gurdjieff's feelings, for example:

> ... this particularity of theirs, namely their predisposition to periodic reciprocal destruction is such an unimaginable horror that such a hideousness that no name can even be found for it.[10]

In respect of Gurdjieff's feelings of humanity, note that in *Life is Real*, he states that - as part of a specific regime - he would provide his body the food it needed, and:

> ... after satisfying myself and during digestion, to stimulate within myself for not less than fifteen minutes the feeling of pity, thinking of other people who had no means of having such food.[11]

One of the other ideas we discerned in the Epitaph passage was that of unity. I am not suggesting that Gurdjieff created a monolithic doctrine. Gurdjieff's ideas and practices follow principles, but they do not lead to a closed system It is possible, I would suggest, working from these passages above, and from the autobiographical material in the "Prologue" of *Life is Real*, to arrive at this: Gurdjieff's fundamental principles are mystical: the unity of all existence, and its complement, the diversity of all existence. He also brought ideas and practices which facilitate the experiential understanding of both the oneness and the fragmentation of existence. Gurdjieff's ideas and practices do not lead to a closed system. He is placed directly in the mystical tradition, and thus differentiated from the "esoteric' or "occult" worlds. A study of Gurdjieff in fact illuminates the mystical traditions known to us, and brings them within reach of our daily lives. In the spirit of the epitaph to his father, he devoted his life to realizing his aims.

At the end of the day, if I were to choose one word to describe him, I would say that he is a mystic. I choose this word not only because of the centrality of *unity* to his ideas, but also because he showed how to experience and strengthen that unity within oneself and because of the religious, spiritual and philanthropic context of his Work.

---

[9] Gurdjieff (1999) 26-27
[10] Gurdjieff (1950) 1057
[11] Gurdjieff (1999) 44

2. Ouspensky and In Search of the Miraculous

As stated, we need to assess the credibility of our sources. For example, are Ouspensky's reports of remarks attributed to Gurdjieff always accurate? If so why, and if not, which ones can be accepted? Ouspensky (1878-1947) is often considered to be the most important of Gurdjieff's pupils.'[12] Patterson writes: "Without question the place of Pyotr Demianovich Uspenskii in the Gurdjieffian pantheon is unique. He is unrivalled as the chief interpreter of what has become known as the Gurdjieff Work..."[13] Speeth endorses Wilson's characterization of Ouspensky as playing Plato to Gurdjieff's Socrates.[14] The American "Christian" oriented Encyclopaedia of Cults and New Religions, under the rubric "Gurdjieff Foundations", provides the pithy information: "Key literature: *All and Everything: Beelzebub's Tales to his Grandson* and other literature by Gurdjieff and Peter D. Ouspensky." Common too many published assessments is the idea that whereas Gurdjieff scattered ideas with lavish abundance, he lacked the capacity to systematize them. This ability to organize the ideas, it is said, was Ouspensky's unique contribution. Perry takes this idea further, making the unsupported assertion that "Gurdjieff envied Ouspensky's abilities as a writer…"[15]

Writers can go beyond this by referring to a "Fourth Way", and treat Ouspensky as if he were equal to Gurdjieff in that both were seekers on this "Fourth Way".[16] This is reflected in Nicoll's *Psychological Commentaries on the Teaching of Gurdjieff and Ouspensky*,[17] and Reyner's reference to "the Gurdjieff-Ouspensky philosophy".[18] This view has respectable antecedents: its first attested proponent was Ouspensky himself, speaking in 1923. Ouspensky must have provided the material used by the *Daily News*, in the following extract from an article of 19 February 1923 under the sub-heading:

> KINDRED SPIRITS
>
> Before meeting Gurdjieff at Moscow in 1915, Mr. Ouspensky had made a special study of the psychology of art during travels in Central Asia, Egypt and India, and had also specialised in certain branches of higher mathematics. In Gurdjieff he found a kindred spirit who had gone further on the same road, and the two enthusiasts joined forces,

---

[12] This assessment, at least in an absolute form, is not so marked among persons who are acquainted - directly or indirectly - with the work of Mme de Salzmann. Vaysse (1979) 3, for example, notes and praises Ouspensky's contribution, but adds: "It was Jeanne de Salzmann's achievement to preserve and transmit in all their original authenticity not only the written part, but also the oral and practical parts of the teaching given by Gurdjieff."
[13] Patterson (1996) xi
[14] Speeth (1989) 12
[15] Perry (1978) 42
[16] Note the sub-title &Hunter (2000), *P. D. Ouspensky: Pioneer of the Fourth Way*.
[17] Nicoll refers often to the 'Fourth Way", not only in the *Commentaries*, but elsewhere.
[18] Reyner (1981) 10

> travelling and teaching in Russia as they were driven hither and thither by the tide of war or famine.
>
> After some years of this wandering life they found themselves in Constantinople, and from there drifted across Europe till they pitched their camp in the famous forest near Paris.
>
> "My book telling of our discoveries so far as they have gone, should be out this summer", Mr. Ouspensky stated. I am thinking of calling it *Fragments of an Ancient Teaching*. In the meantime I am lecturing before small private classes, which is as much as my command of English permits.
>
> "When students have once got over the initial difficulty of thinking along new lines and grasping the meaning of the terms employed - which may sometimes take a good many weeks - they make steady progress in quickness of perception and understanding, even without taking a course at the Institute.
>
> "The difficulty on our side is to translate our discoveries into modern forms, but I hope that there, too, progress is being made."[19]

I have only seen this passage cited for this purpose by Webb.[20] I think it must be accepted as reasonably accurate, allowing only for some tidying up of Ouspensky's English, should this have been necessary. The photograph of Ouspensky which appears with this passage was taken by the *Daily News*, so one need not doubt that they did have access to Ouspensky, and his cooperation. Indeed, if Ouspensky had not delivered himself in these or similar terms, it is difficult to know how they could have correctly reported the title of his proposed volume.

I do not accept that Ouspensky was, in any significant sense, Gurdjieff's peer. A perusal of *Miraculous* and the transcripts of his group meetings in *Fourth Way, A Further Record* and *Record of Meetings*, makes it transparent that the vast bulk of the ideas Ouspensky taught in these classes were - contrary to what he told the Daily News - the ideas of Gurdjieff. But, beyond this, I contend that Ouspensky's teaching of Gurdjieff's ideas, even as Ouspensky had learned them, was unbalanced. First, Ouspensky gave undue importance to concepts such as "eternal recurrence" and the "Table of Time in Different Cosmoses". Recurrence introduced an element of fantasy which was, to a significant degree, antagonistic to Gurdjieff's ideas and methods. The Table is very impressive: an intellectual *tour de force*, but something of a dead end from the point of view of Gurdjieff's more practical aims. Another aspect of Ouspensky's lack of balance is that he violated

---

[19] *Daily News*, 19 February 1923, p. 7
[20] Webb (1980) 382

certain principles he himself espoused, and these lead to an overly intellectual and thus skewed presentation of Gurdjieff's teachings.[21]

I shall return to these ideas. However, the first step in dealing with Ouspensky is to consider the question of the proper genre of *Miraculous*. This work is the central text for this part of my enquiries. As with any work, it covers several genres (or to use the vocabulary of modern genre theory, it includes several forms).[22] For example, some of *Miraculous* reads as a straight autobiography. Other parts strike one as practically extended philosophical discourses. But I contend that its true overall genre is none of these. There are autobiographical elements, and the book can properly be called an autobiography. But we can be more precise, for these autobiographical elements really all are concerned with, or lead up to or away from, his encounter with Gurdjieff. Major autobiographical details are omitted or disguised. For example, his personal life is almost entirely unmentioned. Ouspensky's wife was a formidable woman with an impressive intellect.[23] She was deep, incisive, concise and witty.[24] But not only is she not mentioned in *Miraculous*, she is lightly but effectively disguised in one instance where it would have been perfectly proper to name her. Patterson was told by Lord Pentland, who knew both Gurdjieff and Ouspensky, that the anonymous person in *Miraculous* who states their aim in the terms Gurdjieff best approves,[25] was in fact Madame Ouspensky. When he wrote the book he changed the gender to say "master" not "mistress" because - in Lord Pentland's words - "It would be objective."[26]

The sort of personal details one can find in Butkovsky-Hewitt's essay length book are simply missing. For example, she often mentions the time of day or night at which a conversation took place, and gives details of remarks by not only Gurdjieff and herself: but also by Ouspensky and others. St Petersburg, its social life, and its white nights are more vividly presented in her short volume than in Ouspensky's 389 solid pages.[27] This is not to criticize Ouspensky: it is merely to point out that Miraculous cannot be described as an "autobiography" *simpliciter*. It would be

---

[21] I also would challenge the use made of the term "Fourth Way", especially if it is intended to imply that Ouspensky had the understanding of the "Fourth Way" that Gurdjieff did, let alone Gurdjieff's status as a teacher of the "Fourth Way".

[22] Longman III (1991) 10: "... the classification of a text as a whole is here considered its 'genre', while 'form' is reserved for the individual units within the text."

[23] Whether Ouspensky married her or not, she was known as "Madame Ouspensky": see Webb (1980) 136-137 and Patterson (1996) 52 n. 34.

[24] Personal communication by Mr. Adie. The details are confirmed by numerous accounts, of which see chiefly. It is interesting that several people have been prepared to go into print with criticisms of Mme Ouspensky: see for example C. Lewis and C. S. Nott.

[25] Ouspensky (1949) 100 and 103

[26] Patterson (1992) 248

[27] Butkovsky-Hewitt (1978). Pages 16-49 alone bring out the strong contrast with Ouspensky's austere work

better to speak of the bulk of its pages as "an autobiographical account of Ouspensky's learning from Gurdjieff."

But while this is arguably true of the majority of the work, to my mind, *In Search of the Miraculous* as a whole is an apologia in the sense of a defence or vindication of one's actions. The book opens with the words: "I returned to Russia in November, 1914" and proceeds to state that this was his return from a journey through Egypt, Ceylon and India to "seek the miraculous".

Despite not having found the "miraculous" he was convinced of the rightness of the search, and, indeed, that: "I felt that my search, and everything connected with it, was more important than anything that was happening or could happen in a world of 'obvious absurdities'."[28] The book ends by referring to his farewell to Gurdjieff in January 1924. The final words are: "On returning to London I announced to those who came to my lectures that my work in the future would proceed quite independently *in the way it had been begun in London in 1921*."[29] (Ouspensky's italics).

In both instances Ouspensky has returned after a voyage. In both cases he has been searching for "the miraculous" and in each there is a certain disappointment. There is, however, a substantial difference between these bookends. In chapter 1, Ouspensky can only speak of "his search". At the close of the book, he can speak of his "work" and of people who attend his lectures. In between, we have the Gurdjieff ideas he had absorbed (and perhaps even some like the Diagram of Everything Living, which he had not), with a certain measure of Ouspensky's own ideas, such as the Table of Time. Not all of Gurdjieff's ideas are presented here: the concepts of triads of forces is found only in *Fourth Way*,[30] as is the delightful story of the devil and the sly man. The concept of the centres was given out in such a manner that Ouspensky opted for a compromise, whereby he would try and reproduce some of that information in *Miraculous*, while "endeavouring to avoid what has already been given in the first and second series of lectures."[31]

This is not to deny a certain validity to Pentland's statement that *Miraculous* was "intended to preserve the teaching in as pure and impersonal a form as possible."[32] But even this is subordinate to Ouspensky's apologetic purpose. Had this been the only intention in Ouspensky's mind, how do we explain his criticisms of G., and the details of his separation from Gurdjieff? These might show that Ouspensky had drawn a distinction between Gurdjieff and his ideas, but even this contradicts the notion of preserving "the teaching in as pure and *impersonal* a form as possible."[32] (my emphasis).

---

[28] Ouspensky (1949) 3
[29] Ouspensky (1949) 389
[30] And in other records of Ouspensky's meetings.
[31] Ouspensky (1949) 56
[32] Pentland (1979) x

If one accepts that the most apt description of *Miraculous* as a whole is an *apology*, this explains another interesting fact, that Ouspensky told the *Daily News* that he would be publishing *Fragments* in the summer of 1923, and yet did not do so. There is no doubt that Ouspensky backed away from his statements to the *Daily News*. Thus, in *Miraculous*, he ingeniously states:

> Soon after its opening the Institute attracted the attention of the press and for a month or two the French and English papers were active writing about it. G. and his pupils were called the 'forest philosophers', they were interviewed, their photographs were published, and so on.[33]

From this, the use of the third person plural "they" and "their" definitely implies that Ouspensky was neither interviewed nor was his photograph published. Yet both occurred. The only conclusion I can draw from all of this is that Ouspensky was embarrassed by his interview. And why did Ouspensky not publish *Fragments* in the summer of 1923? We cannot how now. But I doubt it was because it was not ready for publication. Further, Ouspensky made a point of saying only a few pages earlier that Gurdjieff had authorised his publication of the projected book "to expound his St. Petersburg lectures and talks with commentaries of my own".[34]

I think the key to this puzzle lies in the reference to "commentaries of my own", and the gap between their respective roles as Ouspensky stated it to the *Daily News* and as it appears - and had to appear - in *Miraculous*. That is, I conjecture that Ouspensky did not publish in 1923 because the book would have shown Gurdjieff as the teacher and Ouspensky as the pupil. Why did he not wish this? Because Ouspensky had already started groups in London and wished to continue with them.

To my mind, this strengthens the conclusion I had already arrived at, that the proper genre of *Miraculous* is that of the *apologia*. This brings us to another question: how does *Miraculous* stand as a record of the Gurdjieff teaching? Is it the reliable and authoritative tome it is often taken to be? Few books have been as influential in the development of modern, Western, extra-ecclesiastical notions of spirituality as P. D. Ouspensky's *In Search of the Miraculous: Fragments of an Unknown Teaching*. Since its publication in 1949 it has been lauded as a source for the study of Gurdjieff and his ideas. There have been more qualified assessments. Webb observes that:

> Because *In Search of the Miraculous* seems to be the clearest existing account of Gurdjieff's teaching, it is widely read, and some of the results have been very odd. The hieratic-religious tone which provided the background to Gurdjieff's talks belongs entirely to the Russian phase of his activity and is directed to the people among whom he was working. It belongs particularly to Ouspensky, whose personal preoccupations naturally influenced the questions he asked Gurdjieff and the items of Gurdjieff's conversation he snapped up.[35]

---

[33] Ouspensky (1949) 386
[34] Ouspensky (1949) 383
[35] Webb, *The Harmonious Circle*, Thames and Hudson, London, 1980, p. 139.

As we shall see later, this insight can be developed even further. I would like to suggest that although *Miraculous* is undoubtedly a magnificent achievement because of its exposition of Gurdjieff's ideas, it is yet a limited treatment of those ideas. There are several aspects to this issue. First, there is Bennett's recollection that:

> (Gurdjieff) had been asked by Madame Ouspensky to decide whether or not Ouspensky's own book, *Fragments of an Unknown Teaching*, should also be published. He remained undecided about the latter for some time, pointing out when he heard it read aloud that certain of his ideas were far more clearly and strongly expressed in Beelzebub. He finally agreed on condition that it should not be published in advance of his own book.
>
> ... he praised Ouspensky for the accuracy of his reporting. Once I read aloud in front of him an early chapter of *In Search of the Miraculous*. He listened with evident relish, and when I finished he said: "Before I hate Ouspensky: now I love him. This very exact, he tell what I say."[36]

In *Gurdjieff: Making a New World*, Bennett again presents some of this information, with a slightly stronger emphasis on the importance of Beelzebub:

> When in 1948, Mme Ouspensky sent over the typescript of *Fragments of an Unknown Teaching*, as it was then called, and Gurdjieff had this read out in front of him, he constantly remarked that the presentation was not as satisfactory as Beelzebub and insisted that we should turn to the latter as the authentic source.[37]

There can be no doubt that, by and large, *In Search of the Miraculous* is an accurate report of what Gurdjieff had said between 1915 and 1918 to and in Ouspensky's hearing. Louise March, writing of Gurdjieff's last visit to New York (commencing December 1948) remembered:

> After every luncheon a chapter from the draft of Ouspensky's *In Search of the Miraculous* was read...Mr. Gurdjieff praised it often, "Very exact is. Good memory. Truth, was so." Sometimes Gurdjieff was dissatisfied, "Is too liquid. Lost something."[38]

It can be seen that there is no contradiction between these two accounts. However, Bennett, who was more frequently in contact with Gurdjieff at the time *Miraculous* had been sent over, reports the very telling comparison which Gurdjieff made between that book and *Beelzebub*. Further, it appears to me quite possible that Gurdjieff was content to have a pupil's accounts of the ideas as he had taught them at an earlier time circulating, at least when the account was of the quality of

---

[36] Bennett (1997) 205

[37] Bennett (1973) 177. Bennett reiterates here that *Miraculous* should not be published until "*Beelzebub* had appeared and had been on the market for a number of months. This wish of his was ignored after he died..."

[38] March (1990) 74-75

Miraculous. Gurdjieff was able to contemplate the possibility that some people would find Ouspensky's format a helpful supplement to *Beelzebub*.

The superiority of *Beelzebub* is one qualification of *Miraculous'* eminence as an exposition of Gurdjieff's ideas.[39] But one can extend this, for the relationship between the "system" Ouspensky purported to teach, and the ideas and practices of Gurdjieff - especially those which he was using at the end of his life - is another matter. Further, and particularly in respect to the idea of Recurrence, I do not accept that Ouspensky's reports of remarks attributed to Gurdjieff are always accurate in the sense of "the truth, the whole truth, and nothing but the truth".

But more vitally, there is a striking difference between Gurdjieff and Ouspensky in that whereas Gurdjieff's teachings and practices were always developing, Ouspensky's remained static except for two occasions: when his wife arrived in London and reinvigorated his practices, and at the very end of his life, when he "repudiated" the "system". But the overall contrast between these two men is the difference between a master and explorer, and a gifted pupil who leaves the master after too short an apprenticeship, and sets himself up as teacher. This was unfortunate, because there are indications that the gifted pupil's limitations were of such a nature that he left his master just when he had come to the lesson he most needed. It was additionally sad, because the pupil missed out on the further explorations undertaken by his master. As one person who knew Gurdjieff as a child, said to me: "Gurdjieff was an ongoing surprise".[40] Without wishing to be unfair to Ouspensky, it appears that he could only accept a certain quota of surprises, especially where they held him back from setting himself up as a teacher.

Bibliography

Part One: Gurdjieff

Gurdjieff, George Ivanovich

(1950) *All and Everything: Beelzebub's Tales to His Grandson*, Two Rivers Press, Aurora (first published in 1950 by Harcourt, Brace & Company)

(1985) *Meetings with Remarkable Men*, Arkana Penguin Books, London (first published in 1963 by Routledge)

(1999) *Life is Real only then, when 'I Am'*, Arkana Penguin Books, London (first published in 1975 and 1978 by Triangle Editions Inc.)

---

[39] Insert a reference to Vaysse's point
[40] Personal communication in 1989 by George Adie Junior.

All & Everything Conference 2003

Part Two: Authors other than Gurdjieff

Ankerberg, John and Weldon, John
(1999) *Encyclopedia of Cults aid New Religions*, Harvest House Publishers, Eugene

Bennett, John Godolphin
(1997) *Witness*, Bennett Books

Butkovsky-Hewitt, Anna
(1978) *With Gurdjieff in St. Petersburg and Paris*, Routledge and Kegan Paul, London

De Hartmann, Thomas and Olga
(1992) *Our Life with Mr. Gurdjieff* (definitive edition), ed. T. C. Daly and T. A. G. Daly, Arkana Penguin Books, London

Hunter, Bob
(2000) *P. D. Ouspensky: Pioneer of the Fourth Way*, Eureka Editions, Amsterdam

Longman III, Tremper
(1991) *Fictional Akkadian Autobiography*, Eisenbrauns, Winona Lake

March, Louise
(1990) *The Gurdjieff Years: 1929-1949*, The Work Study Association, Inc., Walworth

Ouspensky, Pyotr Demianovich
(1949) *In Search of the Miraculous*, Harcourt Brace Jovanovich, New York and London

Patterson, William Patrick
(1992) *Eating the "I"*, Arête Communications, San Anselmo

(1996) *Struggle of the Magicians*, Arête Communications, Fairfax

Pentland, John
(1979) "Foreword" to Vaysse (1999)

Perry, Whitall N.
(1978) *Gurdjieff in the Light of Tradition*, Perennial Books, Bedfont

Reyner, J. H.
(1981) *Ouspensky the Unsung Genius*, George Allen & Unwin (Publishers) Ltd., London

Speeth, Kathleen Riordan
(1989) *The Gurdjieff Work*, Jeremy P. Tarcher / Putnam, New York

Vaysse, Jean
(1979) *Toward Awakening*, Harper & Row, San Francisco

Webb, James
(1980) *The Harmonious Circle*, Thames and Hudson Ltd, London

Wilson, Colin
(1993) *The Strange Life of P. D. Ouspensky*, The Aquarian Press, London

© Copyright 2003 - Joseph Azize - All Rights Reserved

A Macroscopic View of the Two Fundamental Cosmic Laws in Relation to the Motion of the Trajectory of One's Search

Will Mesa

I repeat, my boy: Try very hard to understand everything that will relate to both of these fundamental cosmic sacred laws, since knowledge of these sacred laws, particularly knowledge relating to the particularities of the sacred Heptaparaparshinokh, will help you in the future to understand very easily and very well all the second-grade and third-grade laws of World-creation and World-existence.

Beelzebub's Tales To His Grandson, P. 755

Introduction

The importance of the study of the two fundamental cosmic laws, namely, the Law of Seven and the Law of Three, is reflected in the third being-obligolnian-striving, "the conscious striving to know ever more and more concerning the laws of World-creation and World-maintenance."

In this article, I intend to study these two laws by describing their practical applications to the important question of one's own search. I will first review the two fundamental laws, emphasizing the action of the fifth Stopinder of the Law of Seven, and the intervention of the third force of the Law of Three. I then present a macroscopic view of the operation of the two fundamental cosmic laws in relation to the motion of the trajectory of one's search. Two aspects are emphasized, namely, the active participation of the second being-body or Kesdjan body during actualization in us of our own Sacred Triamazikamno, and the critical action of the fifth Stopinder or Harnel-Aoot during actualization in us of our own Sacred Heptaparaparshinokh.

The emphasis of the article is on the practical application of the material covered in its effects on Work on one's self.

The Two Fundamental Cosmic Laws

All throughout his many years of teaching, Mr. Gurdjieff always asked his disciples to put in their own words what he had taught them. For example, in search of the miraculous we not that he once asked Ouspensky, "try to discuss all I have said just now, from the point of view of your dimensions." In what follows, I show how, following Gurdjieff's indications, I have tried to put the Law of Seven in my own words.

The Law of Seven as it appears in the *Tales*:

The-line-of-the-flow-of-forces-constantly-deflecting-according-to-the-law-and-uniting-again-at-its-ends.

The Law of Seven as I have formulated it:

The-movement-of-substances-and-the-action-of-the-forces-resulting-from-the-exchange-of-substances-following-a-discontinuous-interactive-nonlinear-trajectory.

The reformulation I have introduced follows very closely certain recent discoveries of the workings of Nature. It is now a well-known fact that all the forces in the universe arise from an exchange of particles or substances. For example, the force between two interacting electrons arises from the exchange of one photon, and in the process light is emitted. One may say that the force coming from the work of a community or a group will result from the exchange of substances among the members of the community, and in the process light or understanding will be emanated from the community or group. The exchange of substances is known in the Teaching as Iraniranumange or common-cosmic-exchange-of-substances. Therefore, the reformulation above incorporates in one sentence both the main characteristics of the Law of Seven and the fact that all the forces result from the action of the common-cosmic process of Iraniranumange.

We can now look closely at the three characteristics involved in the formulation above, namely, the discontinuous, the interactive and the nonlinear characteristics.

The discontinuous characteristic is the result of the cyclical and segmental manner of the first cosmic law's operational mode. Each complete cycle of the law is composed of seven segments (Stopinders), connected one to the other. It is from this composition that the law derives its name. The realization of one complete cycle is known as an octave, in that there is an entire period between the beginning of one cycle and the beginning of another. The point of union of each segment is named as a point of deviation or center of gravity. Thus, there are seven segments and seven points of deviation in one complete cycle or octave. The first point of deviation corresponds to the union of the octave with the last segment of a preceding octave and the last point of deviation corresponds to the beginning of the last segment of the octave in its way to a new octave.

The interactive characteristic is the result of the manner in which the segments (Stopinders) interact with each other during actualization of a complete cycle or octave of the law. Each segment has its own subjective properties, which are measurable in terms of its vibratory quality (rate of vibrations) or vivifying factor and its relative position in the cycle. These subjective properties depend, in part, on the subjective properties of preceding segments and, in turn, affect the subjective properties of subsequent segments. This characteristic accounts for the fact that the "Whole" or any other integral totality is always formed of seven independent aspects with distinct and well-defined subjective properties that in their interactions result in the "Whole."

The nonlinear characteristic is due to the subjective action of certain segments of every cycle or octave of the law. To be precise, there are three segments (Stopinders) with very specific subjective properties. These are the third segment, which is the segment located between the third and fourth points of deviation, the fifth segment, situated between the fifth and the sixth points of deviation, and the last or seventh segment located between the last center of gravity of a given cycle and the beginning of a new cycle or new octave.

Both the third and the last segments have properties of retardation. They are responsible for the fact that the movement of substances and the action of the forces do not follow a linear trajectory. The fifth segment has subjective properties that are the result of its relative position between the third and last segments. It is the most important in the cycle or octave because of its oppositional effect within the totality of functioning in the cycle or octave.

The totality of functioning in each complete cycle of the law is dependent upon many factors. Some of these are external to the process in which the law is operating, while with others, the internal factors arise from within the process itself. Specifically, the totality of functioning of each octave is dependent upon the relationship between these external and internal factors, the vibratory quality of each segment, and the particularities of each of the three already mentioned segments.

The particularity of the third segment is that its subjective action - the operational action that it exerts on the totality of functioning of any complete cycle of the law, in relation to a given cosmic process - is dependent upon the automatic affluence of all of the forces external and near to the process itself. That is to say, the subjective action of the third segment is only a function of the automatic affluence of forces external to the cosmic concentration in which the law is operating. It is because of this particularity that this segment is called the mechanically actualized segment.

Since the automatic flow of all of the conditions external to the process where the law is operating is a helping factor in the operation of the law, the third segment is similarly named the segment of external-help. It must be noted here that for the benefit of the totality of the law's functioning, the subjective action of the third segment is the more prolonged of the two segments with properties of retardation.

The particularity of the last or seventh segment is that its subjective action - that which it exerts on the totality of functioning of any one complete cycle of the operating law in relation to a given cosmic process - is dependent only upon the affluence of forces obtained from the outside through that segment from the results arising from the actualization of all of the efforts occurring within the process or within the concentration in which the law is operating. Because of this particularity, this segment is known as the intentionally actualized segment.

A Macroscopic View of the Two Fundamental Cosmic Laws

In this case, because the helping factor in the operation of the law is a result of the action actualized within the process or within the concentration in which the law is operating, the seventh segment is also known as the segment of self-help. In order to facilitate the transition from one cycle to another in the operation of the law, the subjective action of the last or seventh segment is the least prolonged of the two segments with properties of retardation.

The particularity of the fifth segment (fifth Stopinder) is that its subjective action flows by itself from the action of the other two. Its action does not depend on the affluence of forces from outside but rather on its asymmetry in relation to the completing process of the Law. It is this asymmetry the one that produces a disharmony in the action or functioning of the fifth segment. Because of this disharmony, the action of this segment achieves results that can be diametrically opposed, that is to say, it can give "opposite results."

More specifically, within a given process in which the Law of Seven is operating, results arising from the subjective action of the fifth segment can vary from a benefit directed, in its totality, to the exterior of the process up to a benefit directed, in its totality, to the interior of the process, all dependent upon the internal conditions existing within the process.

If the internal conditions within the process are in a state of total chaos or disorder, the benefits resulting from the subjective action of the fifth segment are directed, in their totality, to the exterior of the process. If those conditions are of total calm or order, the benefits are directed, in their totality, to the interior of the process. In conditions intermediate to total chaos and total calm, the benefits resulting from the subjective action of the fifth segment of the law are apportioned between the exterior and the interior of the process within which the law is operating.

The fifth segment is known as the Fifth of the law. It is the action of the Fifth one that is the most important key to understanding the Law of Seven, and it is the action of this segment that is the most difficult to understand.

The subjective characteristic of the fifth segment guarantees the common exchange of substances or exchange of energies continuously and constantly taking place among cosmic concentrations. The subjective action of this segment is therefore responsible for the formation and transformation of cosmic substances. Here we have the importance of this segment within the totality of functioning of the law. This characteristic can be inferred from the following statements taken from the *Tales*:

> Thanks to the new particularity of the fifth Stopinder of the sacred Heptapararparshinokh, these emanations issuing from the Sun Absolute began to act at certain definite points of the space of the Universe upon the prime cosmic substance Etherokrilno from which, owing to the totality of the former and the new particularities of the sacred primordial laws, certain definite concentrations began to be concentrated. (p.757)

> At this very place in the process of the first outer cycle of the fundamental sacred Heptaparaparshinokh, namely after the formation of the Third-order-Suns or planets just here, owing to the changed fifth deflection of the sacred Heptaparaparshinokh, which as I have already said is now called Harnel-Aoot, the initially given momentum for the fundamental completing process, having lost half the force of its vivifyingness, began in its further functioning to have only half of the manifestation of its action outside itself, and the other half for itself, i.e., for its very own functioning, the consequences of which were that on those last results, i.e., on these said Third-order-Suns or planets, there began to arise what are called, 'similarities-to-the-already-arising.' (p.758)
>
> And as after this, surrounding conditions of actualizations were everywhere established corresponding to the manifestation of the second particularity of the fifth Stopinder of the fundamental sacred Heptaparaparshinokh, therefore from then on the actualization of the fundamental outer cycle of the sacred Heptaparaparshinokh ceased, and all the action of its functioning entered forever into the results already manifested by it, and in them there began to proceed its inherent permanent processes of transformation, called "evolution" and "involution." (p.758)

The following are other statements taken from the *Tales* where the importance of the fifth segment (fifth Stopinder) is pointed out:

> And these subjective properties of theirs (active elements belonging to seven independent classes) and likewise their what are called 'properties of vivifyingness' are actualized firstly, according to what form of functioning of the fifth Stopinder of the Sacred Heptaparaparshinokh was flowing during their arising, and secondly, whether the given active elements arise owing to the conscious intention on the part of some independent individual, or whether they arose automatically, merely owing to the second-grade law called 'Attraction-and-Fusion-of-Similarities.' (p.785)
>
> Just these same substances in beings, according to the fifth deflection of the Sacred Heptapaparaparshinokh, have the free possibility of giving, in the manifestations of the common presences of three-brained beings, results not similar but 'opposite to each other. (p.791)
>
> That is why, in respect of these being-substances, the beings themselves must always be very, very much on their guard in order to avoid undesirable consequences for their whole."(p.791)

The relative importance of the fifth segment within a given cycle or octave of the law, is also a consequence of the fact that the possibility of evolution towards the completion of the cycle of the law, or involution towards the origin of the cycle being developed, is dependent upon whether or not the actualization of the fifth segment is realized. This fact is clearly indicated in the following statement taken from the *Tales*:

A Macroscopic View of the Two Fundamental Cosmic Laws

> It is necessary at this point in connection with the actualization of the fifth Stopinder of the sacred Hepataparaparshinokh to trace a parallel between two processes which externally have nothing in common with one another, namely: in the same manner as the first being-food cannot acquire its vivifying power until after its transformation into being-Piandjoëhary, in the same manner on this piano the vibrations of a chord do not acquire a corresponding vivifying power until they have been fused with the preceding vibrations produced, starting from the center of gravity of the totality of the vibrations of the note 'sol.'(p.869)

In other words, a cycle cannot complete its trajectory before having passed through the actualization of its own Fifth.

The actualization of a complete cycle or one octave of the Law of Seven for any given process is dependent, then, upon three conditions. The first is that the process may receive external help emitting from the automatic flow of the totality of conditions surrounding the process. The second is that the initial impulse of the movement of substances or action of the forces, after having received the help necessary from the exterior through the third segment, may actualize the fifth segment and in this way may evolve towards the last segment of the cycle. The third and last condition is that, once clear of the Fifth of the law, the results arising from the totality of efforts actualized exclusively within the process are such that they may assure the transition to a new cycle through the last or seventh segment of the law.

The above-described sequence is for an evolutionary or ascending trajectory, that is, for an evolutionary movement or ascending action of the forces: initially, the mechanically actualized segment or segment of external-help, then the actualization of the Fifth of the law, and finally, the intentionally actualized segment or segment of self-help.

For an involutionary or descending trajectory, that is, an involutionary or descending movement or action, (as in the case of the Process of Common Creation), the sequence is as follows: initially, the intentionally actualized segment, then the Fifth of the law, and finally the mechanically actualized segment.

The operation of the Law of Seven or first cosmic law, explicates the reason for phenomena observed in Nature, as well as those occurring in the process of life shared in common among men, and even to those of man's inner world, which are discontinuous or fragmentary, cyclic and do not conform to a simple movement or progression of linearity. One such example is the way in which many of man's actions become deflected from their origin due to the nonlinear characteristics of the law, often to such a degree that they end up being their very opposite. Another example, one that is more easily detectable, is the curvature of space. It is only when many strong constraints are introduced to purposely simplifying the analysis of such phenomena, that the possibility of arriving at a simple description based on the suppositions of continuity and linearity, can be attained.

The discontinuity resulting from the operation of the Law of Seven is easily observable in certain processes, while in others it is more difficult. The difficulty is mainly due to the fact that in a great majority of the processes occurring in Nature, as well as in the collective and the individual lives of men, many cycles of the law intervene which interweave among themselves, or develop parallel to the fundamental octave of the process, or results in a combination of interwoven and parallel octaves. The fractioning in these processes can only be observed in bold strokes.

The Law of Three as it appears in the *Tales*:

Every New Realization Derives Itself from Previous Realizations through a Process of Fusion in which Participates Three Orders of Independent Substances.

The process of fusion occurs in this way: the substance of higher or first order (carrier of the active principle) unites with the substance of lower or second order (carrier of the passive principle) resulting in the substance of middle or third order. For a new realization, the substance of middle order becomes either the substance of higher order for the preceding lower or the substance of lower order for the succeeding higher. The process is continued in this manner in a chain of realizations, along a trajectory that conforms in its totality of aspects to the operation of the Law of Seven or first cosmic law. The description above is for an evolutionary or ascending trajectory.

It is because of the manner in which the Law of Three operates that it can also be formulated as "A law which always flows into a consequence and becomes the cause of subsequent consequences, and always functions by three independent and quite opposite characteristic manifestations, latent within it, in properties neither seen nor sensed."

It is of the outmost importance to understand that the substance of this third order not only is the result of the fusion of the other two, but it is also the intervening factor in the formation of new realizations.

The three independent substances participating in every new realization have been known as: the first order substance as positive substance; the second order substance as negative substance; and the third order substance as neutral substance. Each of the three independent substances is the carrier of each of the three independent forces -the positive substance is the carrier of the positive force, the negative substance the carrier of the negative force, and the neutral substance the carrier of the reconciling force.

The prime emanation of our Most Holy Sun Absolute also acquires the characteristic operation of the Law of Three. The Holy Force contained in this prime emanation manifests itself as three independent forces known as: Holy-Affirming or Holy First Force; Holy-Denying or Holy Second Force; and Holy-Reconciling or Holy Third Force. No one of the three forces is superior to the other two. Their relative importance abides in the fact that when they participate concurrently a complete realization is obtained. More specifically, and this point must be emphasized, is that it is the presence of the third independent force—the Holy-Reconciling—that is the determining factor in the arising of a new or complete realization or phenomenon.

For instance, in the artificial formation of bread, three independent substances serving as sources of the three independent principles of the Law of Three participate. The affirming principle is carried by the totality of substance composing water; the denying principle is carried by the totality of substances composing the flour obtained from the wheat grain; and the substance resulting from the process of burning or from fire carries the neutralizing principle. The mixtures of water and flour alone will produce a temporal mixture or dough, which in the given case results in a partial realization. If this mixture is baked over fire, then, because of the intervention of the neutralizing principle of the Law of Three, a permanent fusion is obtained as a result of which the new totality of substances derived from the water, the flour and the fire, namely, the bread, becomes a new or complete realization. It is also important to notice that the quality of the bread produced will depend on the subjective quality of the Stopinders through which the process must move through in order to bring about a manifestation.

Another example that clearly shows the intervention of the actualized middle in the formation of new realizations is the process of Nature known as the continuation of the species. The male sexual substance (carrier of the active principle or first substance) blends with the female sexual substance (carrier of the passive principle or second substance) to actualize the middle or third substance. This middle or third substance is in the form of a new being. If the third substance or new being is male, then it becomes the active substance or first substance for further realizations. If the third substance or new being is female, then it becomes the passive substance or second substance for further realizations. In either case, continuation of the species is ensured.

Macroscopic View of the Two Fundamental Cosmic Laws in Relation to the Motion of the Trajectory of One's Search

The operation of the two fundamental cosmic laws can be examined at different levels. By microscopic view, I mean the two laws operating on our lives, as compared to a microscopic view where the two laws operate at a smaller scale such as is the case of the transmutation of the first being-food. We can also view the two laws operating at a megaloscopic scale such as the involutionary process of creation.

Before proceeding to the examination of each law individually, it is important to keep in mind that it is the interaction of the two laws that brings actual manifestation of phenomena on the plane of matter-energy (see my article in Stopinder Number Ten). However, for the sake of simplification, it is convenient to study the operation of each separately, always keeping in mind their mutual interaction.

The operation in our lives of the Law of Three can be viewed in different ways. One way is how the law operates in the interaction of the three bodies of three-brained beings, namely, the planetary body, the second being-body (body Kesdjan), and the higher divine part (higher being-body). This interaction is clearly stated in the following two statements taken from the chapter The Holy Planet "Purgatory" of *Beelzebub's Tales*:

> In other words, every wish of the planetary body is taken as undesirable for their higher divine part which has to be coated and perfected, and therefore all three-centered beings of our Great Megaloscosmos constantly carry on a relentless struggle against the wishes of their planetary bodies so that there should be formed in them, in this struggle from the what is called 'Disputekrialnian-friction', those sacred crystallizations from which their higher Divine being-part arises and is perfected in them.(p.802)

> In this constant struggle of theirs, the equilibrating harmonizing principle is their second being-body, which in their own individual law of Triamazikamno represents the neutralizing source; and therefore this second being-part always remains indifferent to their mechanical manifestations, but for all their active manifestations it always tends according to the second-grade cosmic law 'Urdekhplifata' to unite with those desires of which there are more whether in one or the other of the two mentioned opposite being-parts. (p.802)

It is obvious from the statements above that in our own individual Law of Three the second being-body represents the neutralizing principle. Furthermore, it is also obvious that in our struggle for self-perfection, the second being-part tends to unite with either the desires of our planetary body or the desires of our higher divine part. Therefore, it follows that our Law of Three can be viewed as either an involutionary movement or as an evolutionary movement of the second being body or body Kesdjan. What follows is a schematic diagram of both the involutionary movement resulting from the second being-body uniting with the desires of the planetary body and the evolutionary movement resulting from the second being-body uniting with the higher divine part. The movement is always initiated by an active participation of the second being-body, which always involves a conscious struggle, something worth noticing in relation to our personal struggle for self-perfection. The process of activation, however, can lead to either a downward movement, an involutionary path, or to an upward movement, an evolutionary path, something also worth noticing. One may say that the involutionary movement leads to a wrong crystallization of man number five, while the evolutionary movement leads to a correct crystallization of man number five.

Because the diagram shows the interaction of the Law of Three with the Law of Seven, as the three principles moves through the Stopinders of the Law of Seven, it can be referred to as a Triagram. It should be observed that the Triagram does not show the details of the operational characteristics of the Law of Seven, something the Enneagram, when correctly understood, does show. What the Triagram does show is the fusion or Harnel-miaznel of two substances, emphasizing how the resulting substance or actualized middle becomes either a higher or a lower substance in further actualizations. (See the Trigram on the following page.)

A Macroscopic View of the Two Fundamental Cosmic Laws

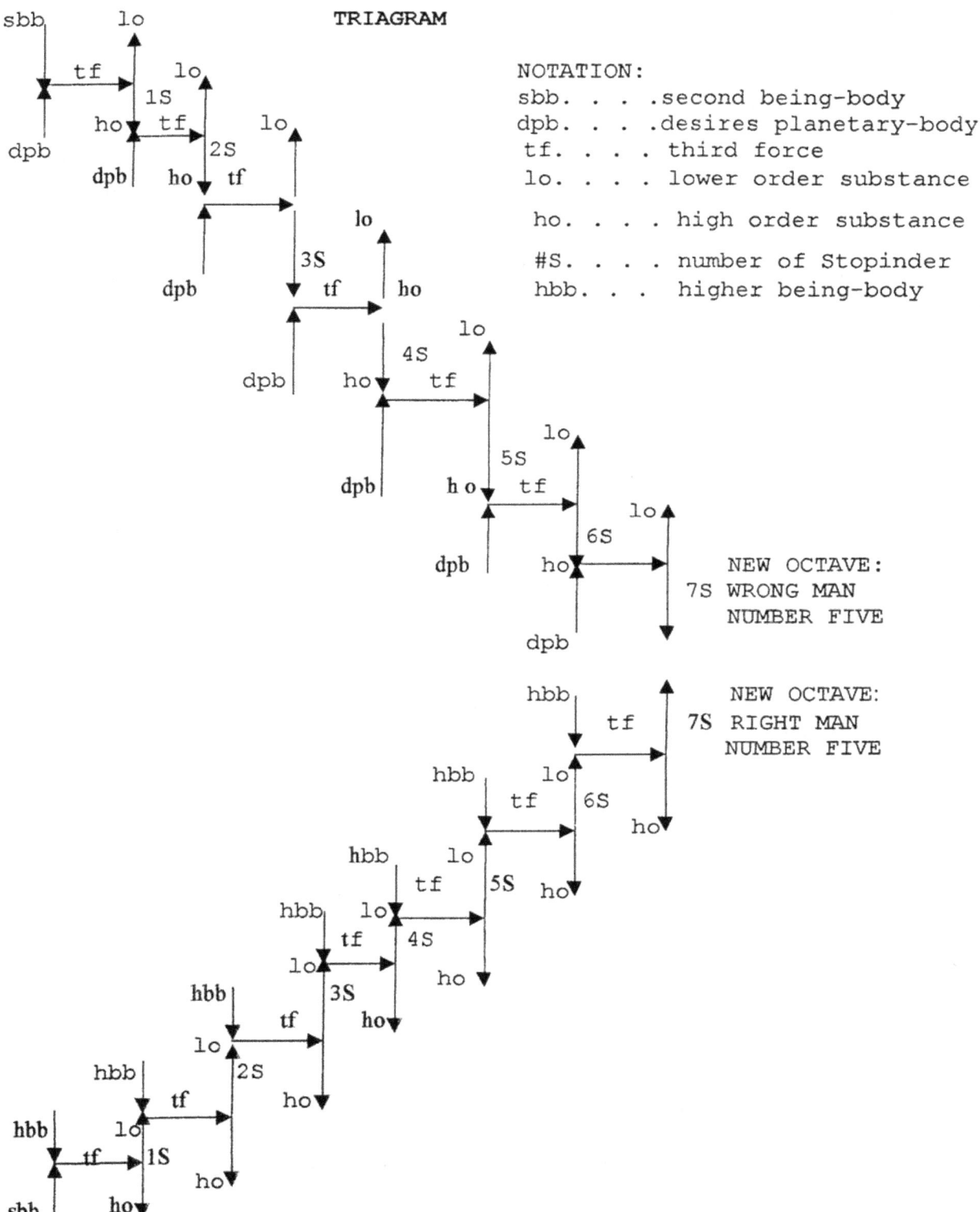

An important question immediately arises in relation to the diagram shown above. What kind of knowledge can be derived from it? The diagram shows very clearly the difference existing between the actualized middle when the movement is one of involution or when it is one of evolution. In the former case, the actualized middle becomes either higher for the succeeding lower, or lower for a preceding higher; in the latter case, the actualized middle becomes either higher for the preceding lower, or lower for the succeeding higher. This latter case, the one for a movement of evolution, corresponds to the formulation of the Sacred-Triamazikamno given in *Beelzebub's Tales*, p.751.

The most immediate practical impact of this knowledge is the fact that if one's actualized middle becomes the higher for a succeeding lower, one then follows the way of involution or the way of descent into the lower planes of existence. Conversely, if one's actualized middle becomes the lower for a succeeding higher, one then follows the way of evolution or the way of ascent towards the higher planes of existence. In other words, on the way of evolution each step we take to advance takes us up because we are lower; on the other hand, on the way of involution each step we take to advance takes us down because we are higher. One may say that the way of evolution is the way of humility and service, while the way of involution is the way of pride and arrogance. The formulation for the Law of Three in *Beelzebub's Tales* is not capricious; on the contrary, it describes the correct and proper way, the way of evolution, the one the true Seeker must follow.

The operation in our lives of the Law of Seven can be viewed as the law governing the motion of the trajectory of one's Search.

Although the trajectory or motion of the search differs with each Seeker, the operational characteristics of the law are always the same. The Seeker must arrive at a solid understanding of the first cosmic law's general operation just as he/she must also thoroughly understand its operation as it relates to his/her Search. This understanding is essential to the person seeking his/her objective position among the inevitable conflicts arising from the processes of common shared existence.

The first thing to understand is the fact that the Search does not follow a linear continuous trajectory. It takes place in discrete stages, along a nonlinear or curvilinear trajectory, under conditions that are sometimes dependent or not on the Seeker. The understanding of this characteristic of the law is very important because if there is one aspect of the Search that is very discouraging, is the existence of long intermittent intervals during which the Search ceases to progress or seems to regress.

One may say that the geometry of the Search is step-wise ascending spiral. This contrasts with the geometry of life in general which is a circle.

Then, the Seeker must strive to understand the operational characteristics of the three segments discussed in the previous section, as it relates to his/her Search. In this sense, the Seeker must pay close attention to those moments and situations in which the factors of external help become apparent. According to the operation of the law, these factors are required to achieve mastery over the third segment of external-help, the mechanically-actualized segment of the evolutionary cycles as generated by the Search.

The Seeker must then be very attentive to those moments when, after actualization of the segment of external-help, the Search calls for actualization of the segment of self-help. In accordance with the operational characteristics of the Law of Seven, these factors are necessary for giving mastery over the last segment or the segment of intentionally-actualized/self-help characteristic of the evolutionary cycles brought about by the Search. These moments require very specific efforts and they are different for different Seekers. They must come from the Seeker's self.

Then the Seeker must pay very close attention to those moments when, in conformity to the first cosmic law, the fifth segment or Fifth of the law makes its appearance. According to the law, the subjective action of the fifth segment (fifth Stopinder) flows by itself from the action of the other two. The Fifths are intrinsic to the Search. In other words, the Search itself generates the Fifths.

The moments of appearance of the Fifths of the law are moments when extreme care is demanded. For the simple reason that the action of the Fifth achieves results that can be diametrically opposed, that is to say, it can give "opposite results." Since this is always the case, the appearance of the fifth segment always involves a choice.

The Fifths are the moments of truth in the Search. They are those situations in the face of which the Seeker is required to make the choice on which rests the future as well as all possible outcomes of the Search. The Fifths are the Search's trials and temptations. If the Seeker falls during realization of any of the Fifths, the Search, in the best of cases, must be reinstated from its very beginnings. At worst, the Search stops or something catastrophic occurs in the life of the Seeker, accident or illness, which makes continuation of the Search impossible.

The Fifths or temptations are then those events (or event) in the Seeker's life that drastically change his/her life's course. The Fifths exists only for those who have direction, who follow a path and who have a goal. Falling into temptation is a sin in the real sense of the word, which is, "missing the mark." If there is no direction or goal, there are no temptations; and if there is no temptation, there is no fall. What fall could possibly exist in the life of a person without a goal or direction?

The Seeker must understand that the Fifths of the law are inevitable. The law can only manifest itself in one form. However, just as the Fifths are inevitable, they are also indispensable because of the fact that as a result of its actualization, the trajectory of the Search can accomplish complete realization. In other words, it is from actualization of the Fifth that the trajectory of the Search can acquire its vivifying power to move to the complete realization of its evolutionary cycle. Because the temptations and the trials are inevitable and indispensable, the Seeker must be attentive to the moments and situations when the Fifths of the law are occurring in order to assiduously proceed during these opportune occasions.

Two striking features characterize the moments and the situations corresponding to actualization of the Fifths. The first is that these moments correspond to times of great tension and great intensity within the life of the Seeker as his/her attention is totally consumed by his/her Search.

The second feature is that these moments and situations are always the same. As the Seeker repeatedly goes around them, the Fifths also repeat themselves causing the Seeker to continuously address the same decisions and choices.

This characteristic of repetitiveness of the Fifths is subject to both objective as well as subjective rationales. From the objective point of view, the repetition of the Fifths of the law is the representation of the mechanicity characterizing the life of ordinary people. From the subjective point of view, the repetition of the Fifths is the actual representation of the particularities proper to each Seeker's individual Search. Each Seeker having his/her own trajectory observes the same situation repeating itself over and over again and they have to continuously face and make decisions and choices. When the Seeker thinks that they are finally out, the obstacle of the Fifth rears its head yet another time. In fact, it is the Seeker's arrival at the recognition of his/her own Fifths that heralds the Search's real beginnings.

The Fifths corresponding to each Seeker's trajectory, are manifestations in conformity to the laws, of the adversary that each person secretly carries within himself/herself, the overcoming of which is essential to the fulfilment of his/her highest destiny.

In fact, paradoxically intrinsic to the Search, the adversary is the actual carrier of the Seeker's possibilities and potentialities. However, because they are only possibilities and potentialities, the adversary is capable of destroying the Seeker or, even more significantly, the Seeker can allow itself to be destroyed by it.

The Seeker must understand at the very outset that his/her struggle with the adversary is his/her own battle. The Seeker must fight this battle within the summit of his/her own consciousness, addressing the Search as he/she does death, alone. Just as nobody can die for him/her, nobody can fight the battle for him/her. The Seeker's only consolation may be the realization that other warriors have engaged in a similar or greater battle.

The Seeker must repeatedly face his/her hidden adversary as well as his/her own Fifths. They are the moments of trial, preceding advancement to a new stage of the Search. The Seeker must rely again and again on the Divine Impulse of Objective Conscience to successfully overcome the adversary.

Eventually, repetition of the Fifths tends to fade. The Seeker having escaped the repetition now feels liberated from the chains that had pitilessly encumbered his/her progress.
Through the Grace from Above, by his/her own being-efforts, and the fundamental universal binding force of the ever-present-ever-flowing Force of Eternal Love, the Seeker is rescued from the powers of destruction.

A Macroscopic View of the Two Fundamental Cosmic Laws

The Seeker is given the secret password, the magic word, which alone permits access to the Real World or World of Above: The World of Divine Objective Reason.

The Search has now reached the intentionally actualized segment of its cycle of realization.

The Seeker has now become the intentionally actualized segment (Stopinder) of the cycle of return to the Prime Source or Most Great Foundation of the Great All-embracing of everything existing.

Such a person, such a man or such a woman, transformed in an intentionally actualized segment of the evolutionary cycle of return to the Real World, is the Real Man.

Thankfully, by the Grace of God, this is possible.

Such relatively free and independent cosmic units of the "Great Whole" are known within the entirety of the Universe as Cosmic Individuals, the consciously, active, and voluntary agents of our COMMON FATHER ETERNAL CREATOR.

And only such relatively free and independent cosmic units of the "Great Whole" in the service of the whole have the objective right to call themselves and to be called "Sons of the Living God." "A particle, though an independent one, of everything existing in the Great Universe."

At this moment, in addition to the service that he/she is obligated to render to Great Nature through his/her inevitable participation in the Universal-Process-of-Common-Cosmic-Exchange-of-Substances, as well as the service he/she is obligated to render to his/her own existence and being, he/she possesses the joyful and glorious possibility of consciously and voluntarily serving, through his/her completed individuality, the Process of Common Creation originally initiated by the CREATOR of everything existing in the Universe.

© Copyright 2003 - Will Mesa - All Rights Reserved

A Macroscopic View of the Two Fundamental Cosmic Laws - Questions & Answers

Question 1: Can you assign a vector direction to either one of the two trajectories depicted in your Triagram?

Will Mesa: I see two vector directions. One follows the way of involution and the other follows the way of evolution. The inclination of either vector depends on the interrelation between the three bodies, the planetary body, the Kesdjan body, and the higher being-body. I once met a group of people who were working on the way of involution at a very accelerated speed and the inclination of this group's trajectory was very steep. The body Kesdjan of some of the members of this group was very much in the direction of the desires of the planetary body. They were working the wrong way, working towards the wrong crystallization. In them the actualized middle became the higher for a succeeding lower; each step they took to advance took them down because they were higher. They followed the way of pride and arrogance. We must strive for an actualized middle that becomes the lower for a succeeding higher; in this way, each step we take to advance takes us up because we are lower. We must strive for the way of humility and service because it is the only way that leads higher.

Question 2: Why do you put so much emphasis on the fifth Stopinder or Fifth of the Law, as you call it?

Will Mesa: Because the Fifths of the law are the moments of crisis in relation to the trajectory of one's search. They correspond to what we call temptations. These Fifths or temptations exist only for those who are engaged in a serious search. Without temptation, there is no fall; but without temptation, there is no rise either. We need the temptations and we find them in the life of each and every serious seeker. It is by the action of the Fifth of the law that we move up or down. These Fifths are generated by the search itself: We need them, as much as we need the two lad shocks of the law. There is no way we can avoid them. The law is the law and we cannot escape the action of the law.

Question 3: What do you mean by the Grace of God?

Will Mesa: I mean the presence of the mystery of the intervention of the Holy Third Force, what we call the Holy Spirit in the Christian tradition. This is a total mystery that we cannot totally and completely comprehend. It is the mystery of the Holy Trinity. We can see the operation of the law of three but we can neither sense nor perceive how the law operates. In relation to the two fundamental cosmic laws, the law of seven and the law of three, there are two mysteries. One has to do with the intervention of the Holy Third Force and the other has to do with the appearance of the Fifths of the law. We can experience the manifestation in our life of these two mysteries but we cannot understand how they come into existence. We have to accept the Grace of God.

A Forum of Those Who Knew Gurdjieff

Forum Panel: Adam Nott and Matthew Thring

Facilitator: Keith Buzzell

"What has Gurdjieff given to you?" (and) "What has he asked of you?"

Keith Buzzell: Two years ago we had a most informative and truly delightful visit with Professor Thring and we are all very happy that he was able to come and be with us again. So we will begin with Professor Thring and he will have some things to say and invites anyone to interrupt him at any point. I would like us to be as informal as possible.

Prof. M. W. Thring: I will start standing up but I may sit down in the middle if I get too weary. What I thought I would do is try and give you a brief autobiography of the effect of Gurdjieff and his teaching, the message he brought back from Asia, has had on my life. Because, I fist came in touch with Ouspensky's lectures, J G Bennett took me to Ouspensky's lectures in 1937 and my future wife had been with them since 1934 and so I went to Ouspensky's lectures. I had at Cambridge had always argued against the chaplain that there could be no Creator because I accepted the Cavendish-scientific view that science was everything, and scientists still believe this, that science is all knowledge. Which is what my second book is going to be totally against. So I went to Ouspensky's lectures and I was very impressed because he talked to us about 'many 'I's' and about mechanicalness and about Self-Observation and he told us about Self-Remembering but it was a completely unknown quantity. We had no idea what Self-Remembering was. Then I worked with Bennett when Ouspensky went to America and then Bennett took me to Paris, allowed me to go to Paris, in 1948, July 1948, just after Mr Gurdjieff had had his second car accident. And he came to the meals. We were invited to meals for lunch and evening and I went altogether for about eight or ten long weekends during the period until a year later, when I went to America for my first trip. I came back from America with ten copies of In Search of The Miraculous which had just been published. Ouspensky would not allow it to be published until this time because he had seen a copy of *All & Everything* from Stanley Nott. (sits down)

Gurdjieff had his second accident, and the first time I went to a meeting he was so ill that he was effectively dead, and yet he was making enormous efforts. He couldn't eat anything yet and he made enormous efforts to be a host. I am absolutely convinced that he kept himself alive for, that last eighteen months or so, in order to bring together all the groups that had started with him and had separated, and that this was his aim and this was what he achieved. Jane Heap and all the American soups and J G Bennett's group and half the Ouspensky group went to those meetings and so we had English weekends or English speaking weekends. Now what I got mostly from those weekends, the first was hope. The second thing was the enormous benevolence of Gurdjieff He really was the exponent of 'Love everything that breathes', which is what he puts into All & Everything. The other thing that I really got was that he and Mme de Salzmann were people living on a different plane from anything I had ever seen before. They were very special people who had developed themselves by their own Work and it gave me hope that I could possibly come this way. Another thing that I got particularly impressed with was the toast which was 'He who does not Work upon himself will perish like dog. He who works on himself may become candidate for honourable death' and this was tremendously valuable to me, this impressed me and it has been with me ever since, that particular expression.

So there was hope, you see? Under Ouspensky I had learned that I 'couldn't do' and I had no idea what doing Self Remembering was, and I had never learned about Self Sensing, never learned about it under Ouspensky, not a bit! So that was one of the main things that I got from Paris, the idea of being alive in your own body. And then we learned the idea, instead of Self Remembering only, we learned doing I AM. It replaced Self Remembering.

Doing I AM, again I didn't have a clue what it was, and indeed I had very fortunate episode. I finished, that is, I got the last drink out of a bottle of Armagnac and Mr Gurdjieff said to me, 'You have got that bottle, with a little bit to drain in it to take away'. So I took it away and J G Bennett said, 'well if you get it to take it away you've got to bring a dozen bottles of Armagnac in its place'. So I borrowed some money from somebody richer and bought the cheapest Armagnac I could find in a shop and took it along. Mr Gurdjieff opened the door to me and said, 'Come in'. He sat me down in his little room and he said, 'Now, what do you want?' And I think I probably said something like 'To be a candidate for honourable death', you see. Anyway, he was happy with my answer. Then he said, 'Well, do I AM at least once in every hour'. Now, I didn't have clue what doing I AM was. Though I tried just to remember the idea, for quite a while, for a few weeks, and only missed one hour when I happened to be giving a lecture and couldn't summon any attention. But it wasn't until about thirty years later when I got the *Third Series* that I found I had a bit of a clue what doing I AM was. In the *Third Series* he speaks about a vibration or a sensation or a feeling in the Solar Plexus and he also speaks about breathing in, and then as you breathe out, feeling something flowing to a part of your body. Those two clues are both in The Third Series and I began to get some feeling of what it meant and I am still working on it, still trying to get somewhere properly with that.

So the other thing, a great thing from Paris was that we met the Movements. We were allowed to take part in the Movements in the Salle Playelle with the French groups. I remember one occasion when Mme de Salzmann told us all to lie on the floor and then picked up our arms and legs, and they should collapse like a sack of potatoes if we were properly relaxed and that memory is with me ever since.

The other thing about the Movements was I couldn't possibly do them! For one thing I have got no sense of rhythm anyway, no natural sense, and it made it almost impossibly difficult for me even to begin it. But I got the feeling of how, if you had all three centres, or brains, connected with attention on the movements, and all the different rhythms with the different parts of you, and so on, then there was no room for the wandering thoughts which informed my ordinary consciousness. And then if they crept back everything went. And again that is something that I am with. What he (Gurdjieff) calls fictitious consciousness, and whenever I try to open myself I have to fight that.

So, all those things I got. Then Margaret saw that I was about to have a nervous breakdown. She took me over to Paris and we had a meeting with Mme de Salzmann, and Mme de Salzmann definitely said 'You have got enough material, go and Work by yourselves and look after your family properly'. Because it was I wasn't looking after my family properly. I had two young children and a third on the way.

Now, some other things about Paris, we took our daughter Susan out, when she was six, and we took her to lunch and then, in the evening, she (Margaret) put her to bed in the hotel and left her in the charge of the lady keeping the hotel. And later in the evening Mr Gurdjieff said to Margaret 'Go and fetch child' and Margaret said, 'No, I won't. The child is too tired' and he (Gurdjieff) just said nothing. And then afterwards she asked Peggy Mensch about this because she was very worried about it, and Peggy said, 'No, he likes somebody who knows what is right,' and that Lady Pentland had been told to do same thing and had brought the child in and he had given her a sweet and sent her to bed. It is a very interesting story.

Another interesting story is about when Margaret was watching the Movements and Margaret was heavily pregnant with our third child. Mr Gurdjieff saw that she was getting over-excited by the movements, because she is a very rhythmic person, musical And he gently came and turned her head away. Because he could see it was dangerous.

Oh, and the other story that I haven't told you is about what happened to the wine, you see. When I took the bottle, he gave me the bottle and he said, 'Drink that when you are in real trouble and I will come and help you.' Now we kept it for about thirty years and then it got lost in a move. Then about another ten years later I suddenly realised what he meant by real trouble which was when I realised that I was a machine, was totally without will and that I could not get out of this situation without help from above. Then I knew what he meant by 'I will help you'. And in a way, I mean he didn't come and help me, but the memory of it somehow gave me hope again.

And hope was the important thing, but with Ouspensky there was no hope. Poor Ouspensky, I mean, he died without hope! Ouspensky was a brilliant man; he did a marvellous job in his book, In Search of The Miraculous. It is a wonderful account of the theoretical side of Gurdjieff's teaching. And I think it and All & Everything, and the Second series and Third Series should be all be taken together. Because the way, for example, the Laws of Three and Seven are dealt with in

Ouspensky's In Search of the Miraculous and then in Beelzebub is entirely different and yet they fit together. And it is worth thinking about how they fit together.

Now what happened after Paris? We worked for a little while with Henri Tracol and Mme Lannes and then I got this Professorship in Sheffield in 1953 and so we adopted what Mme de Salzmann had told us to do 'go off and Work by ourselves, you have got enough material'. And in a way we formed a school between us, for about thirty years. And then in 1981, when I retired, we made contact again with the London Group. We had always kept contact through Catherine Murphy, who had shared a flat with Margaret before I got married to Margaret. She was Secretary of the London Gurdjieff Society and she told us about all the books as they came out and we got hold of them and read them immediately. We must we have read together All & Everything at least twenty times, once a year, for twenty years and it sinks in. And we appreciate the value of his deliberate 'burying bone deeper' which he does all the way through *All & Everything*. And how it forces you make an effort to pick the meaning out of that whole-page sentence. A tremendously valuable exercise, and it shouldn't be spoilt by over simplifying it.

Then in 1981 we got back in touch, we met Henri Tracol and we met Mme de Salzmann and we have been in touch ever since. In 1982 Henri Tracol told me to write a book relating Gurdjieff's Ideas to Modem Science and that book is about to be published this year and it is called *The Seven Riddles of The Universe*. It is all ready; we are just correcting the proofs.

And then I am going to write the third book which is applying Mr Gurdjieff's idea of Conscience to try to solve the terrible mess that the world is in at the moment by educating the conscience of the young which to me is the only hope.

That is about all I have got to say, really.

Keith Buzzell: Could you comment any more specifically? Because you have certainly made mention of some of those things. But the second question, what has he asked of you?

Prof. Thring: Well, it is to try to become candidate for honourable death, which is a life-time quest.

(Tape-break...) (Speaking of Gurdjieff's Question...)

...The question that drove him (G) all over Asia. What is the purpose of Life? Trying to understand what is the purpose of life.

Joseph A.: Did you ever hear Mr Gurdjieff say anything about Mr Ouspensky or the book, *In Search of The Miraculous*?

Prof. Thring: I didn't, but Bennett heard it and he recorded in his book that (G said) 'Now he is my fiend!' And that is right you see, I mean, because he recognised at once that although it is different, the two fit together as two sides: two halves of one apple. Whereas, Ouspensky just refused to publish it because he had heard about All & Everything, he had seen the manuscript of it; and this is because Ouspensky was a smaller man than Gurdjieff Ouspensky had a brilliant mind but he did not have real depth of feeling of that kind. This is my opinion.

I mean, I had an interview with him once and I asked him a question. I will tell you what it was. I was terribly worried by my tremendous sexual urges I asked him what to do about it and he said, 'there is no answer.' Fortunately I married Margaret six months later. I had no question any more! (Laughs)

Joseph A.: I heard the story once that some of Mr Ouspensky's pupils went to Mr Gurdjieff and after Ouspensky had died and started asking him questions about The Hydrogens and Gurdjieff didn't answer those questions and so instead he said to them, 'I have a question for you. Are you a good son? How do you look after you mother?'

Prof. Thring: Yes. On the other hand I found the Hydrogen Table extremely valuable, because I have got that kind of a mind. I can understand saying that because it very quickly becomes formatory, but it is what he calls mathematics, true mathematics. You see one of the points I am making in my new book is that the awful thing of scientists is that they even think we could find a Mathematical Theory of Everything. But fortunately, actually in this week's edition of The New Scientist, what's his name, Stephen Hawking has finally come out with the idea that I don't think we can find The Theory of Everything.

I have a very good analogy. If you take Reality as an elephant, scientists only look at the feet, four feet, Biology and Physics and so on... Mathematicians only look at the footprints! But people with genuine spiritual knowledge and religion and poets can all see the elephant, perhaps the head of the elephant. It is the story of the blind Men who feel an elephant and they feel different parts of it, which is wonderfully apt.

Adam Nott: Med, you said Ouspensky said nothing very useful about Self Remembering or Sensation. Do you remember that last night you mentioned the double-headed arrow...?

Prof. Thring: That's right, I did.

Adam Nott: ...Which is found in *In Search* and which I think is very valuable and don't want to skip past it because it is just a double-headed arrow and you carry on reading... But it is really a key symbol. Can you say something about that?

Prof. Thring: Well, the idea that I and the thing that I am looking at are both together, so to speak, that the arrow points to both, so I am connected. The important thing about Self Remembering, from my view, is that my head and my body are connected, they are sharing attention. And then you say, well 'but where do the feelings come in?' but if the head and the body connect together deeply enough the feelings come in too. That is how I understand it. Yes, thank you for reminding me of that.

Ron B.: You say that Ouspensky was quite shocked when he was told that *All & Everything* was being published. At what stage did Ouspensky actually know that Gurdjieff was actually writing the books of *Beelzebub's Tales*?

Prof. Thring: (Turns and addresses Adam Nott) Well I think your father was responsible for that. He had a copy in manuscript. There were a lot of copies in typescript. He had a copy and he showed it to Ouspensky. Now exactly what date that was I don't know but it must have been in the thirties some time, I think. Do you have any knowledge about that?

Adam Nott: No, but I remember him carrying that book around before the Second War.

Prof. Thring: He describes it in his book, doesn't he? In fact he does mention the date and I think you will find it in one of his two books. One of Stanley Nott's two books.

Barbara S.: How do you understand Mr Gurdjieff when he spoke about remorse?

Prof. Thring: Talk about remorse... Well he had a wonderful phrase. 'Use the present to repair the past and prepare for the future.' That contained it all because only remorse can repair the past.

Sy G.: Could you say something about how Ouspensky himself saw himself in relation to Gurdjieff. Did he see himself as an equal, or as the pupil?

Prof. Thring: I think he saw himself fundamentally as the pupil, but one who could not get on with his master, as it were. That is how he describes it in his book; you see. I don't think he was the teacher or anything, except that he admits that he had got the knowledge from Gurdjieff. But he just couldn't accept Mr. Gurdjieff's very strange methods. Gurdjieff would deliberately shock people, you see, in all kinds of ways such as swearing. Another thing I remember was that he told us that he had two hundred children. He said it many times. At the time I thought it meant purely that he had two hundred pupils that he had brought into the Work. I'm not so sure about it now. (laughter) But he would deliberately shock. At the same time these were intentional shocks, they were meant to shock. He meant to shock Ouspensky out of his thinking and the shock he produced in the 1930s to Orage's pupils was a fantastically powerful shock. Orage told Stanley Nott that he had totally upset his life but he still thanked God every day that he had met Gurdjieff But that was a shock and so was the shock he gave to the De Hartmanns, a tremendous shock, but he could see when a shock was necessary. And there is nobody now who can see when a shock is necessary. That is one of the problems. A shock is necessary in any life of any group and it requires somebody of a different level to be able to give the shock and know it is right and to know how to do it. The other thing I would say is that I feel that, there is a message that Henri Tracol gives in his book and it is that the time comes when it is necessary for the pupil to leave the master and to stand on his own feet. The shock is necessary at that point.

John S.: Could you speak a little about the meals at Mr Gurdjieff's flat and the Toasts of the Idiots in particular?

Prof. Thring: I can indeed! You see I drank honourably and I was actually sick in Mr Gurdjieff's sanctum in Paris. That did me a lot of good! That was a real shock to me and it shook me out of my vanity, really effectively.

Well, the toasts were very important and the man had to drink a third of a glass of vodka or Armagnac at every meal and there would be ten toasts at a meal, so that was quite a lot of alcohol. And I think myself that the alcohol was meant to serve the same function as the drug that Ouspensky describes which put personality to sleep and left only essence there, but I think it did do that. And it was probably because of that that I always came back from Paris with a feeling of having lived in a different world where all my ordinary worries had disappeared and it was something where I had an aim. And that is to me one of the most important things Mr. Gurdjieff said, 'Must have aim.' Must have aim, and in a way Margaret and I kept our aim alive for all those thirty years we were working alone.

John S.: Can I ask a further question? Do you think that the Science of The Idiots ended with Mr Gurdjieff's death as an aspect of Mr Gurdjieff's dispensation?

Prof. Thring: I don't know. I've got a list of the toasts that my sister collected when she was there and I don't know that anybody but Mr Gurdjieff could use that science, you see, this is the problem, because it was a very mysterious science and he claimed it was thousands of years old. Ancient knowledge, but it was very mysterious, you had to go down, then you had to work back up again and various things, but it was important. We had to choose our own idiots and I chose zigzag idiot. I am not sure it was the right choice but, I chose it because I felt I couldn't keep on one aim all the time.

John S.: Did Mr Gurdjieff ever accord an idiot to you, apart from the idiot that you had chosen?

Prof. Thring: No, I think there were too many of us, you see, so he just told us to choose our own idiots.

John S.: Did Mr Gurdjieff ever dispute with people the idiot that they had chosen for themselves?

Prof. Thring: No, but he did once say to somebody, I think it was to Stanley Nott, that he could now go up to a Higher Idiot which means going down. But undoubtedly it had a very deep significance and I cannot say I have anywhere near got to the bottom of it, except that the twenty second Idiot was God.

Ron B.: Could I just ask another question about those feasts and the heavy drinking? I have seen the effects of drink and alcohol can have upon myself and colleagues and people. So can you take your mind back to that period because you probably had quite a view, not only of the toasts but the heavy drinking and remember the sort of action it had on the people around you. Because the table was crammed, wasn't it? I mean some people were standing up, so there were a lot of people in the flat, so all drinking like that, some would go side up. Did you see anyone get bad tempered or moody. You were sick and that is the kind of thing that happens lots of times to people. Did you remember anything at all like that? Because "Drink makes a man more so," and I think that Gurdjieff knew that.

Prof. Thring: I mean it is as I say. It is the one (thing) that gets rid of your personality, gets rid of your mask, so that you are what, you are underneath. I think, as far as I can see, that is what happened to everybody. But the women only drank a sixth of a glass. But it was a medicinal ritual. It was intended and if Gurdjieff had noticed that one person was having trouble he would have told him not to drink any more. Because although he was suffering he was keeping an eagle eye on all of us.

Ron B.: He himself could drink an enormous amount, couldn't he?

Prof. Thring: He did drink but he also had Monsieur Egout who had to take his drink if he (G) didn't want it just as there was Monsieur Poubelle who had to eat his food if he didn't want it, and eat it. I was once made Monsieur Poubelle, the time after I had been sick. Mme de Salzmann said to Bennett, 'Are you sure it's alright?' and Bennett said 'Yes, yes, my people are alright!' (laughter) And I was all right, but only just.

Joseph A.: Did you ever hear Mr Gurdjieff say anything, or did you ever get an impression from him about whether he wanted his ideas and books spread or maybe even his attitude to publicity or how to go about it.

Prof. Thring: This is a very important question. I know that he said at one point that he would like to see the Pope reading his book and that he would like to see it read in every church. And of course he believed that all the great religions were founded by messengers from God. This is where I personally feel that only way out of the World's present trouble is to bring the various Religions to concern, make some kind of film or something, to teach the attitude of their religion to the Three Questions of Conscience:

One is - What is the purpose of Life?
One is - What is Compassion?
One is - What is the proper attitude toward my own body?

That is what I am going to put into my third book as being the only hope of our civilisation to survive, if all the religions, and I mean the non-fanatical people in those religions, because the fanatical people say, 'Our religion is the only one and everyone else must die!' And unfortunately there are fanatics in all religions. But that is how I am trying to develop the idea of conscience that is the key to the message of Ashiata Sheimash after whom wars stopped all over Asia. I mean that is a tremendous parable, isn't it!

All & Everything Conference 2003

I don't say it happened but it is a key, to me it is vitally important.

Keith Buzzell: I will now turn to Adam and ask the same two questions.

Adam Nott: Well I intended to try to address these questions. But I think I should make excuses for my presence here as 'one who knew Gurdjieff.' Because I did meet Mr Gurdjieff, but at the time, unlike Med, I knew nothing of his teaching. I was eighteen years old, staying with the De Hartmanns in Paris but on my way to a Work camp in the south of France where I was looking forward to meeting people of my own age and doing physical work with them building a school. And my father insisted that I should go and visit Mr Gurdjieff in such a way that I refused. And he said 'Well, you know, you could look him up as an old friend, and I knew that he wasn't an old &end, although I had heard his name all my life. I didn't know, but I knew he was important. But at that age and even now, I am quite shy and the idea of going into Paris and meeting an unknown person, especially someone who, well, there was a feeling about him. In fact I can remember as a child, struggling, I must have been about six, writing a letter which began 'Dear Uncle George'... It was to thank him for some sweets he had sent via my parents. But my mother said. She made me feel it might be interesting and worthwhile to meet Gurdjieff. So the big obstacle was the telephone call in French to Mme de Salzmann's secretary, but having discovered where to go, I then went there. Now the reason I knew nothing of his teaching was, first of all, there was nothing published. Secondly, probably because my mother was the child of converts to Roman Catholicism, she had had an overdose of what her parents believed and she wanted to avoid this for her children. But in any case, I think she realised, I think they both realised that one has to discover the Work for oneself. It is not a help if one's parents are following the same path. So I went in complete ignorance and on meeting Mr Gurdjieff it was quite obvious who he was, and I said 'Je suis Adam Nott. '

I was then ushered into a corridor where there were some people standing waiting silently, and I thought, very tense. But I now know why. I have been in the same situation. This was in the summer of 1947 so there were not a lot of people there, and I am very grateful to have actually had a meal with him when there were about twelve or fourteen people there and it was a comfortable number of people to take in, as a visitor.

The meal proceeded and there were these toasts and I was provided with a tumbler of Armagnac, and when that was empty another tumbler which I found very acceptable. And I can remember very little of what was aid, but, what stays with me, and I find that impression can be evoked when I am reading *Beelzebub's Tales* is the impression of the man. It is difficult to put this impression into words, but I would say there was something big about him and I felt warmly welcomed by him. And at the end of the meal I was invited to go for some coffee by some of the people there, in a cafe, and one of the people said 'Do you always speak to Mr Gurdjieff in French?' and I hadn't realised, well I guess actually the conversation at the meal was in English and in French. So I went back. I was invited to come back. I got the message telling me I could come 'whenever you want' but I was interested in other things. I think I felt a great excitement from that visit but I think I wanted to join my friends in the south of France.

A Forum of Those Who Knew Gurdjieff - Matthew Thring & Adam Nott

And this, I'm not sure of the chronology, but I made several other visits to the flat.

(tape change)

I would like to address the question. I would like the question to be 'What did he leave?' which has been of value to me, and the most important thing is that he left pupils. Because those pupils became my teachers and then the forms within which they worked. The form of working in a group and the forms of the movements and of course his writings, and his music. Now I thought, partly because I thought it would be interesting for me, in the face of this demand, to try to understand why it was necessary to Work in a group. Or what does group Work consist of? I think the necessity is due to this situation of multiple 'I's or that is one of the reasons. In a group one is sharing the same aim, for example, the aim could be the question why am I here? Or, how is it possible to see the truth about myself? Now that immediately provokes another question. How is it possible to see the truth about oneself when there is no oneself? So, in a group questions are asked and answers are given and obviously I am speaking about a group under somebody who is more experienced who gives a direction into the group. But my own experience of group Work is that one is just as likely to learn from one's colleagues in the group as from the one leading the group. One of the things that happen in a group is that questions are asked, a response is given and some people may register the response, or the question. The following week the same question may be asked by someone else and in the end they are all basically the same question. But because I am, within me, continually changing it takes a long time for anything to register. And so as one pursues this search with colleagues there are moments when one is more receptive to the material and there are moments when one isn't. This is not an easy path to follow. There are occasions when one can become very discouraged but then when you hear another person with exactly the same problem as you this gives you courage, in fact. I think one can learn more from recorded failures than from reported successes. Because when somebody has a glimpse of something true then you think 'I wish I could have that, whereas where they have 'failed', in quotation marks, one tends to empathise and to realise that one is not alone in this struggle. Now what is the difficulty about seeing ourselves? I think that the most obvious difficulty is that at 'the moment when one glimpses some aspect of oneself; which one could learn from, there is a reaction, either pleased or disappointed. Probably rather usually disappointed or shocked at the behaviour that I see then I am taken by the reaction, and so what I have seen doesn't leave an impression. So then a question is, 'How is it possible to see and not react. Now, as I understand it this is only possible when the centres are connected. The level of reaction is a level where one centre has predominated. So in order to see it is necessary for the centres to be connected. So how is this possible? Now this brings us, I think, to the fundamental question. How is it possible for the centres to be connected? And experience shows that before three can be connected, two need to be connected. That is quite logical. So which two? Well Med has already given a clue but if I try to connect my emotions with my body or if I try to connect my emotions with my mind the emotions are so strong that there is no possibility of a relationship. If I try to connect my body to my head there is a possibility of a relationship. Now then if that relationship can be maintained the feelings can come in. So how do I connect my body with my head? Now this is something I know how to do; but that doesn't mean I can do it. And if I told you how to do it... Well I would tell you how to do it if I thought it would help you, but it is a discovery that has got to be made. Now if those connections are made there is quite a different possibility which I have experienced, but I can only speak about experience and from memory. That experience is that one again sees something of oneself; but instead of this approval or disapproval, the experience is of something being fed, or nourished, to be given energy and than at that moment I see that this life, or my way of living my life, which on an ordinary level I am continually trying to improve, and of course not doing so, that I don't need to change that. On the ordinary level there is always this feeling that I must do something better. But seeing from that other point of view I see that my life is material for my Work. If there is somebody there who can transform their impression then of course fit only happens when things are together. So the question is how do you bring them together? And I think you could say this is what Gurdjieff asks. I think it is what is meant by Being-Partkdolg-Duty and I think it is also what is meant by Remembering Oneself.

Now the movements are a wonderful medium because the kind of experience that I have been describing can actually take place if one submits to the demands of the movement. In other words one is helped towards an entirely different experience of oneself without realising it. You how, one is not looking for the experience, one is trying to meet the demands of the movement helped by the rhythm and the music, and the times you reach something and when you reach it you realise what it is. And that, for me, offered hope and assured me that by my own efforts there was somewhere that could be reached. But there is always the difficulty that if you have a good experience the experience of something like being present, being all there, the centres being together this can put a blight on one's own efforts. Because you then have this memory of how things could be, and instead of starting from scratch, starting from now, where is where you have start from, you are looking back and saying, 'well you are starting now but it is not quite like that!' And then you are not here any more, so that is another of the obstacles. Now I won't speak about Mr Gurdjieff's writing because probably from what I have heard this morning you are better acquainted with them than I am But I would like to ask you a question in their relation. If what Mr Gurdjieff left is designed to be a three centered activity, how can reading Beelzebub be a three centred activity?

End of Session

Papers Written to the Forum "Those Who Knew Gurdjieff"

Papers written by the following Contributors to the Forum were read.

Paul Beekman Taylor

What did Gurdjieff give to me? What did he ask of me?
What Gurdjieff gave me was the image and functioning of a "normal man."

I was in a sense "born and raised into the Work". That is, my mother, and all those who played fatherly roles in my education - Jean Toomer, with whom I lived for a considerable amount of time as a member of his family, Nick Putnam with whom I spent a good deal of time in Connecticut and New York City, Orage followers Sherman Manchester and Daly King - exercised Gurdjieff's ideas to the extent that they seemed to me for several years to be a rule of conduct instead of an exception. I remember very little consciously of my time with Gurdjieff at the Prieuré and in Paris or my time with Orage in London, but since December 1948 I have been in continuous touch with and in the company of those who had lived with Gurdjieff. In short, what Gurdjieff has given me has come to me through the two interlocked channels of his personal pupils and himself. Both channels carry the same message, but Gurdjieff himself was the "real thing"; that is, he incarnated the ideas that others could only follow. Knowing Gurdjieff "in the skin," as he said, has made an impression upon me far beyond the records of his systematic teachings and writings. Gurdjieff told me (and I include in the "me" all the others in his presence at the time) never to trust myself until I knew myself. He told me to question whom I was whenever I made a decision or a judgment. "Not until you discover who you are not will you be able to begin the journey to discover who you are." Gurdjieff made me acutely aware of my multiple identities before him. Whatever I said to him raised the question in his eyes: "Do you know who is saying these words?" Doubt yourself; he taught, and whenever I feel that emotions are governing my actions, I question what center in 'me' is in control.

Gurdjieff gave me a sense of urgency to know how to concentrate, not just mentally, but psychically, physically, and rationally at once. He taught me to feel any or every part of my body at any given time. Awareness is control, he taught. Awareness of pain, for example, seemed to facilitate understanding its sources. Taking pills was an abdication of responsibility for alleviating, not eliminating, pain by will power. One can learn more from pain that from pleasure.

My earliest memory of Gurdjieff was his throwing biscuits at me from his seat in the conservatory at the Prieuré, after I had pestered him for some sweets while he was taking his afternoon tea or coffee. He threw insults with the biscuits, "bolda, svoloch!" I learned from that moment that words need not eliminate or reduce pleasure of acts.

Later, when I was a young man, Gurdjieff taught me that nothing need bother me unless I let it do so. But, it was the lesson from witnessing his reaction to circumstance that taught me the most. He was able to not hear things that might tax his patience or waste his time. He was able to not feel pain or discomfort.

In his direct teaching, he counselled me to avoid at all costs doing what was expected of me, first by my mother, and secondly by my school-teachers. Fulfilling their expectations would forfeit my own possibilities to be what I might become to be what others wanted me to be for their sake, to realize their plans for me. Education is a factory turning out servants for a social system, when it should be, as it once was, an avenue toward a realization of self. He said that his own teaching was not dedicated to changing anyone's "actual" today, but in awakening in him a potential that might be developed into tomorrow's actual.

Gurdjieff gave his pupils a means of developing potential. A step in the process was a conscientious scan of one's false selves. One's "real" self is perceivable, he said, only when all the false ones are exposed and disdained. What then is left is one's essence. So, one must learn to recognize the false in order to find the real. One method of discovering the false is to play it, to play the role one thinks is the real self. "Play what you think you are and you will see how shallow is that role." I remember him saying that the best way to see myself was to observe and assume his perception of my self.

Gurdjieff taught these things, and the words he used were understood in as many different ways as persons who heard them. He knew that I was incapable of "objective understanding," but he said that I might be capable of realizing conscientiously what factors in my consciousness determined my understanding.

Such precepts are easily repeated in varieties of forms to a wide audience with different effects. What makes them particularly resonant for me is the example of the man himself. Knowing Gurdjieff personally was an experience that gives a force to his teaching that I cannot put into words. Gurdjieff was at once the exemplar and the denying example of everything he said. He was to me a Dostoiesvkian figure, one who reveals truth by displaying the false. He seemed demonic, but suggested that though God can play the devil, the devil cannot play God. He exemplified the man who reveals himself capable to reach as high as low he can stoop. He was slovenly in habit, dressing in disordered fashion, smoking and drinking in apparent excess without any display of refined manners. He swore, ranted, and insulted. He had not a whit of patience, cutting off the speech of others as if they had said nothing. Once, reaching a railway crossing with the barriers lowered, he simply turned and drove in the opposite direction from where he intended to go just to avoid the wait. He arrived finally at his destination as if there was no time or day expected for arrival. He did not reserve rooms or dining table in advance, but always got service, one way or another. His display of uncontrol was sublime control! He manifested anger at trifles and treated disasters as amusing trifles. He displayed negative emotions as playthings of an unshakeable positiveness. There were lessons to be gleaned from such behavior, and finding the lesson was itself a lesson. To me, a young man, Gurdjieff was everything, but at no one moment could I be sure what he was. He was an example of all things one could be. In memory he remains the highest human being I have known or have been able to conceive of.

© Copyright 2003 - Paul Beekman Taylor - All Rights Reserved

Dushka Howarth

The Gurdjieff Heritage Society
c/o Dushka Howarth, Coordinator
East 70th. St., (Apt. 3E), N.Y., N.Y 10021
Tel: (1) (212) 734 5757
Email: info@gurdjieff-heritage-society.org
Website: www.gurdjieff-heritage-society.org

To Our Friends... Present and Future:

More than fifty years have passed since that compassionate, special human being Mr. Gurdjieff left in our keeping a valuable teaching, with clearly defined principles, fresh stimulating "ideas", and, most important, precise practical suggestions for "living" them.

But in recent years we have begun to see that this priceless legacy is increasingly being allowed to deteriorate, become neglected or lost, and Mr. Gurdjieff's carefully considered, specific instructions are being ignored, misunderstood or misinterpreted. Distortions of "The Gurdjieff Ideas" and "The Fourth Way" proliferate in the public marketplace, and even the meticulously constructed and jealously guarded "Movements" are being deformed, forgotten, or used inappropriately.

A large number of people here and abroad don't accept that "all this is inevitable!" They share a sincere wish to preserve, practice and pass on Gurdjieff's teaching undistorted and are pooling their efforts in this direction.

(P. D. Ouspensky warned long ago that: "Ideas become distorted when people begin to invent their own explanations and theorize, but so long as they work sincerely and try to verify anything that comes into their minds, and work according to rules and principles, distortion is not at all necessary." *A Record of Meetings*, p.367)

For such tangible materials as recordings, films, photos, letters, etc. (and increasingly emerging treasures of unpublished exercise notations, music manuscripts, teaching suggestions, memoirs, etc.) there are proven modern methods which can, and must, be used to arrest and reverse deterioration, and, unfortunately, theft!

Once properly preserved and copied, (by digitizing, scanning, put onto CDs etc.,) these items require a small fraction of the previous storage space--and, as added insurance, can then be duplicated and distributed to other locales to ensure their safety, and longevity.

Papers Written to the Forum "Those Who Knew Gurdjieff" - Dushka Howarth

Such techniques also mean that, without jeopardizing the irreplaceable originals, these materials can then be accessible to Foundation libraries and sanctioned Work groups for use in their activities...And, important to the future of the Work, to authorized Movements instructors, pianists, and group leaders for "verification, arbitration and inspiration."

What started simply as numerous lengthy phone-calls, countless emails exchanges and occasional personal visits developed into an active community of "right-minded", "like-minded" people (several hundred have made themselves known so far.) which we provisionally called "THE GURDJIEFF HERITAGE SOCIETY".

A nucleus was formed to protect and administrate the results of all this work, and various personal estates, assets, book rights, etc. Now there are already many encouraging fist results-- hits of much research, on-going expert technical work, expenditures of time, energy and funds--, and, of course, many heated discussions, sharing of personal experiences, etc. but all in a climate of common goals, deep respect, warm humanity, and, hopefully, joy and satisfaction!

Legal advisors have suggested a more formal organization of the Society so this is now being implemented. Non-profit corporation status would facilitate donations and bequests of invaluable book collections and other Gurdjieff materials, which at present are often simply abandoned or discarded.

Notably we have found that, unbelievably, out of the approximately 3000 Gurdjieff books and articles currently available, (refer: The Gurdjieff Annotated Bibliography) the entire New York Public Library system contains only 61 examples (which do not even include "All and Everything"). However we remember that Mr. Gurdjieff wrote to us all (in his Circular Letter January 13, 1949): "I intend that the first series of my writings shall be made freely available without payment to all who are in need of their help." So, at our instigation and with our cooperation, an extensive Gurdjieff division is now being created in the central research section and Randy Berenek (Director of "Planned Giving") and Beth Diefendorf ("Chief of Research. Departments") will coordinate, evaluate and channel material we gather to appropriate research (and lending) departments.

A few of our other varied "preservation projects" are: Full orchestra recordings of Gurdjieff's music. His "Seid Dance", "Song of the Aisors", "Song of the Fisherwomen", "Duduki", and "Tibetan Masked Dance", scored into an "Oriental Suite" by Thomas de Hartmann were beautifully recorded by the Dutch State Radio Metropole Orchestra which also performed them live (with Gurdjieff's "Great Prayer") in Amsterdam last June before an enthusiastic audience of 1500. The Gurdjieff Heritage Society had located and preserved the scores, acquired the proper permissions, paid for the parts to be copied, meticulously confirmed tempos from de Hartmann's own piano recordings, etc. all in close cooperation with de Hartmann's heirs, Tom Daly Sr. and Jr. The entire project was initiated and produced by Gert-Jan Blom. (subsequently appointed Artistic Producer of the Metropole Orchestra, and Musical Advisor of the Holland Festival). And even more important, all the orchestrations Gurdjieff himself dictated for the Paris Movements

All & Everything Conference 2003

Demonstrations in 1923 are also being recreated by the Metropole Orchestra, the recording taking place this week. (March 31 - April 4).

As for Gurdjieff's unique harmonium recordings: Though literally melting away with age, the original tapes were coaxed back from the Gurdjieff heirs. These together with wire recordings made in New York, copies of missing tapes salvaged £tom amongst effects of the late Tom Forman, and from the NY Foundation's (mildewed) closets, from private collections, etc. all have been salvaged, data-based, and transferred to CDs. Thus we have accomplished the urgent first step - everything that Gurdjieff himself ever recorded has been saved for the future. The second step, the accessibility and usage of this material, is still to be "pondered" and arbitrated... hopefully with respect and good will! A limited edition boxed set is envisaged for the use of authorized groups containing all 160 or so recordings on approximately 19 CDs accompanied by a detailed, well-illustrated book. (a Blom/Daly/Howarth cooperation.) Being scanned to CDs are definitive notes for the "finished and set by Mr. Gurdjieff" "39 MOVEMENTS", compiled, and corrected during many summers of intensive cooperative work by Jeanne de Salzmann,, Marthe de Gaigneron (the original note-taker), and Jessmin Howarth, the original set of notes (impeccably translated to English by J. Howarth) was confided to the NY Foundation but by 1984, when Mrs. Howarth died, they were found to have disappeared. (Recently reported: "In San Francisco"!!?). One other copy, sent to Mme de Salzmann, was promised us by Michel "once he went through his mother's papers!" However, with huge effort we have recovered and reconstituted (from handwritten or carbon copies, etc.) most of these invaluable notations and a team is transferring them (with verifying photos and other unique material) to CDs for safe, practical storage. (There are still several lacking that we need help replacing! From Paris or California?)

Also being scanned onto CDs for preservation-storage and carefully considered sharing is definitive material on the "SIX OBLIGATORTES" as noted by Jessmin Howarth, acknowledged by Mr. G. and Mme de Salzmann as the final authority on all the early Movements. This includes notations, photographs, history and teaching material (with special hints for beginner's classes, and "inhibition" exercises for advanced), corrected music, suggestions to pianists, etc.

We have developed a lively, mutually beneficial cooperation with the Gurdjieff International Review (and other serious journals) and attempt on-going surveillance, investigation and documentation of the many other, (mostly aberrant) "Gurdjieff" web sites. Our amicable relationships with heirs of Gurdjieff, Ouspensky, and many others have made it possible to collect and preserve a treasury of old photographs and drawings, videos of current group activities and movements from various countries, recordings of lectures and broadcasts, etc.

We continue our best efforts but would welcome suggestions, participation, criticism, information, etc. from everyone (especially those who had contact with Mr. Gurdjieff himself or can bring forward additional material to be preserved or suggest projects that need doing).

As for a motto for us? Let's consider this! Almost a century ago Mr. Gurdjieff climaxed his first ever written exposition of his ideas (which, one often forgets, was the scenario of his ballet) with this blessing which is the White Magician's curtain line at the end of The Struggle of the Magicians: "May reconciliation, hope, diligence and justice be ever with you all.

"Amen!"

Sincerely,
THE GURDJIEFF HERITAGE SOCIETY
(c/o Dushka Howarth, Coordinator)

P.S. The forthcoming joint memoir *IT'S UP TO OURSELVES, A Mother, a Daughter, and Gurdjieff*, by Jessmin and Dushka Howarth (containing 700 photos), opens with these quotations:

Jessmin Howarth: "Remember, dear, you don't have to judge 'the ideas' by the people who believe in them."

Dushka Howarth: "We were blessed in our lives to come close to some special human beings. Special, yes, because they had more Being than the rest of us. But that doesn't mean that they were any the less Human. Quite the contrary."

G. I. Gurdjieff: "I cannot develop you. I can only create conditions in which you can develop yourselves."

Sophie Grigorievna (Mme. Ouspensky): "You sit around waiting for pearls when what you should actually be doing is not to be swine."

Olga de Hartmann: "Mr. Gurdjieff could hit you over the head and catch you before you hit the ground. These people only know how to hit you over the head!"

A. R. Orage: "Religion without humanity is more dangerous than humanity without religion."

© Copyright 2003 - Dushka Howarth - All Rights Reserved

Kathleen Riordan Speeth

"What has Gurdjieff done for you? What has he asked of you?"

I am a child of the Work. My parents met because of their interest in the ideas as presented by Mr. Orage. Before I was seven Mother read me the manuscript of Beelzebub, chapter by chapter, as a bedtime story. Did it form magnetic center? Perhaps so; or it could be that I was born with one. Nestling near her, listening to her voice, I was aware that I had the power of 'yes' and "no" in me. What I learned then has, for better or worse, framed my thinking, my life. When I first saw Mr. Gurdjieff he was sitting on a low couch. I leaned over and kissed his right cheek. He smiled and said to Mme. de Salzmann, "Elle a des possibilités." At that moment I experienced myself not only as a little girl in a blue dress with puffy sleeves but also as someone (or something) quietly watching, deciding, and even though I might be irresponsible, I knew I was answerable for my life. Did Mr. Gurdjieff do this for me or ask it of me? I think so. During World War Two, when even Americans had to do without, I ecstatically put a chocolate covered cherry in my mouth from the big box Mr. Gurdjieff gave each child. He was an indulgent grandfather; I was divinely satisfied. When we toasted the idiots with Armagnac and milk, and my little cordial glass was refilled after each three gulps, I was even happier. I used my power of "yes" and by choosing eight silver dollars, then using them unwisely. Was this a lesson? I believe it was. When I was about twelve I was sitting next to Mr. Gurdjieff's chair, on the floor of the stage in the Wellington Hotel. In front of us masses of people were doing movements. Their unison shook the hall. The piano that supported the rhythm was almost drowned out. He shouted directions. Then he looked down at my spindly legs ensconced in their first long stockings, and he made a laughing remark. I became conscious of my vanity. Did he do that for me or ask that of me? No doubt. The experience of someone who was part of the Work since birth has to be different than that of converts. Until I was thirty I was part of the Gurdjieff Foundation. I made efforts to strengthen my wish not to give in to life nor run away from it. The movements strengthened my attention. In groups, it seemed to me, students were being encouraged to suppress emotion instead of learning to use the energy behind them to produce any emotion they wished. Lives became serious in the wrong way, as I saw it. Did the contrast with Mr. Gurdjieff's energy help me to see this? Indeed it did.

At Mendham I pruned tomato plants, washed windows and chopped parsley in the big house, hushed because of me. Ouspensky's failing health. My daughters stayed in the children's house, where there were no parties, just lessons and readings. Mr. Gurdjieff was gone by then, but the experience there, and in the New York Gurdjieff Foundation, seemed to me to be a demonstration of his teaching about descending octaves. Many (not all!) teachers and students had become repressed, suppressed and superego-controlled, producing a sort of esoteric-high-church ambiance complete with traditions and dogmas. The kindness and joy had drained away. Did having been in Mr. Gurdjieff's presence sensitize me so that I could have that insight? Of course.

Papers Written to the Forum "Those Who Knew Gurdjieff" - Kathleen Riordan Speeth

In 1975 I published a little book called *The Gurdjieff's Work*. I was severely criticized for daring to express myself on a subject that had been part of my life since birth. Since most of my critics had been lifelong family fiends, this amounted to being sent to Coventry. It was a test of my development. It confirmed my sense that I was alive, well and answerable for my life even though what once was had come to an end. Did Mr. Gurdjieff prepare me to be a black sheep? I believe he did, and I am forever grateful.

© Copyright 2003 - Kathleen Riordan Speeth - All Rights Reserved

Nicolas de Stjernvall

Never follow the pock !
Do all that you can also not do!

It is precepts like these which I heard often in G. I.'s close entourage, and which I tried to put into practice myself.

In being with him for the first time in 1937 I lost no time to get acquainted with his place. The apartment seemed spacious at the time. Nevertheless, when I saw it again years later after the death of Georges Ivanovitch, I was surprised to imagine how I could have moved about, slept and served G. I. over a period of several months in lodgings which I found now surprisingly small and uncomfortable. When I arrived I found Valentin, alias Valia, Gurdjieff's nephew, who showed up a few times each week. Needless to say, the greater part of our work consisted in buying, preparing and serving the midday and evening meals. Food occupied an important part in the life at rue Colonels-Renard.

My workday began normally at 8 in the morning and ended often around 11 at night because, in the beginning, I slept in the salon of the apartment, set off by a screen. Georges Ivanovitch neither frightened nor put me off in any way. He was perfectly relaxed in my company. He slept most of the time in his underwear. Each time I saw or heard him go toward the bathroom in the early hours of the morning and blow his nose in the oriental fashion, that is to say loudly, pinching his nostrils alternately, I couldn't restrain a shrug of the shoulders. When later in the morning he went again to the bathroom and gargled, close by, I showed my disapproval with a stiff look. He didn't care the least.

In the morning, Gurdjieff was usually satisfied with just a cup of strong black coffee, sometimes with a biscuit and a glass of water. That didn't hold him back him from lighting his Russian cigarettes even before eating. He was as demanding a schoolmaster when it came to the way his bed was to be made, which surprised me because I deemed this detail absolutely secondary. A fine appearance and clothing fashion were the least of his concerns. He attached no importance whatsoever to what he wore, though he changed his underwear often. His wardrobe was reduced to the bare minimum. The same was true of his shoes, socks ties, hats, handkerchiefs, etc. He disliked shaving and did it only by a sense of obligation. I pressed his trousers from time to time, sewed on buttons, and did even the little daily tasks of mending. I carried out the dirty linen and his shirts to the local laundry, and he gave me full leeway to carry out domestic chores. Little by little, I groomed myself into being his executive right-hand man.

This is the way things would go, for example, in the evening. I would park his automobile, a current model Hotchkiss, on the rue Brunel. Then I would fetch his mail from the box, read it to

Papers Written to the Forum "Those Who Knew Gurdjieff" - Nicolas de Stjernvall

him, and sometimes translate important official letters. In the beginning, my sleep was troubled by the murmurs or the giggles of women who took part in the almost nightly parties which G.I. seemed to appreciate so much as any connoisseur of nocturnal pleasures. His sexual potency absolutely astounded me. Apropos, about once a week I would cross paths in the apartment with a certain Olga, who had a sly and furtive look, and was obviously the recruiter of pretty young girls. Before going to sleep I always left a thermos bottle full of mocca by his bed. In the salon, as I retired graciously from the scene behind my screen, I'd catch a sight of the attractive faces, tableaux vivants in the process of being prepared for the evening. More and more bothered and at the end of my patience I took Gurdjieff aside one day before his afternoon nap and told him without equivocation that I would prefer to spend my nights anywhere else than rue Colonels-Renard. At fist he gave me a look of irritation but then the lines of his face relaxed almost immediately into a smile full of affability. We had perfectly understood one another! The same day, I moved my meagre belongings to the Hotel d'Armaille, a modest hotel on the street of the same name, a few metres away.

I have already spoken of the importance meals played in the daily routine, and the shopping for goods for their preparation. I wondered often how Georges Ivanovitch managed to have so many people every day at his table both for noon and evening meals. He needed this unbroken flow of conviviality, loud voices, toasts, etc. From all appearances, he fled solitude and acted genuinely unhappy when he found himself at the table only in the company of one or a few boring relatives.

Soon after my arrival in the apartment, in my company, Gurdjieff charged his nephew to roast four appetizing capons in the oven. 'Uncle' was expecting some important guests at noon. I enjoyed joking with Valia, and while the master was out somewhere, we relaxed in the salon where we got along like old buddies. What was to be avoided at all costs that day unfortunately came about when we forgot completely about the capons in the oven. I saw Valia leap straight up from his seat and run to the kitchen, only to return with a disconsolate face. At that very moment I heard the key turn in the lock. G. I. came in through the entry with his guests without the least pause. Valia, eyes ablaze, grabbed me by the shoulders and begged me to tell his uncle the bad news. It had to be done quickly. Without changing the expression on my face, I went up to Georges Ivanovitch and whispered in his ear: 'There's bad news. We forgot to take the chickens out of the oven!'

Mastering his rage and his disappointment, Gurdjieff strode off toward the kitchen. "Triple assholes you are. Take the chickens out of the oven immediately" he roared. With a quick twist of his hand, G. I. tore off the skin which stuck to the burnt carcasses of the birds. A few spoons of butter, some creak onion; garlic powder and some spices transformed into a delicacy what was a hopeless disaster a few moments ago. I couldn't believe my eyes. Turning to his nephew, he said 'Serve this in a crown of basmati rice. This will be a Georgian specialty like 'chokhom bili'. Gurdjieff and I often did our shopping in the local markets not far from Place St. Ferdinand. We were a sight at the butchers when G. I., oblivious to others, sliced directly out of sides of beef and lamb the cuts he wanted, without in the least shocking the proprietor of the shop. At that time, whole carcasses hung at the butcher's for the clientele to see. You can imagine the looks on the faces of those who witnessed such behaviour for the first time! Georges Ivanovitch liked most of all lamb and veal.

Nonetheless, we often bought fowl and fish according to our moods. The boiling and roasting ritual in the kitchen was virtually invariable at Gurdjieff's.

Before leaving his apartment for the Café de la Paix, G. I. would ask for a large sort of basket, which he'd fill later with large globs of butter, add some meat specialties of the day, and some spices to go with it. The rest, the vegetables, salads, snacks, were my business. Like most Caucasians, Gurdjieff adored fresh herbs and asked for them year-round. I discovered a good Corsican green grocer on Pereire Boulevard where every day I'd find fresh mint, estragon, parsley, large round onions, garlic, etc. I served him all these things on a large platter at each meal.

One day, despite my searches in the area I couldn't find the fresh mint he particularly liked. He called me out of the kitchen and began to berate me, fury in his eyes. I confronted him straight-faced without blinking, clenching slightly my teeth (I add parenthetically that for a long time I had built up an emotional armour, and it took the worst thrusts of G. I.'s rage). He usually stopped yelling, realizing that his cries were futile once the torment he had intended for me had been inflicted. Be it as it may, he was the fist to turn away, realizing apparently the futility of continuing the exercise. I guess that my detachment and calm disarmed dear Georges Ivanovitch a bit more each time he let loose his anger.

Each day I tried continually to make the most of the good principles which he had instilled in me. I had, so to speak, assimilated the essential core of his teaching. With a poker face, Georges Ivanovitch observed and encouraged me in my efforts and in the exercises which I performed on my own. I invented them myself and I was able to do them well, leaving aside the pleasures of idle reading, stuffy theories and abstract reasoning. My exercises were as much mental as physical, and were directed above all to make my acts conscious and subordinate to my will. The exercises in question would certainly seem quite modest and simple in the eyes of some. I regret that.

It was generally in the morning that I would tell Gurdjieff everything I had accomplished, whether the results were successful, half-successful or, in a word, failures. I never had the impression that G. I. listened to me only for my pleasure. He followed attentively my accounts, nodding his head, smiling, asking questions, etc. I began passing notes to him which summed up my little secrets. For example, and very generally, the exercises can be reduced to a few acts of self discipline as follows:

'You put on your left sock instead of the right one when you get up'.

'You make three steps forward and one to the side, your toothbrush behind your ear (ten times)'.

'You serve the table with your left hand all day'.

'You keep a stupid smile on your lips without stop for two hours'.

'You speak your fist words of the day at a particular time'.

Papers Written to the Forum "Those Who Knew Gurdjieff" - Nicolas de Stjernvall

'You take upon yourself to fast completely for two days', etc.

In the beginning, the presence of Valia at his uncle's was mainly to assure meals abundant enough for he or six persons, and which were served on G. I.'s return from the Café de la Paix. After a couple of false starts on Valia's part, Gurdjieff charged me with the fixing of a midday meal to which he had invited a number of people. In the course of doing the shopping rounds, I was chagrined to note that most of our habitual suppliers had changed their policies toward us. One would even say they had banded together. Despite promises and my insistence, all of them who had sold us things on credit, refused categorically to serve me, because, it seems, we were in debt up to our necks. Under these circumstances, I decided to go willy-nilly to the Café de la Paix to bring Gurdjieff up to date on the situation.

"Oh, shit!" he groaned, and then recomposed himself quickly, and said to me:

'Postpone lunch one hour, or more if necessary. We'll serve meatballs. Buy some ground meat and improvise the rest'. He handed me 60 francs, adding that he would shear two or three sheep before tomorrow to put us back in the swing of things. I should mention here that Gurdjieff had set himself a principle that he followed scrupulously. 'You see', he would tell me from time to time, 'Ill go broke today and tomorrow I'll make some more money'.

It wasn't unusual to see Gurdjieff borrow money from the waiters at the Cafe de la Paix, all of whom had known him for a long time. These discrete transactions did not at any time seem dishonourable or even indecent to them. They knew too well Mr. Bonbon, his sumptuous gifts as well as the lordly tips which had become legendary. The waiters at the cafe could only congratulate themselves, since their modest loans would reap huge gains.

I was able to get Valia to give up everything and come to help me. Together we were able to prepare dozens of meatballs in record time, and the hors-d'oeuvres were all ready. Everything went without a hitch that afternoon. Gurdjieff was in particularly good form. There were six guests at the table. With his eyes sparkling with malice, G. I. joked continuously, making suggestive and amusing gestures. There was a young Turkish woman at the table with lovely eyes, and she broke out in bursts of laughter at regular intervals as she listened to Gurdjieff tell her short anecdotes m her native tongue.

I was able to witness a similar episode another time with a beautiful Greek who also seemed to delight in G. I.'s jokes in her own language. Nonetheless, the master had an enormous linguistic handicap which prevented him from expressing himself as he would wish. It is true that he mastered Armenian and Russian perfectly, though he spoke with a decided Caucasian accent. He had undeniable familiarity with Turkish, Greek, Georgian, and, to his great credit, I've been told by others, rudimentary knowledge of various Asian languages. But, alas, his knowledge of English and French was restricted to a scant few words and expressions. His grammar, syntax and vocabulary were unique to him alone.

We would often go to the Turkish baths or a sauna on the rue des Rosiers, along with Valia and other acquaintances. Georges Ivanovitch liked to relax and have a massage in these places where he felt pleasurably at ease. For grand occasions we directed our steps to the well-known restaurant Chez Prunier to eat crayfish. To be sure, G. I. was unmatched as a giver of his famous bonbons which he kept in reserve in his pockets. Mr. Bonbon was notorious. Those delicious bonbons, often with fillings, sometimes pure chocolate, were made in Estonia and imported by Fazer, a well-known Finnish connoisseur. In France, in Paris, they could be found at Fauchon's, or Petrossian's and at other deluxe sweetshops.

All guests who had the honour of crossing the threshold of the apartment at rue Colonels- Renard knew perfectly well the celebrated closet displaying an inimitable assortment of foods and drinks which Georges Ivanovitch never stopped supplementing with purchases of new specialties. In fact, this closet display-case became a genuine attraction. One could begin with sight of bakhlava, rahat-loukoum, and halvah; and a few were those who knew of the innumerable exotic fruits which Gurdjieff had discovered who knows where. One couldn't find such rarities ever on display on the street. Their price was high, of course. Few people at that time had seen or tasted litchis, paves, kumquats, papayas, kiwis, and so forth, which arrived from the four corners of the earth, carefully wrapped in wadding or even in jewellery boxes! At certain meals, in presence of particular guests who were pointed out to me by G. I., by a prearranged order or cryptic sign, I would bring in for dessert the most rare produce from Mars or from Mount Ararat. According to the circumstances, after a blow with a wooden mallet in the kitchen to liberate them, I had the privilege of serving on a tray, with infinite care and ceremonial flourish, exotic fits found nowhere else in Paris. You think I am serious or kidding? Believe it or not isn't my problem. The point is that the effect looked for was achieved: Wide-eyed wonder and squeals of surprise. Stifling my own laughter, I would see it every time.

Four or five times, satisfied with my service, Gurdjieff would exclaim to me as I left him for the night:

'Take the car and go have fun'.

He had entire confidence in me, knowing that I wasn't prone to alcohol or drugs, and that I smoked only irregularly. Despite the fatigue accumulated throughout the day, I would go sometimes by foot to the amusement park at Porte Maillot and mix with the thick crowd idling there. The spot was noisy, amusing and offered all sorts of attractions. I remember one modest show, but quite exciting for all to see. It consisted of a quite cute young girl lying in a bed placed on a platform. We could only see her face between the blankets. The man who ran the show passed out cloth balls to whoever wished to throw at her on the platform Each time one of these balls hit the target, a good distance away, the young girl would leap from her bed m the skimpiest of dress, wiggle her hips a few moments before the aroused spectators, and then disappear again beneath the blankets.

Papers Written to the Forum "Those Who Knew Gurdjieff" - Nicolas de Stjernvall

I would also go by car to Pigalle, Montparnasse or Montmartre to relax in my own fashion. I was drawn to the Russian cabarets, less expensive and more authentic in those days. I went occasionally to 'Monocle', a lesbian nightclub where I wasn't at all ill at ease. It was a place to where I drifted almost without thinking of it. The atmosphere was pleasant and calm. Outside before the entrance, there stood a sort of female huckster, dressed in a smoking, who rustled up a clientele with a tipsy voice. Seeing me arrive, she'd greet me every time with a very friendly smile. Inside, I had fun watching pairs of succubi and incubi tenderly twined together, dancing unprovocatively with languid grace.

Naps after meals and drinks at lunchtime were sacrosanct for Gurdjieff. Everyday, I would see him go to his bedroom and fall off into a deep sleep almost immediately after his guest had departed. One day, unexpectedly, around three in the afternoon I heard the doorbell ring again and again, and then an incessant knocking on the door of the apartment. Angry, I raced to the do&, opened it carelessly and said to the intruders that Gurdjieff was not available. I was about to close the door when one of the men (there were three) blocked the door with his foot and with excellent French in an arrogant tone, said:

'The master has fixed a rendezvous for us. Let us in at once'.

Without waiting for a reply they stormed into the salon and took places at their ease. I wasn't the kind to recognize any celebrities of the day, or even know their names. From all appearances, though, these were important people. After a few seconds musing over their possible identities, I was able to attach tentative names to the three guests, but since I was not absolutely certain, I restrained from judgement on the spot. It seemed likely that these were two writers and a famous actor. Without my heart in it, I went to waken Georges Ivanovitch. I had to shake him for some time, but as he came to his senses, with his eyes opening, I explained that there were three visitors in the salon who were waiting impatiently to see him. Since he was wearing long underwear, I handed him his slippers and a bathrobe. Seeing him enter, the visitors got up as one, bowed with respect and glued their eyes to him.

'Tell them to join me at the Cafe de la Paix late in the afternoon', Gurdjieff said to me. I did this and the three left immediately. G. I. seemed still somewhat asleep after his nap, a bit pathetic and vulnerable.

The few rare occasions when I saw him return alone (usually when he went out alone in the evening, he would let me off much earlier), he was in a bad mood. Under such circumstances the bonds between us were much tighter, marked by simplicity and, I am sure, reciprocal affection. He was visibly ill at ease staying in one place. Sometimes he took his little portable harmonium, isolated himself in the salon and spent a good hour improvising melodies which were always a little sad. He had, all the same, retained many oriental habits. This is to say that I saw him pace back and forth, hands clasped behind his back, fingering his beads. I rarely saw him with a book in his hands. I had often to remind him of down-to-earth matters. I had to point out the suppliers whose accounts were to be paid right away. I brought him up to date on our debts in the area, etc.

Once he asked me to give him an injection in the buttocks. I had a very limited talent in that sort of thing. 'Give me a shot', he said, pointing out with his finger the exact spot for the needle. Despite my desire to do the job, the needle just wouldn't go in correctly. It hurt him and drew blood.

'For God's sake!' he screamed and tore the syringe from my hands. Lying on his stomach he wiped the discoloured spot with ether for a while and plunged the needle in his buttock. It remained for me only to empty into him the contents of the syringe, which I did. His mood softened immediately, and he asked me where I was with my *pomni sebia*.

From: Nicholas de Stjernvall, *Daddy Gurdjieff*
Paris, Rue des Colonels-Renard

© Copyright 2003 - Nicolas de Stjernvall - All Rights Reserved

The Great Theme: An Analysis of One of Gurdjieff's Hymns

Wim van Dulleman

(Note from the editor: The following pages are copies of the two 'overheads' which Wim used during his presentation. While it is not possible to provide the reader with a comprehensible representation of the presentation, since it would be out of context in the absence of a piano, we felt that the content of these pages may be of interest.)

"... the conviction that the cosmos is a sublime and harmonious construction, guided by a higher intelligence, in which man has its own, subordinate position..."
As defined by Jamie James, *The Music of the Spheres*, 1993 Grove Press, New York

In the Timeaus, the Demiurge constructs the world in accordance with the diatonic scale.
See: Comford, F.M., *Plato's Cosmology*, London, 1937

In *A&E* the creation is based on the same diatonic scale, however the calculation through which this scale is reached is different.
See Russell Smith, *Cosmic Secrets*, The Dog, Texas, 1993

Concept and structure of the diatonic scale should not be confused with the Greek scales, f.i. Gurdjieff's favorite scale the Aeolian-scale.

Geometrical and/or mathematical patterns play a dominant role in all so called "visions" and/or psychotic hallucinations.

NUMEROLOGY AND MUSIC

The importance of the number 9 in Western Symphonic Music.

There is an overlap between mathematical and musical genius.
see: Aldous Huxley's novel *Little Archimedes*

The numbers 3 and 7 in Gurdjieff's "program" music
(Yet Gurdjieff was not dogmatic, story of 12-tone scale)

PROGRAM - MUSIC An important but almost extinct form of music.
Folk-music.

All & Everything Conference 2003

Possible use of onomatopy.

Thorns De Hartmann-S approach towards music.

The "edited" and "unedited" versions compared.

The role of existing orthodox music in Gurdjieff's hymns.

The Religious Ceremony.

MEASURES AND COUNTS, Theme A,B,C

A27

B37 double timing

C37

sounding of "E"

A27

B28

C3(4)7

sounding of "E"

A16

B38

sounding of "E"

variation: theme D37

A27

B37 double timing

C17

The Great Theme: An Analysis of One of Gurdjieff's Hymns

Interlude of seven measures introduces another tonality. Measures are defined very precisely (not common in De Hartmann's sheet-music of Hymns, occasionally these are without any measure-divisions. This interlude looks like a reverse of the ABC-structure, but now the C-section is no longer an "echo" but a very pronounced "call".

The apotheosis, 1 of fourteen measures, in which a struggle leads to the C majeure-chords, reminiscent of the C-sections and the "call" in the Interlude.

Conclusion of music with twice three measures, C majeure quietly descends to A-minor.

© Copyright 2003 - Wim van Dulleman - All Rights Reserved

The Unfolding of a Symbol of Law

Keith Buzzell

In all of the Great Traditions and in many of the great Philosophical Systems there is an intentional use of symbol. Symbols, similar to the Akhaldan symbol, often make use of portions or representations of living forms. Symbols may be in color. They may be of quite a variety. Many of the traditions have symbolic representations that take geometric form In 1987 I was engaged in reading in the literature on sacred geometry. Also at the same time I was reading in chapter Purgatory, especially those portions that Len read out last night that have to do with the creation of the Universe. At the same time a third pole was Volume 2 of *The Dramatic Universe* wherein Bennett unfolds his way of looking at the worlds and the laws as they begin to appear. I was reading in all three of these areas (I can't really remember when the notion occurred to me) wondering whether it would be possible to try to develop a symbolic representation that would incorporate aspects of all three of these focal points of my interest at that time. Sacred geometry, Volume 2 of *The Dramatic Universe*, and Purgatory chapter.

I wanted to keep this as coalescent and simple at its beginning and see whether it would be possible to unfold, if you will, (like the petals of a flower - that kind of unfolding) that would go on progressively from that nidus, from that germinal point, and which would contain everything. In other words, all of the laws, all of the Will, all of the patterns that are going to guide the unfolding of this form would have to be contained in this primordial state, in whatever this representation was going to be. Then it would simply unfold itself. If you put all the rules, all the laws of this unfolding into this initial state, and then simply say 'go' then this would begin to unfold. What kinds of patterns would it generate? That was the question I had.

I decided that, and I'm sure this was primarily because of Bennett's influence in the *Dramatic Universe*, that the triad was the first starting point. So much of the thinking that later became point, triad and circle started with triad. Why I have no idea, my own prejudice I suppose toward trying to see things triadically or Bennett's approach which is so clearly triadic in the unfolding of the laws. So I suspect it was more that than anything. A bit further along in this unfolding process I decided on the point, because it is dimensionless, because you can't say anything about it in terms of its unfolding attributes because it is in a state of absolute unity, so you can put anything you wish into it. You can put attributes, you can put qualities, you can put anything you wish into it, but in terms of discussion, elaboration, you can't take anything out because you would begin to infer that there were parts to this singular state. It seems really important to say, if the Will is one, and that's what the point seems to represent in this symbolic representation, the point is the state of absolute unity, then it is the state of absolute oneness and it doesn't have parts. You can't talk

The Unfolding of a Symbol of Law

about parts because as soon as you talk about parts, it has already begun to unfold. So, we have this state of absolute compression of all qualities and attributes into this very difficult-to-conceive-of state of oneness in the point.

The two simplest two dimensional forms that show evidences of absolute symmetry are the equilateral triad and the circle. The circle actually comes first. Think of constructing a circle and a triad. I've read in some Sacred Geometry texts that you can construct the triad with only one step more than it takes to construct the circle. It takes two steps more as I understand it. But in any case the simplest then would be the circle and then the next simplest would be the triad. So I decided on the point in the center of the circle. That would be, and what I subsequently began to refer to, as the Will point. The triad would represent the triune characteristics that unfold from the Will, so we go from one to three. The circle interestingly is, when you look at the history of its use symbolically in the Great Traditions and in many philosophical systems, it seems that it's used in both ways. The symbolic representation of point, circle and triad became the simplest initial expression of the state that I was trying to give some dimension to:

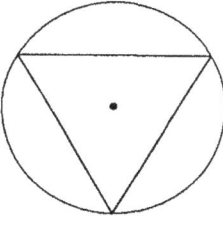

Figure 1

The circle, as I said earlier, seems, in different traditions and in different philosophical systems, to represent both the whole, the one, but it also is a premier representation of process, of things happening, of things going in a circular pattern. It seems simultaneously to be a way of representing one or the other or both. It could be the first step beyond a point when you want to get at some dimension in order to keep with its absolute symmetry. What's the dimension of the circle? Whatever you want. Make it as small as you want or as big as you want. The important thing is that it is completely symmetric in its relationship with the point and it is the simplest design reflecting that state of unity. But it also reflects completion, also reflects function, if you will, the process function that has to do with the unfolding itself. So this seemed to be as point, triad and circle, an adequate beginning.

So I decided that this representation was going to unfold as the petals on a flower, progressively. I would have to consider three unfoldings. It would have to unfold by point, there would have to be some representation of that movement of the Will but still considered as point. Similarly there would have to be an unfolding of the triad, the triad as representing the Law of Three. The circle then became the representation, the symbolic representation in my mind at least, of the law of seven. Now you see why I put a little emphasis on what appears at first as a symmetric representation. From point you go to circle, law of seven, then it goes to triad, law of three. So

115

which is the first law, it is the Law of Seven, not the Law of Three. So, how can we have this unfold from itself, how can it generate from itself?

We'll go quickly through one way of doing this. There are a number of ways in which this works out. I'm going to give you a view of the triadic unfolding because it visually is much easier to follow and to see exactly the fundamentals of how this can generate itself and what is implied in that generation. I'll give you a little representation first and then you'll see what I'm driving at. We'll take a triad, an equilateral triad:

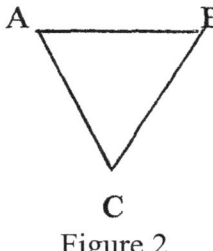

Figure 2

Now we are going to consider, in the unfoldment this triad, with this line here (AB) as an axis me a hinge). Then we can fold this point (C) here through space to form this triad ABC'. We can then, by the same thought process, use the other sides as an axis, (AC&BC) since this is in a state of absolute unity, symmetry or equivalence of law or potency. They are co-equal with respect to the potency of unfolding, so this then would produce:

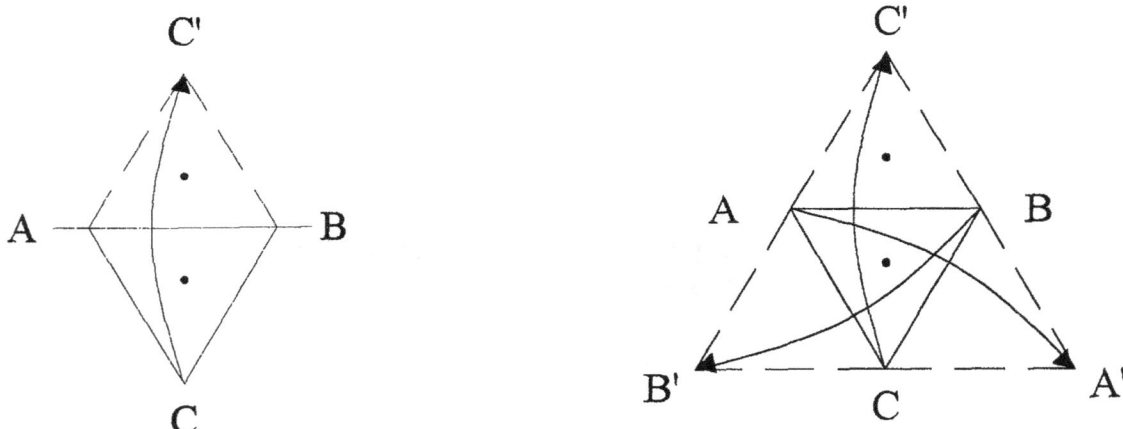

Figure 3

Now, as this unfolds, AB is now the axis and in the upper triad the sides AC and BC are not used as axes. So their potency, if you will, within the other triads, is undiminished. We can say that that potency of AB is used up or is used in order to accomplish that degree of unfolding. But in that unfolding the AC and the BC have not been used. What I'm trying to establish here is that the sides in this fist unfolding retain a potency to serve as a further axis of motion because the next step is obviously to unfold each of these. Keep in mind this is a state of simultaneity (three triads)

The Unfolding of a Symbol of Law

that has unfolded from this state of simultaneity (one triad). These are simultaneous with each other. They are equipotent - but different.

One of the great mysteries that occur in many of the Great Traditions and some of the great philosophical systems is this enigma of the three and one, of the three becoming one. How can one be three, the paradox of the Father, the Son and the Holy Spirit? This is one way, symbolically, of representing that because if these three powers simply fall over these multi-potent axes it becomes one. You could say very clearly it is one, but it is three in its unfoldment at this point. But at any point you could also consider that it will fold back in and re-establish and then conceptually we would be back in this situation of being able to say this is the state of absolute unity and therefore we can't take it apart because we can't climb inside of it. In order to begin to take it apart, in order to begin to talk about it, it must manifest, it must unfold. That's what I'm establishing here as far as the actions are concerned.

The second order or the second step in the process of unfolding is this:

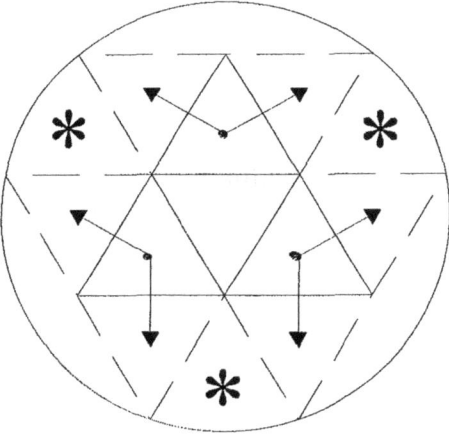

Figure 4

The next unfolded step will be this:

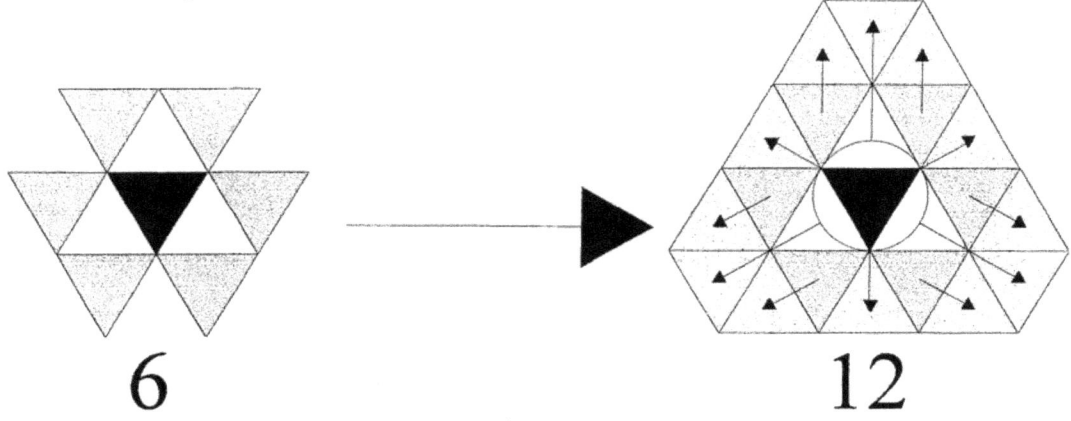

Figure 5

All & Everything Conference 2003

The point I want to get at is to establish the unfolding process. Notice that one goes to three but then its going to double itself'. The three are now going to become six. There are six second-order triads here. When the next unfolding takes place, we have complications and this is one of the most interesting aspects of the symbol. I tried to stay with the notion of symmetry, that all motions coming from a singular source would have to be absolutely symmetric. I had to try to stay with this notion of this unfolding from the state of simultaneous unity so everything is equal that you get this mirror imaging, this unfolding that is going to be coequal in all respects.

Now at this level all the sides have been used in their primary potency as axes. So now we can say, with respect to the first triad that the sides have got to take on different characteristics because they have already been used as a primary unfoldment and that would apply to the exterior two sides of all six of these triads here. The complications that come in, because of the symmetry requirement that I mentioned, are that here are these spaces (in the spaces of the asterisk) that have to be accounted for (See Figure 4).

This brings us to a second principle of the unfolding process, that which considers that the point can also be taken as an axis of rotation. The points AB &C in the original triad world 1) can now produce the 12 triads of law of World 12 (6 by unfolding over side axes, and 6 by unfolding over 'point' axes).

This brings us to a second principle of the unfolding process, that which considers that the *point* can also be taken as an axis of rotation. The points A, B & C in the original triad (World 1) can now produce the 12 triads of law of World 12 (6 by unfolding over side axes, and 6 by unfolding over 'point' axes).

The unfolding principles, of side and point axes, remain the same for the appearance of World 24, World 48 and World 96. The particulars of each unfolding are too complicated to go into here but the resulting triadic forms are these:

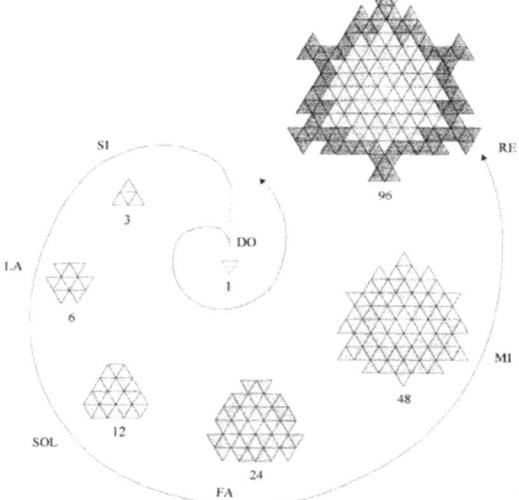

Figure 6

The Unfolding of a Symbol of Law

Keep in mind that what is represented here is only the triadic unfolding. If each of the triads has a point at its center and a circle around it you can see the complexity and subtlety which arises quickly. Any given circle passes through adjacent circles of other worlds, and this establishes a way of asking questions related to the successive vibratory levels of the 'Unique Cosmic Element'. Unfortunately we don't have time to consider these features further.

The last feature I'd like to point to concerns the form of the 6 Laws of World 6 and the fact that they appear in a consistent manner:

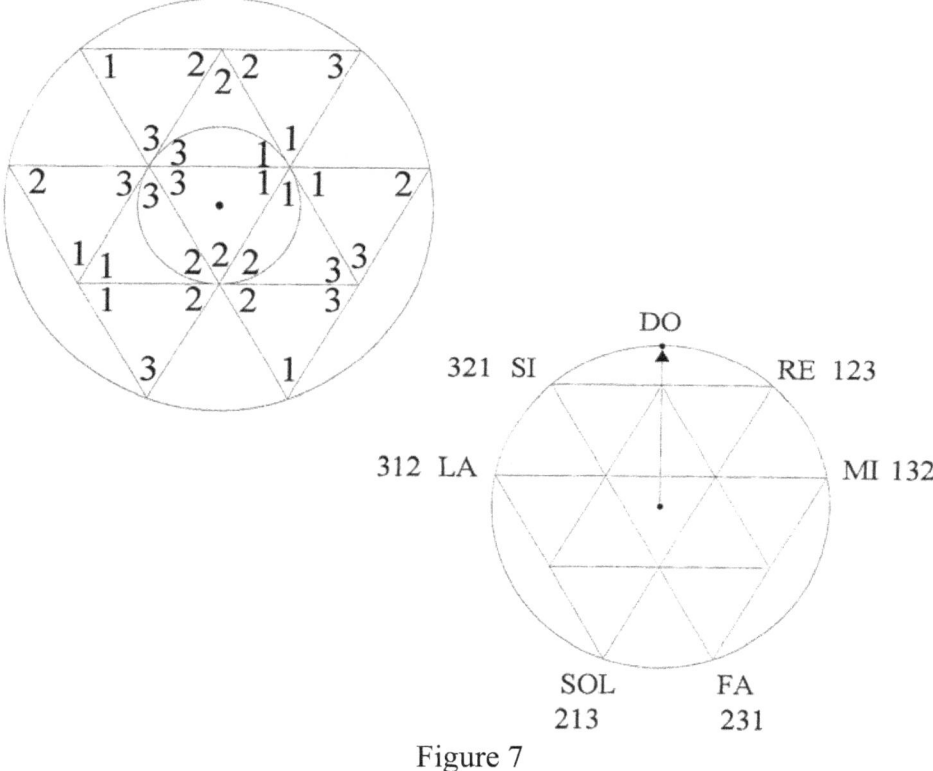

Figure 7

This connects up to John Bennett's Volume 2 of *The Dramatic Universe*. I assigned numbers. This is not a trick. I had someone, one of the first times I presented this, say, 'that's just a trick'. It isn't a trick because you could say that the apices are alpha, beta, gamma, red, blue and white, anything you wish it to be as long as it differentiates the fact that those three angles are not the same. They have the same angle in measurements but they are different because they are three different angles within each equilateral triad. However you identify them, call them whatever you wish, I put numbers on them for clarity. You could put something else. My meaning then becomes pretty clear. Notice that in World One you have a simultaneity of the three forces and the law of seven is absolutely contained within itself. We'll get back to it, but this is Autoegocrat in a symbolic representation, Autoegocrat. The laws, before the laws are changed. Now if you take this and now carry it through the second step in the unfolding process. If you do that by the numbers then you end up with an interesting situation which gets more complex. You will be able to number all of the angles in the triad. Now preceding down here, what I've done, I've derived six numbers and want to go over how we derived them The highest potency is going to be with reference to World One. So in deriving the form of these numbers here, this is 1. It starts with 1 because it is an unfoldment of this aspect closest to the Will or to the World One representation. The second number (2) is closest to World Three or to the unfolding that has gone up. The number 3 is unfolded out into what we could call a symbolic representation of *function*. We have then Will, Being and Function, 1, 2, 3 in the form of the upper right triad. Over here (321-upper left) is the mirror image. It must begin with 3 because 3 is the highest relative to World 1, and then again going to World 3 equivalent it is a 2 and then the unfoldment for the most functional expression is now in the outer apex. That is why we can name these as I have named them here. Always it starts from what is closest to World One and moves to what's closest to World Three and then the final functional expression completes the triad itself. So we generate six forms. All of you who are familiar with Bennett's elaboration of the laws will see the correspondence to the same place that he ends up, but from a somewhat different approach. There are six possible combinations of this three number system. If we now put a circle around it, and here what I've done is try to give you some notion of where this symbol began to go as it unfolded in its point, triad, circle form Suddenly we have what you could call the World Six level we have the Form of all Laws, we have the form of the six Laws (from Bennett's perspective - Creation, Interaction, Identity, Transformation, Order, & Freedom). This is how Bennett labelled the six Laws. We can also ask some interesting questions of this enneagram-like form I am not saying this is an enneagram I am not saying this is the way to derive the enneagram or where it came from or any such nonsense. All I'm saying is that this becomes an interesting representation of an enneagram-like form that we can then ask questions of. The Do, notice its placement here. It has emerged from inside, Always this question comes up. Why? Because it's always like that. If you think of the simplest kind of decisioning process that we take up in our We, say from the decision exercise, from the decision to go to work or to get the job done, or to clean the bathroom or whatever. That decision does not take place in the outer world of manifestation. The steps in the process the (re-mi-fa-sol-la-si), those occur in the outside world. But the decision did not occur in the same world. That came from inside, always comes from inside and when the process is completed it goes back inside. If you put circles around all of these triads, they produce a very complex diagrammatic form. The symbol is a symbol of *Law*. The World 'out there' that we are aware of is *not* this. World Six is the pattern, the pattern that emerges that is going to condition and qualify everything that will emerge beyond it. Those six great laws are going to compound themselves as you begin to descend into manifestation. We're first going to see one aspect of those laws moving, in Bennett's terms, from absolute essentiality to existentiality and this happens when you unfold into the world of Sun (World 12). This is parallel in Purgatory chapter to the first condensation that then leads to Suns (Deuterocosmos). So this is then World Twelve in its representation and there are twelve triads and there are ways to discuss that which we won't go into because that would take until 10 o'clock tonight. To talk about the form of each of those laws and why with symmetry, with the requirement of symmetric outer motion it produces this form World 24 in law then becomes this form (See Figure 6). World 48 becomes this form here and finally World 96. At each point there is a doubling of the laws.

The Unfolding of a Symbol of Law

So even up to the World Six representation it gets to be very complicated when you try to look inside of it and ask what's going on, especially when you start talking about motions. Put motion in each of these circles and you see this immensely complex and subtle relationship between these triads. Lot's of other interesting questions come out of that.

I want to back up now and discuss an idea that's related to symmetry. In the classic representation of the enneagram each step is 40° all the way around. That's an ideal representation but, as a number of people have said (from physicists to philosophers to spiritual teachers) our world, if it were absolutely, absolutely symmetric the laws would be locked one into the other and there would be (as Bennett put it) no holes and nothing would happen. You must have small degrees of asymmetries that emerge in order to allow process, in order to allow one level to relate to another. One world will not relate to the one below it in the Ray of Creation unless there are openings, unless there are ways for energy to flow down into and flow back up into. I sat down with one of my step-sons and we constructed this unfolding out to World Six and I asked him to measure the angles from one outer triad apex to the next on the circle. It looks very symmetric. I would imagine that none of you picked up on any asymmetry in that circle where the triads unfold, but it's slightly asymmetric. One of those angles produces three intervals that measure 39.44° not 40°, and the other three are 40.56°. So it all turns out to be symmetric. As the red of a symmetrical unfolding it introduces the first asymmetric elements in *function*. So things can now happen. Looking at this symbolic representation what can this possibly mean? How I've interpreted it is that this is a very direct corroboration at the level of World 6. We have this pattern of all laws in the Universe, all the great six cosmic laws and they are so aligned that they are going to allow the whole of the universe to occur. So they have to be slightly misaligned. There has to be a degree of asymmetry to allow that process to go on. When my step-son measured these out that was one of these interesting moments. When you look at it visually it looks equal and yet measure it and it is a little off.

I want to return to when I mentioned the circumstance of Autoegocrat. Again, these are impressions that come from seeing the symbol and trying to be as specific about holding to the requirement that I established in the first unfolding in the representation (See Figure 8). Here, aspects of the Will are represented by that triad whose apex is down and aspects or attributes of the Being are those which apex up. The Seal of Solomon form was quite accidental as fir as I was concerned. In fact, as unclear as I was at this point in time, I didn't really see it that way. Someone else had to actually point it out. But what became interesting when we were talking about the Do coming always from inside leading out and then going back inside. Well here is Do, as the point is the Will. This is the one Will, the Will of the absolute. Recall what Len went into in detail last night with the line of the flow of forces constantly deflecting according to law and meeting again at its ends.

A geometric generation of an enneagramatic form

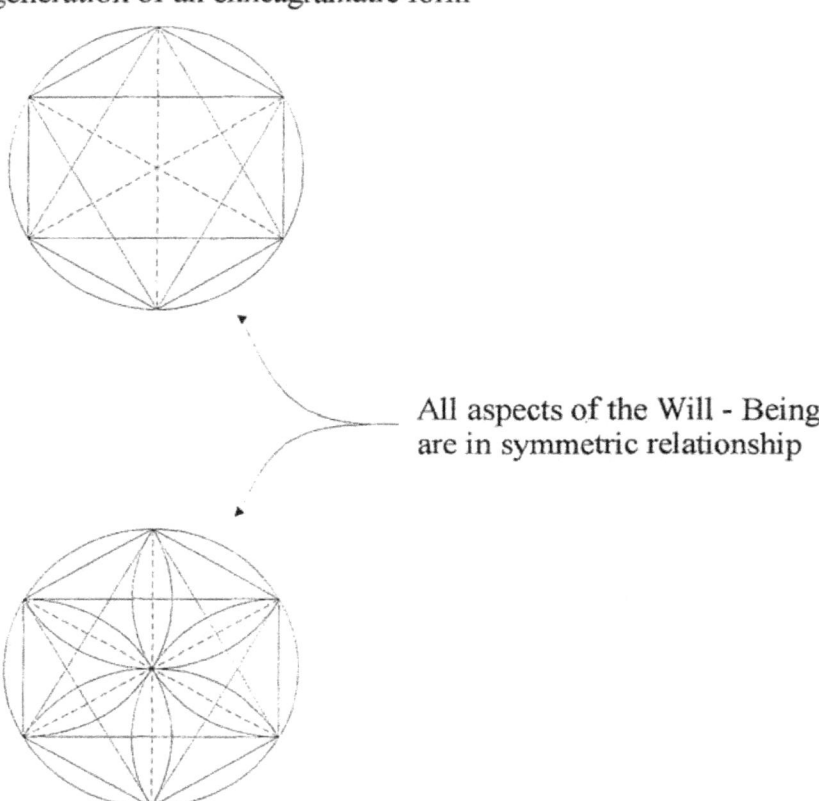

All aspects of the Will - Being are in symmetric relationship

The Will points (centroids) of the World 6 triads

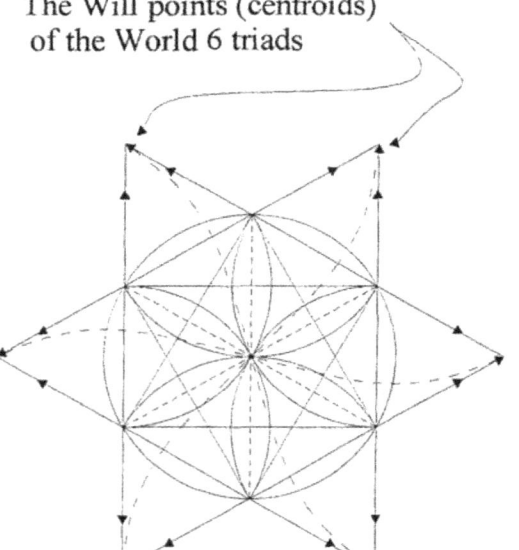

The Will Points of World 6 are 'reconciled' in the outer form

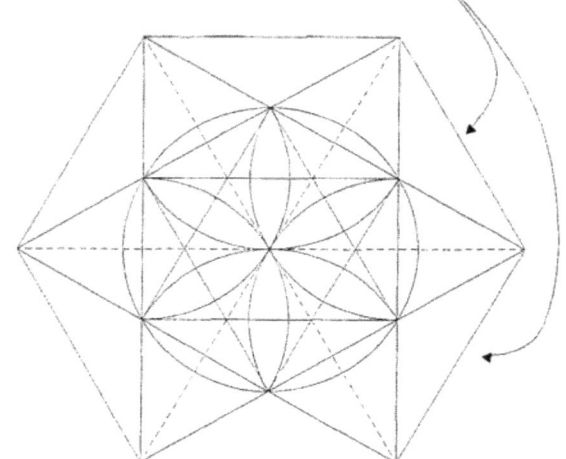

Figure 8

The Unfolding of a Symbol of Law

What we are really pointing to here is the "I Am". Remember that in the Hebrew Tradition that "I Am that I Am". That's the state that we are trying to symbolically represent here. In that case there is no differentiation in form between the attributes of Being, the capacities of Being and the attributes of the Will. So they are in a state of complete symmetry. The Do that starts in the center can go Do-Re-Mi-Fa-Sol-La-Si, and if you go backwards it can go Do-Re-Mi-Fa-Sol-La-Si. In other words the state of simultaneity and the state of relationships within this form of the law has to be absolutely symmetric. This means there is no such thing as a fixed Do-Re-Mi-Fa-Sol-La-Si-Do. They are all the same and simultaneously so. I find it interesting that there is an expression in Murray Gell-Mann's, *The Quark and the Jaguar*, where he makes a statement about the world of matter and the world of anti-matter. He says if matter is running in time forward into the future, anti-matter runs, according to law backwards in time. It runs backwards in time. An interesting thing here is that for it to be symmetrical the Do-Re could be Do-Si. You see what I mean. In this state of Autoegocrat there is absolute symmetry/simultaneity. You cannot differentiate that it's going to go this way or this way. It must go all ways. All possibilities have to be there in that state. Those possibilities begin to appear only when we go one step beyond, to World 6. World 6 then establishes in law the pattern of what is to emerge, and what emerges is World 12, the world of Suns. The laws that now are in existence begin to play a role. Our asymmetries begin to pile up and we find that at each step the external form that I showed you looks quite symmetric. When you try and establish the Do-Re-Mi-Fa-Sol-La-Si in World 24, it looks quite symmetric and it is, externally, quite symmetric. But the Stopinders vary, they are not the same, at least not in this symbolic representation. They are not the same as they are in World 48, not exactly the same. The relationships, relative to the Mi-Fa and the Si-Do and the dis-harmonised fifth, those remain. But it varies, it changes from one world to another when I put in the overlapping of the inner circulation.

Well, that's a real compressed version of something that's been in motion now for about sixteen years. The enneagram appears, or an enneagram-like form appears. At World 48 level there are interesting representations of the lateral octave. The whole sequence of the lateral octave, with the appearance of Microcosmos, Tertartocosmos, one-brained beings, two-brained beings, and three-brained beings. They all appear, and the surprising thing to me is how symmetrically they appear. No, symmetry is not the right word here, - rather how *consonant* the requirements that are there in law are to Gurdjieff's elaboration in *Beelzebub's Tales*.

© Copyright 2003 - Keith Buzzell - All Rights Reserved

The Unfolding of a Symbol of Law - Questions and Answers

Questioner 1: Keith, there's a symbol on a temple in Egypt that someone is calling Flower of Life. Have you looked at that and have you reverse engineered that to see what the source of that symbol might be, what it contains in it?

Keith Buzzell: Which temple are you referring to?

Questioner 1: Well it's a symbol that looks a lot like these flowers that develop inside the perfectly symmetric World 6 that you had up there. Inside the Solomon Seal you have these little fleur-de-lys kind of things.

Keith Buzzell: A portion of a circle?

Questioner 1: Yes they overlap and they kind of look like a flower a little bit. Well there's another symbol that's on a temple in Egypt that's in some books that are out published right now. Some people must have seen these books, no?

Keith Buzzell: I don't know

Questioner 2: I thank you very much for your presentation. Now, Sacred Geometry as I understand, is a tool in this instance to formulate some ideas or some concepts that have been formed in your mind that relate to Work, and Sacred Geometry is the way to express them, right?

Keith Buzzell: Maybe. That was my question, going way back to the beginning. The astonishing thing, has been along that way in both the particulars (when we look very closely at a very small part of it or in its enlarging forms) how resonant it is with so many different Work ideas. So it has been very helpful from that perspective to ask questions.

Questioner 2: I see in what you have done that there is the need that we can not be rid of expressing these things through some kind of model. I think it always happens this way, even the language that we use is a model of sorts, of ideas and the way that this model is unfolding, the model presented in Sacred Geometry or that kind of language. That model, it needs some words as it unfolds, like for example, the word unfold. You say the Will from the Point unfolds. I think this is inevitable when we are using models. When we are using models, we are using a frame of concepts, that we're looking at the concepts themselves from the outside. They help us look, right? At the moment we are using the word unfold. It cannot be of World 1 because if it were from World 1 they would be in the Will and there would be no way of using another word except that or - do you see what I'm trying to say?

The Unfolding of a Symbol of Law - Questions and Answers

Keith Buzzell: Yes, this is the power of abstraction but also it's the weakness of abstraction.

Questioner 2: Exactly, that's the power. That's exactly what I'm trying to say. Thank you very much. So there's a question there. Would there be models that minimize this kind of contradiction?

Keith Buzzell: The Akhaldan symbol has always been a powerful symbol, it's especially direct experientially. I put that inside of me in terms of the values and capacities. It is experiential. This symbol is not like that. This is a different kind of representation. It's much more, in a sense, austere or abstract and you can say that's a negative. It is, but that's not my question.

Questioner 2: Okay, fine. That's exactly what I want to say. What would happen, for example then, if in this model you substitute the Will of the Absolute for the Will of the Being? Would it unfold like the Being is moving in this direction of unfolding worlds?

Keith Buzzell: Yes.

Questioner 2: This is my question.

Keith Buzzell: Yes, that's how I understand it. And again I think this follows a perception that Bennett put into words very well, that Gurdjieff talked about in many different ways. That is that in moving down the Ray of Creation you can relate three successive worlds with respect to Will, Being and Function. As you move down it becomes again Will, Being and Function with respect to the lower world. A world that represented in law the Will at one level is Being for another level and Function for another level. For instance, and there is considerable beauty in this, if you take World 6 as the representation of law or the pattern of law. If we take this here (pointing to the World 6 triadic form) what I've drawn has this very symmetric inner circulation. This is now the pattern of law. Will is World 1, World 3 would be Being and World 6 would be Function. But think of it for a moment. If you're sitting in the place of Endlessness, you have the world of Being as a representation of capacities. So I have the Will and here (World 3) are the arena of capacities the, attributes of that and now, at World six triads I have the functional expression of that with respect to creating an entire Megalocosmos. It's not going to be anything in existence, it's going to be the laws that will guide that expression. That's Function. A Function of what? A Function of the Megalocosmos. This is what's going to guide the functional expression of the entire universe. So in that respect it's Will, Being, Function. If you take World 6, 12, 24 then 6, relative to World 24, becomes the Will. World 12 becomes Being and World 24 becomes Function. World 12, for us, and Gurdjieff says this, it seems to me, in a number of ways, World 12 for us is the world of Will. We don't go all the way up to the galactic level. So what if there are a thousand million galaxies. Our pattern, the expression of that pattern into the whole of our potentialities seems very adequately represented in this galaxy. Why? Because this galaxy is, in the formed sense, a representation or an outer manifestation of World 6. It's not World 6 but it's an outer manifestation because it's all World 12. It's all Suns and that's what we see, and that's certainly not world 6. But what is it that holds it in the form that it has, the spiral form etc.? We look at that and we see the form, but what are the energies? What are the laws that say "it must be like this"?

Questioner 3: If I have a second, I'll tell you the law. There is no Sacred Geometry. That is the Golden Cut, the law with which plants are grown. Like the seeds of the sunflower form a spiral and they respond to this one point six rule. One plus one is two, two plus one is three etc.

Keith Buzzell: But that's not true.

Questioner 3: That's the importance of this expose. And if you show back the spiral of evolution you will see that it corresponds more or less to the Golden Cut. I was very surprised in analyzing figures of companies that the Golden Cut came always as a maximum. I will try to establish the mathematics form for it, but it is the maximum that we can evolve if you consider personal evolution. You know yourselves that one plus one is two, two plus one is three, three plus one is five, very important qualifier. That is the law of evolution, the Golden Cut. Everything in nature grows that way. You can see that pattern in any flower. You can see that pattern in the enneagram

Questioner 2: May I say something? I think that Jacque has moved in another direction than your concept. I'm sorry to say, this is what I believe. I believe that you are talking about growth in things that happen in an already existing world. Keith is trying to have an image of the way the worlds unfold from World 1 to World 3 and so on. I see this as a description of the creation of the world rather than as functions, of processes, within the world.

Keith Buzzell: There are many proportions. The Golden Proportion is only one that appears out of many relationships within the symbol form. It's not true, and you cannot say that because many forms have this that therefore that is the rule, because I can show you a hundred that don't follow that rule and then you say okay, what's the principle there? And that's my point. The principle has to be more abstract, more abstract than that, I think.

Questioner 4: I just want to make a comment and it has to do with the lecture Joseph Azize gave us yesterday about the difference between *In Search* and *Beelzebub*. In *Beelzebub* Gurdjieff abandoned all the symbolic representation, all the symbols were abandoned. He made it very, very simple and so simple that we can use it every day. He invented a very powerful symbol, the Omnipresent Okidanokh, for the law of three. So the Okidanokh is the symbol for the Law of Three in the universe. I'm going to read just a little bit -

"You must also know further that only one cosmic representation existing under the name of Omnipresent Okidanokh obtains its prime arising, although it is also crystallized from Etherokrilno, from the three holy sources of the Sacred Emanation of the Holy Sun Absolute."

Now by inventing this very simple symbol, without going through all this mathematical or geometric abstraction, Gurdjieff made possible for us to use it every day in our Work. How does the Omnipresent Okidanokh manifest the law of three in us and everywhere? Because of one basic

The Unfolding of a Symbol of Law - Questions and Answers

property - Djartklom. When the Omnipresent Okidanokh, which is a symbol of the law of three, enters into any cosmic unit it suffers what is called Djartklom, that is to say, it is dispersed into its three fundamental sources, from which it obtains its prime arising and only then these sources blend again. Now here is how Djartklom happens to us or how can we produce Djartklom when we sit in the morning in meditation or whatever. Well, because there are four ways to produce Djartklom. I'll only give you one, by Conscious Labors and Intentional Suffering Djartklom takes place. So here is the air, the air is full of Djartklom, because Djartklom participates in everything. In every formation in the universe Okidanokh is present, so I can take from the Okidanokh, by Conscious Labors and Intentional Suffering, the three sources of presence in the Okidanokh and I can take them to each one of my three brains. I can take the affirming force which is in the Okidanokh and bring it to my head. I can take the denying force which is also in Okidanokh in the air, its also in the impressions, its also in the 1st Being food and I can bring it to my spine and I can take the Holy Reconciling which is also in the air, impressions and in the food and bring it to my solar plexus. So by abandoning this symbol, and there is nothing wrong about it, and he said it himself, everything that you said here, come basically from inside, and from Bennett, but in *Beelzebub* he abandoned all that. He made it very simple and we can Work on it, we can use it. We can take an impression that comes to me and I can produce Djartklom by Conscious Labor and Intentional Suffering, separate it and bring it to each one of my brains. That is to say Gurdjieff wanted us to be practical.

Keith Buzzell: I would say that all of the quotations, and all the development of terminology here, does not come from *In Search*. They are all from *Beelzebub*. So I object to dismissing - No, I don't care about the symbol. What I'm saying is that the approach, the symbology, when you say that this derives from Ouspensky and Bennett - that's not correct. The primary derivation here comes out of Purgatory chapter.

Questioner 5: My question is, if I understood this, on the part of this unfolding, can be recognized in unfolding all six processes. For example, would there be one of those six processes that I think you mentioned that would establish a possibility for the other combination of the six processes to unfold? For example, you see one of the six processes as growth, digestion, elimination, and crime or corruption, and healing and transformation. Would that be a combination that would give the possibility for the other combination to arise?

Keith Buzzell: Do you mean how do you move from one world to the other?

Questioner 5: No, as I understood it, or as I hope I understand parts of this is that the geometrical representation is also including the movement of the six processes. My question is simply this, is it one combination of these six processes that gives arise to the other combination in the sense that they would sort of, instead of, for example, be represented in two dimensions in all of the combinations sort of unfolding would then be a whole.

Keith Buzzell: My impression is no, that our world is much more interesting and complicated than that. In other words, every expression of the laws, if we take these as doubling at each level or at each world and so forth, then you still have the question of how to speak about a law of World 12 in World 24. It's not going to be the World 12 law in World 12. It's going to be World 12 law in World 24. That presents some very paradoxical kind of issues, especially when we start talking about what's going on inside of us, and when we try to see that relativity in our own Work and I don't believe there is one path in there. The eye of the needle is all around us. The difficulty is in finding it, so I wouldn't see a fixed progression that would link one complex of lawfulness to another complex of lawfulness, if I understand your question.

(tape inaudible)

Keith Buzzell: Yes, that's a pattern, a pattern of law, that is, a form of the octavic principle, but remember that at each step it is open to influences inside or outside. Look at the digestive process. There are times when the body has to break down its own protein in order to survive, in order to do things different so at that particular point because the overall aim of this process is preservation, growth, maintenance, repair and so forth. The overall aim will condition and greatly qualify any of the individual representations, any of the steps in the process. We have to understand that there are ways in and ways out because if we saw only this way, it has to go only this way, then we would be in big trouble.

Questioner 6: I notice that it takes one point straight to draw a point, three to draw a triangle, six to do the next unfolding and twelve to do the next. So my question is, do you think there is any significance in the actual act, you know, of you as a symbologist, doing this and as you do it, you do a certain number strokes in a certain order. Is there any significance there?

Keith Buzzell: I've drawn representations of the symbol, as you can imagine in sixteen years, probably thousands of them and one of the peculiar things is the point of your question. Yes, there are times when all of a sudden there is a question that's coming out of drawing the line that connects this to this and I'll say I wonder if, or could it be, or is the real relationship here that I haven't seen before or whatever. That happens all the time. That's why it becomes so interesting because it starts so simple, it starts in such a simple geometric form and very quickly becomes very subtle and with lots and lots of interesting implications. How close is it to reality? Most important to remember that all symbols are symbols. They are not reality, and all of us fall into that trap. I fall into that trap with respect to this lecture. When I talk to myself, "Is this real?" It's analogous and it's a way of representation. How far does that analogy go and still hold? I think we have to test ourselves, all the time. How far does any symbol go measured up against the reality of this moment, in the effort that I have to try to make or I think I have to make. So I go to the symbol to help me like the Akhaldan on symbol or whatever, but the process, the real event, is not the symbol. So can it be helpful? It's been helpful to us in our group. It's given us a way of asking all manner of questions and seeing relationships and some of them, going back and reading in the *Tales*, we discover that, well - maybe we're misreading it, but we all misread it around whatever our prejudices of the moment happen to be. But its been very interesting how often we've discovered a way of understanding a rather perplexing statement initially and suddenly we see that this is one way of looking at it, like when I read you the quote about the line of forces and so forth and so on. How many of you have ever, I'm sure some of you have thought about it the way I ended up putting it one the board, but most people haven't. They haven't thought that it could come from inside out and go in all directions simultaneously and so forth, so that's an interesting kind of thing. Is it the truth? I wouldn't have the foggiest notion, but as a geometric representation it raises ways of asking questions and that for us has been useful.

His Endlessness and Mr. Gurdjieff

Len Brown

Some time ago, I participated in a Communication Course and we were told that when someone makes what appears to be a statement of fact, the question should be asked:

"What experiences have you had that lead you to say that?"

You might have the same question to ask me.

The title of this paper is "His Endlessness and Mr. G." I toyed with the idea of calling it "God and Mr. G", because of the alliteration, but as far as I can tell, Gurdjieff only uses the word "God" itself ironically. He does write "God-the-Father, God-the-Son, God-the-Holy-Ghost; the three holy forces of the Sacred Triamazakamno". But of "God", he explains to his grandson Hassein:

"Here you should know that your contemporary favorites very often use a notion taken by them from somewhere, I do not know whether instinctively, emotionally, or automatically, and expressed by them in the following words: 'We are the images of God.'

"And indeed, each of them is the image of God, not of that 'God' which they have in their bobtailed picturings, but of the real God, by which word we sometimes still call our common Megalocosmos.

"Although this expression corresponding to the truth exists there among them, yet concerning the consideration of its exact sense, as in general concerning every short verbal formulation, they at best always express with their strange short-sighted mentation - even if they should wish with their whole common presence actively and sincerely to reveal their inner representation and essential understanding of this expression of theirs - something as follows:

"'Good ... if we are "images of God" ... that means ... means ... "God" is like us and has an appearance also like us ... and that means, our "God" has the same moustache, beard, nose, as we have, and he dresses also as we do. He dresses as we do, doubtless because like us he is also very fond of modesty; it was not for nothing that he expelled Adam and Eve from Paradise, only because they lost their modesty and began to cover themselves with clothes.'

"In certain of the beings there, particularly of recent times, their being-Aimnophnian-mentation or perceptible logic has already become such that they can very clearly see this same 'God' of theirs in their picturings, almost with a comb sticking out of his left vest pocket, with which he sometimes combs his famous beard.

…

"And so ... my boy, first of all I must once more and in greater detail repeat that our ENDLESSNESS was forced to create the whole World which now exists at the present time.

"In the beginning, when nothing yet existed and when the whole of our Universe was empty endless space with the presence of only the prime-source cosmic substance 'Etherokrilno,' our present Most Great and Most Most Holy Sun Absolute existed alone in all this empty space, and it was on this then sole cosmic concentration that our UNI-BEING CREATOR with HIS cherubim and seraphim had the place of HIS most glorious Being.

"It was just during this same period of the flow of time that there came to our CREATOR ALL-MAINTAINER the forced need to create our present existing 'Megalocosmos,' i.e., our World.

"From the third most sacred canticle of our cherubim and seraphim, we were worthy of learning that our CREATOR OMNIPOTENT once ascertained that this same Sun Absolute, on which HE dwelt with HIS cherubim and seraphim was, although almost imperceptibly yet nevertheless gradually, diminishing in volume.

"As the fact ascertained by HIM appeared to HIM very serious, HE then decided immediately to review all the laws which maintained the existence of that, then still sole, cosmic concentration.

"During this review our OMNIPOTENT CREATOR for the first time made it clear that the cause of this gradual diminishing of the volume of the Sun Absolute was merely the Heropass, that is, the flow of Time itself.

"Thereupon our ENDLESSNESS became thoughtful, for in HIS Divine deliberations HE became clearly aware that if this Heropass should so continue to diminish the volume of the Sun Absolute, then sooner or later, it would ultimately bring about the complete destruction of this sole place of HIS Being.

"And so, my boy, in view of this, our ENDLESSNESS was then just compelled to take certain corresponding measures, so that from this Heropass the destruction of our Most Most Holy Sun Absolute could not eventually occur.

"Further, again from the sacred canticle of our cherubim and seraphim, but this time the fifth sacred canticle, we were worthy of learning that after this Divine ascertainment of HIS, our ENDLESSNESS devoted HIMSELF entirely to finding a possibility of averting such an inevitable end, which had to occur according to the lawful commands of the merciless Heropass, and that after HIS long Divine deliberations, HE decided to create our present existing 'Megalocosmos.'

"In order that you may more clearly understand how our ENDLESSNESS decided to attain immunity from the maleficent action of the merciless Heropass and of course how HE ultimately actualized it all, you must first of all know that before this, the Most Most Holy Sun Absolute was maintained and existed on the basis of the system called 'Autoegocrat,' i.e., on that principle according to which the inner forces which maintained the existence of this cosmic concentration had an independent functioning, not depending on any forces proceeding from outside, and which were based also on those two fundamental cosmic sacred laws by which at the present time also, the whole of our present Megalocosmos is maintained and on the basis of which it exists, and, namely, on the basis of those two fundamental primordial sacred cosmic laws, called the sacred Heptaparaparshinokh and the sacred Triamazikamno.

"About both of these fundamental cosmic primordial sacred laws, I have already once told you a little; now however I shall try to explain to you about them in rather more detail.

"The first of these fundamental primordial cosmic sacred laws, namely, the law of Heptaparaparshinokh, present-day objective cosmic science, by the way, formulates in the following words:

"The-line-of-the-flow-of-forces-constantly-deflectingaccording-to-law-and-uniting-again-at-its-ends.

"This sacred primordial cosmic law has seven deflections or, as it is still otherwise said, seven 'centers of gravity' and the distance between each two of these deflections or 'centers of gravity' is called a 'Stopinder-of-the- sacred-Heptaparaparshinokh.'

"This law, passing through everything newly arising and everything existing, always makes its completing processes with its seven Stopinders.

…

"And so, our ALL-MAINTAINING ENDLESSNESS decided to change the principle of the system of the functionings of both of these fundamental sacred laws, and, namely, HE decided to make their independent functioning dependent on forces coming from outside.

…

"And in regard to the second primordial fundamental cosmic law, and, namely, the Sacred-Triamazikamno, common cosmic objective science also formulates with the words:

"A new arising from the previously arisen through the "Harnel-miaznel," the process of which is actualized thus: the higher blends with the lower in order to actualize the middle and thus becomes either higher for the preceding lower, or lower for the succeeding higher; and as I already told you, this Sacred-Triamazikamno consists of three in dependent forces, which are called…

"And so, in consequence of the fact that for this new system of functioning of the forces which until then maintained the existence of the Most Most Holy Sun Absolute, there were required outside of the Sun Absolute corresponding sources in which such forces could arise and from which they could flow into the presence of the Most Most Holy Sun Absolute, our ALMIGHTY ENDLESSNESS was just then compelled to create our now existing Megalocosmos with all the cosmoses of different scales and relatively independent cosmic formations present in it, and from then on the system which maintained the existence of the Sun Absolute began to be called Trogoautoegocrat.

"Our COMMON FATHER OMNI-BEING ENDLESSNESS, having decided to change the principle of the maintenance of the existence of this then still unique cosmic concentration and sole place of HIS most glorious Being, first of all altered the process itself of the functioning of these two primordial fundamental sacred laws, and HE actualized the greater change in the law of the sacred Heptaparaparshinokh.

"These changes in the functioning of the sacred Heptaparaparshinokh consisted in this, that in three of its Stopinders HE altered the what are called 'subjective actions' which had been until then in the Stopinders, in this respect, that in one HE lengthened the law-conformable successiveness; shortened it in another; and in a third, disharmonized it.

"And, namely, with the purpose of providing the 'requisite inherency' for receiving, for its functioning, the automatic affluence of all forces which were near, HE lengthened the Stopinder between its third and fourth deflections.

…

"And the Stopinder which HE shortened is between its last deflection and the beginning of a new cycle of its completing process; by this same shortening, for the purpose of facilitating the commencement of a new cycle of its completing process, HE predetermined the functioning of the given Stopinder to be dependent only upon the affluence of forces, obtained from outside through that Stopinder from the results of the action of that cosmic concentration itself in which the completing process of this primordial fundamental sacred law flows.

"And this Stopinder of the sacred Heptaparaparshinokh is just that one, which is still called the 'intentionally actualized-Mdnel-In.'

"As regards the third Stopinder, then changed in its 'subjective action' and which is fifth in the general successiveness and is called 'Harnel-Aoot,' its disharmony flowed by itself from the change of the two aforementioned Stopinders." (BT p. 754 - 775)

There are other Creation Myths but none of these, as far as I'm aware, give a similar description of energy transformations. It is worthwhile at this point to mention the part that our knowledge of these transformations play. In the Ashiatan epoch, seven centuries before the Babylonian era, all the beings of the planet began to work in order to have in their consciousness the Divine function of genuine conscience and for this purpose, as everywhere in the Universe, they transubstantiated in themselves the five being-obligolnian-strivings. The central, third striving was said by Gurdjieff to be:

"The constant striving to know ever more and more concerning the laws of World-creation and World-maintenance".

I find this third, open-ended quest for knowledge to be strikingly different from the other four, number one being to have everything necessary for one's body, number two to have a constant need for self-perfection, number four to pay for one's arising as quickly as possible and number five, to be to assist others in the perfecting of their inner-being. I consider it to be the difference between objective and subjective, a going-out rather than a going-in.

I've plotted both the visible spectrum of light (in terms of wavelength) and the musical scale (in terms of pitch) and both shows the same form of varying increase. In the case of sound, for example, the last step before the next octave has an energy surplus, as you would expect from the shortening of the stopinder, so that this last note of that octave 'falls into' the next note, and so is called a 'leading tone'. The main result is that as energies are transformed to higher or lower ones in the cosmic scale, there are energy surpluses and energy gaps, the one fitting into another. This same process is then applied to the food we eat and the air we breathe so that hitherto unknown (to us) materials are produced by our bodies which go to make a "higher-being-body" when the right sort of practice or technique is applied. This is the point at which the human race has the possibility of creating physical materials (which Gurdjieff called 'Abrustdonis' and 'Helkdonis') that can become a new vehicle for the continuation of consciousness and which link humans to the Universe.

The place for the Gurdjieffian Creation Myth becomes clear. Energy can be transformed upwards as well as downwards - as one writer put it, potatoes are transformed into thought. Physical materials, the emanations from stars in the form of cosmic rays, X-rays, microwaves and so on, materials that in scientific parlance are said to have the characteristic of 'entropy' or scattering, can acquire, via the higher-being-bodies of creatures all over the universe, a focusing of energies or negative entropy, so that the circle of energy is complete. The Sun Absolute is safe!

As far as I know, no present day scientist includes the formation of higher energy substances as part of the possible development of humanity or links this with cosmic processes. The big question in astrophysics today is "The Origins of the Universe".

How does present day knowledge compare with Gurdjieff's insights in *All and Everything*?

I heard a program on BBC TV during February, 2000 on the amazing work that went into fixing the Hubble Telescope, which required four space walks of hours apiece to get the telescope functioning. The Hubble Telescope, with its 2.3 metre reflector mirror, was designed to see into the origins of the universe. It cost 4 billion dollars and as you probably recall, when released into orbit, only gave a fuzzy image because of errors in the primary mirror. When finally corrected it was aimed at a region of sky where no stars appear as viewed from Earth. Clear of the Earth's atmosphere, the Hubble telescope revealed in that small area of sky 40,000 galaxies never seen before. In the last two years more work has been done and I recently downloaded from the Net photographs of a patch of sky, about the relative sky-size of the Moon, in which, again, nothing can be seen from Earth but which are shown to contain 100,000 galaxies seen through a spiral galaxy similar to our own.

The age of these galaxies, as calculated by their red shift, gave a value for the age of the universe as 12 billion years. A truly great puzzle has arisen; many of these new galaxies were found to be mature whereas they should have been very young galaxies given that they must have been formed at the beginning age of the universe, which was found to be 12 billion years old. Previous figures had been calculated to be anywhere between 8 and 20 billion years.

But what is meant by 'Universe'? The origin of our present day theories (or should I say 'knowledge') was work that was started in 1923 by the astronomer Edwin Powell Hubble, after whom the space telescope was named. By 1929 he had identified, by their red shift, certain nebulae that had been thought to be part of our universal starry sky but were in fact distant galaxies. He showed, from their red shift, that they were all moving away from our own galaxy and each other at a rate which was proportional to their distance, in other words, the farther away they were, the faster they were moving. Astronomy now has identified that there are 100 billion galaxies all receding from one another, and the Big Bang theory states that all these galaxies began as an incredibly dense point of matter which suddenly exploded 12 billion years ago to begin the universe as seen today. It took many decades before Hubble's theory was accepted. As recently as the 1950s, Fred Hoyle, the British astronomer, was proposing a steady state theory of the universe in which the universe had no beginning and no end.

Where does that leave *All and Everything* since it was written before Hubble's work became public? I find it difficult to compare the present Big Bang theory and Gurdjieff's Story of Creation and the development of 'stopinders' although I am not a physicist or mathematician but an engineer. Yet if we declare that *All and Everything* is 'symbolic' rather than having a precise physical meaning, I think we throw the baby out with the bath water.

I don't believe that Gurdjieff 'made up' his Story of Creation recounted in *All and Everything*. His work is a 'tour de force' in which he blends his sources, which are and must be many and varied, into a complete whole. But he was writing *A & E* in 1922-25, before Hubble's findings had moved out of pure astronomy into general knowledge. In 1925, the Universe was, and had been for thousands of years, the canopy of stars over our heads and transformations of energy were being discovered. But still there is no adequate scientific account of the physical laws of these transformations of energy.

Incidentally, I heard an expression of these laws formulated in a broad way as: the Law of Three describes "What Is"; the Law of Seven, "What Happens".

The Milky Way is now known as our Galaxy, a spiral type with the Earth's sun situated in the suburbs about two thirds of the way out on one of the spiral arms. When we look at the Milky Way, we look toward the middle of our galaxy and see the dense broad band of stars that make up the galactic centre. Science has shown that the centre of our Galaxy is an immense black hole that pulls all the energy near and consumes it, drawing it all into its completely unknown depths. I heard Stephen Hawking say, incidentally, that a 'black hole' was neither a hole nor black. A 'black hole' is material so dense and with such a great gravitational pull that all objects, including light rays are pulled into it. Using the ideas of space-time, it is like an immense whirlpool in the fabric of space, a huge gravity well. Like a whirlpool it has an 'edge' in which objects with high enough gravity can escape. This is called the 'event horizon'.

Our Milky Way is a 100,000 light years across. That is, if we wanted to visit the restaurant at the end of the galaxy, it would take us a 100,000 years travelling at the speed of Light to get there. Even a Star-Trek type Warp 5 wouldn't be much help.

The numbers are worth repeating. There are 100 billion cells that make up our body and Earth is the place where we have our being. Earth is part of the Sun's Solar System and there are 100 billion suns that make up our galaxy. There are 100 billion galaxies that make up The Universe and it is these galaxies which are speeding away from each other at the speed of light, propelled still by the energy contained in the Big Bang. Astrophysics determined that if there was a Big Bang that started it all, there should be background radiation present of a certain frequency. Recently such background radiation was indeed discovered by sophisticated radio telescopes, a microwave frequency that filled the whole sky. A recent discovery related to the Big Bang is that while all these galaxies are speeding away from each other in an expanding universe, they are not going fast enough. This was determined by measurements taken on supernovas.

A supernova is a star that has reached the end of its life. Its centre has burnt out and it collapses suddenly under gravitational pressure and causes an immense, white-hot explosion that can be seen for millions of light years. This explosion burns itself out in about two weeks and the star dies, cold and lifeless. But the radiation pattern of the light while it still shines out is unique and distinctive. So, if you have the identified supernova lined up in you telescope, you can do a spectral analysis and from the measured red shift, determine how fast it is receding. The problem is that the giant telescopes have a very narrow star field so it's only if you're very lucky can you recognize the supernova, line up the telescope and do the required analysis in the short time of two weeks.

Until a few years ago no one could predict where a supernovas would occur so the use of supernovas was little used, and in order to calculate how fast the universe is expanding, about 50 supernovas would need to be measured. Finally a physicist who was not an astronomer at all but an expert in microwave studies produced a computer program that when fed the star types and locations would then statistically give the location of possible supernovas. It worked.

The result astounded the astronomers. The galaxies were receding from each other as predicted but at a much lower speed than had been calculated by earlier methods. This meant that they were being held back by an unknown gravitational force. What the reason for this is not known although a heretofore uncalculated mass in the universe which can't be seen, known as 'dark matter', is considered to be responsible.

The current picture is a vastness of billions of galaxies at billions of light years distant, receding from each other, with Earth as an inconspicuous speck in this vast array. This is very different from the Universe that Gurdjieff wrote about, a starry sky that human beings have gazed at for thousands of years as the Universe. Gurdjieff's *All and Everything* clearly shows his vision of this starry sky, our Galaxy, as a coordinated universe given life and direction by a divine power. But we, the three-brained beings of the planet Earth, have, as well as all the other beings in this Galaxy, an important part to play. An analogy may make this clearer.

An adult has about a hundred billion cells in the body, some with very specialized actions like muscle cells, others like white cells with a functioning intelligence that enables them to differentiate between friend and foe. These cells also eat, excrete and reproduce, in short they become discrete individuals. But the purpose of this multitude is to serve a mysterious force called 'personality', a personality that can determine their very existence, but of which they can only have a very indirect experience. For example, if the 'personality' went to the movies, the body cells wouldn't have the faintest idea of what was going on, what this sudden influx of neural stimulation was about.

I don't want to push this analogy too far, but the fact is that with the use of our own Reason we can understand our Universe at an appropriate level, which is part of our reason for being here. To point to the situation for human beings, Gurdjieff said that now Ashiata Shiemash is one of the Highest Most Very Saintly common-cosmic Sacred Individuals.

Some years ago, I saw an interview on television with Carl Jung and then, more recently, Joseph Campbell, and they were both asked by the interviewers, "Do you believe in God?". The answer was, in both cases, "No, I don't believe, I know." That would indicate that some individuals have had an experience that transcends the ordinary waking level.

We can call this vastness of billions of galaxies at billions of light years distant, receding from each other, with Earth as an inconspicuous speck in this vast array, the Universe. But if we take the starry sky that human beings have gazed at for thousands of years as the Universe, it gives us just one galaxy to apply our reason, instead of some billions of light years away. Even one galaxy is too big a job.

All & Everything Conference 2003

Then all that happens in this galaxy can be theorized and speculated upon, and conclusions developed that can be applied to daily life.

© Copyright 2003 - Len Brown - All Rights Reserved

His Endlessness and Mr. Gurdjieff - Questions and Answers

Questioner 1: You mentioned the 'red shift' as a tool that astronomers use today to determine whether galaxies are receding from us or coming towards us. Do you feel that there is another explanation possible for the 'red shift'?

Len Brown: Well I know that velocity is equal to distance divided by time so I have often wondered whether time is a factor in the 'red shift' rather than velocity. There was a book written and that was basically the idea behind it.

Questioner 2: At the tail end, when you mentioned the size of our galaxy and the composite number of other galaxies, would it be appropriate to say that the implication is there that Gurdjieff says THIS is our home, that this galaxy is our home? That whether or not there are a thousand million other galaxies is not a question other than something to be in awe of but it, in effect it has nothing to do with the mythology that is analogous to what we must see and try to do for ourselves. Or am I misunderstanding you?

Len Brown: Well one reason that I quoted at length was the fact that G quite clearly writes that at the beginning there was nothing but the Sun Absolute and that was the sole source, the sole cosmic cohesion, and it was because of the changes that His Endlessness made that resulted in our present Galaxy. I can only assume that that applies to OUR present Galaxy and what goes on in another galaxy may not be the laws or be what goes on in another galaxy, other than our own. Now some people would say that limits the power of God. I think it relates it to some scale that is more appropriate to us personally.

Questioner 3: I recently came across a copy of the *National Geographic* from, I think it was from earlier this year and there were many photographs similar to the ones you have shown here. At the time I was reading a copy of *Beelzebub's Tales*. And the two, the combination really, of reading the *Tales*, and the seeing in the *National Geographic*, these kind of photos simply verified for me a true sense of awe and wonder of the reality of this space, and this cosmos. They were complementary basically. All these discoveries just seemed to confirm that type of picture of how all the different worlds had been formed and how one thing leads to another, and the different cosmoses coming and the different sections, so I would thank you for having the opportunity to look at such a magnificent picture again.

Len Brown: I see the situation of Earth as a minute speck of humanity in a vast unimaginably large Universe as something that I cannot comprehend basically. I think that if I bring it down to the Universe as human beings have seen it for thousands of years, the starry sky above then that is something that is vast but manageable in terms of the application of reason.

Questioner 4: I just want to make a comment about the creation of the Universe, because the scientific proof of The Big Bang, because you didn't mention it. A few years ago two physicists at the Bell Labs in New Jersey found with experiment, experimentally, it is not theoretical but experimental what they call the background radiation.

Len Brown: Yes, I mentioned that.

Questioner 4: Oh, you mentioned that, OK. Perhaps I did not hear it. Now the other thing is that going back to the teaching of Beelzebub about the creation of the Universe there is one analogy that we can use for our own Work and on our own self. And here is the situation: His Endlessness had only two choices, either be destroyed by time or create the Universe and suffer. Those were the only two choices. In the same way we have only two choices, either be destroyed by time or decide to suffer.

Len Brown: Nature, red in tooth and claw!

Questioner 4: Right, and then that brings us back to the heart of the teaching of Ashiata Shiemash. We, and all the three-brained-beings of the Universe and the whole of our essence, is and can only be suffering. Is and can only be suffering.

Questioner 5: Not very promising is it?

Questioner 4: Not very promising but here comes the Endlessness's choice, either be destroyed by time or create the Universe and suffer. There is no other possibility.

Len Brown: Well, there is one thing that I didn't understand, I guess I could say, about the changes in Stopinders because the changes in the dis-harmonising of the fifth, which is what your talk was about, and I am still not clear on how that process happens. But that may be the point where you talk about suffering; that may be where it comes in, at that particular point.

Questioner 4: You are right. That is exactly where it comes in, in fact we can say that His Endlessness came out to a fifth.

Len Brown: I'm sorry?

Questioner 4: Our Endlessness came to the fifth of His own Law and that fifth had two possibilities. Either be destroyed, or create and suffer and then, the centre of the teaching, the way I see it, is the teaching of Ashiata. In the sense that, once the Universe…

You see I asked the question the other day, "What did Beelzebub see in the administration of the Universe that was illogical?" And because of that he was exiled. What was the thing he saw that was illogical? There was no answer in the book. Now my answer, and you can have your own answer, is that he saw suffering; and it is not logical. Like you said, 'suffering is illogical'.

His Endlessness and Mr. Gurdjieff - Questions and Answers

Len Brown: But necessary.

Questioner 4: But necessary, you said it. And then he was exiled to the remote corner of the Universe, which is the Solar System. For what purpose was he exiled? To learn what you just said, that suffering is necessary.

(Unrecorded question)

Questioner 6: To avoid suffering, is there an answer in terms of the 48 Laws, which Ouspensky says rule our planet? Is there an exact list of those laws and their content?

Len Brown: I am not aware of that, sorry.

Questioner 6: As you live farther away from the Sun Absolute the more laws you are subject to.

Len Brown: The present world system is set upon the higher eating the lower. I can't see any way out of that. Because it goes on in nature regardless of whether you are a vegetarian or not.

Questioner 7: A question about the current 'Big Bang Theory' being the popular theory, the scientific view of the creation of the Universe. Do you think that we are subject to the laws of suggestibility with regard to this theory? Because there are many other theories which were around maybe ten to twenty years ago. You mentioned the steady-state theory. There have been big problems with the Big Bang Theory; it has had to be revised on many occasions. For example, one thinks that the observations don't quite fit the theory and the theory is modified to make sure the observations fit. One of those variations on the Big Bang Theory was the fact that cosmologists had to put in something called 'inflation' so that when the original Big Bang occurred the rate of expansion of the Universe had to be altered by this theory of inflation to account for the anomalies between what was the previous and what was the new evidence, given by, for example, the Hubble Space telescope. So I wonder whether we are subject to suggestibility?

Len Brown: I think that astronomers try to eliminate their own subjectivity as much as possible. But there is certainly a fashion going on where money and effort are being applied in a certain direction because that is the fashion of the time. What it suggests to me is that the Universe is too big to be part of our Work background. It has to be something more manageable, something more that we can apply our reason to. We can't think of a reason for the existence of billions of Galaxies. I read it in one publication, it might just be the hind-leg of a cosmic dog. That doesn't help us at all.

Questioner 8: First of all I am not terribly concerned about the contradictions between the account in Beelzebub and modern science for several reasons. But putting that aside, I just wondered if you could briefly recap for us what you say the contradictions are? Because I seem to have missed that. The necessary contradictions between what Gurdjieff wrote about the creation of the Universe and the ideas of modern astro-physics.

Len Brown: No, I didn't say there was a contradiction. I said there was a completely different sense of scale. Before, when Gurdjieff wrote *All & Everything*, the Universe was the starry sky above us and now it is a totally different kind of picturing with...

Questioner 8: I'm sorry I misunderstood what you had said, thank you.

Questioner 9: In 1915 when Gurdjieff gave the model to Ouspensky he said that the first model WAS irresolvable so it had to be scaled down to be, it was too big, and then it had to be scaled down a second time, and that is the model we have now. So isn't the original model, isn't that compatible with modern science's view on that, the incredible vastness.

Len Brown: I'm sorry what was the model you are referring to?

Questioner 9: The Ray of Creation that he first explained to the St Petersburg Group in 1915. It was too big to be resolved so it had to be scaled down twice to be acceptable, and the first original model was incredibly vast. I thought that falls in line with the modem scientific view of the Hubble Space Telescope, having surmounted the problems of the atmosphere of the Earth in that it is seeing farther.

Len Brown: I'd have to think about that.

Questioner 2: I want to mention... I don't remember any of that about The Ray of Creation. This is the Hydrogens. The hydrogen Tables get stepped down twice, is that what you are talking about?

Questioner 9: I thought the Hydrogens and the Worlds were compatible.

Questioner 2: No, no, categories of Matter, that is what Gurdjieff calls it. There are twelve categories of matter, actually more, but &he that he deals with.

(tape change)

Questioner 10: Gurdjieff gives some exercises, some specific exercises in the *Tales* and one of them, which I read several times before I realised it, it is around page 79, he says that you need to get up every morning and go and see the sunrise. You must recall this one it is in there. I finally came to appreciate what I think he meant and it was to give us a practical exercise in what you are talking about which is really relativity. It is to get us out of our Earth-centred or personality-centred or ego-centred existence so that we appreciate this whole relativity thing which you were explaining before, the Earth in relation to the Solar System and then in relation to the Galaxy and so on... The thing I am wondering about is what about the idea in this relativity thing inwardly? In other words, in the meditative state, if we can get deep enough is it possible that we become closer in some inner way, let's say some inner dimension or something, to a more inclusive thing. In other words instead of our inner state being at the scale of the Solar System is it possible to be at the level or the scale of the Galaxy? Have you given any thought to that kind of idea?

His Endlessness and Mr. Gurdjieff - Questions and Answers

Len Brown: Quantum Mechanics would seem to apply to the deeper meditative state where the consciousness is becoming on the same the level of the atomic happenings that cause Quantum Mechanics to action. I think that is the area where you have to be able to experience but not to evaluate too much until you have got enough experience built up. Do I make myself clear Sy?

Questioner 10: Technically I don't know a lot about Quantum Mechanics except that it is at the micro-level. I was thinking more in other directions, inwardly, in other words. Does our consciousness in deep meditation expand, let's say the dimension of consciousness expands, as we become less and less identified with our planetary body, with our personality, we become closer to being Endlessness or whatever we want to call that.

Len Brown: But it is possible to have the experience where you are the Galaxy. It doesn't happen very often, it happened twice to Plotinus, for example.

Questioner 13: Although Gurdjieff asks us to look more and more into the laws of world creation and world maintenance it can be also formatory to think that it is just to go on and on, and have this expectation that our investigation doesn't have any limit. I think that when you said that it is not in our being to comprehend the whole Universe I think that is where it ends, and possibly also that what you are indicating, that another dimension can start. And at that edge is, as far as I can see, where we can become silent and not demand more of ourselves than is possible. Through that silence we can recognise the vastness of the Universe which would otherwise not be available to us.

Len Brown: Yes but we have to have the ability of making it susceptible to our reason at some point or other. Either we are at a state where we can't understand it as we are, but we hope that by progression we will. And what I am saying is that it seemed to me that the whole 100 billion Galaxy Universe is not something we could ever come to understand. One Galaxy, our own Galaxy, would be enough, maybe that is too much for us anyway.

Questioner 13: To know our limitations could also be to know ourselves. To recognise how, and in what connections we are limited, it is not a negative response. It is a stop on one level but it is a start in another.

Len Brown: You have to keep on going at it, keep on working at it even though you say, although it is not a good point to start to say this, 'I am going to fail.'

Questioner 13: No, and that is not what I meant. But there is a limitation to how much we can expect to know. And I think one of the prime sources in ourselves to have this goal of the whole Universe is a vanity, at least a form of vanity.
Len Brown: Hmmm.

Questioner 4: I just want to do a little different thing now. I want to ask Sy a question about his last article in *Stopinder*, (*Stopinder* 11, Winter 2003, The High Commission and other Sacred

Individuals - What do they represent? Sy Ginsburg), because I think it is related to this that we are talking about here. In your article you say, and maybe I didn't understand it and that is why I want you to clarify it for me, and maybe to everybody. In your article about 'The High Commission and other Sacred Individuals What do they represent?' and all that you say the names Gurdjieff is using for describing Our Endlessness and describing our Most Most Saintly Ashiata Shiemash and the Archangel Looisos, and all that is a mockery to indicate that such beings don't really exist. They don't exist apart from us. They only exist in an allegorical way. So when you come to the realisation that it is you who are God, I AM GOD, like it is said in the Vedanta, I AM GOD, I am the Self with a capital S, as you say in the article what are you trying to say?

Questioner 10: It is a little bit off, it's not off the subject, incidentally the article emanated from some papers that were presented here at the conference two years ago. It started as a result of an e-mail discussion.

What I was trying to say... is exactly what you said, at a certain very deep level that is who we are and that is what the I AM exercise is about and the whole thing, this is my view, is discovering who we are. And the only real question I have about that in terms of the *Tales* is it seems like on the Holy Planet Purgatory, Endlessness comes there because the beings who have actually crystallised their Higher Being Bodies can never quite merge back into the One. And so he feels badly and he is trying to make them feel better. That is the only question I have. But my view is that it is at a deep level in a meditative state that one gets this feeling, for lack of a better word, that one is, that one is all there is, but I am not sure this is part of this conversation, so.

Len Brown: In another Galaxy there may not be a Purgatory.

Questioner 6: Well then, can we have the address? That would be a good thing. (laughter)

Questioner 11: What I see to be the impulse behind a number of different efforts I have come in contact with relative to knowing more and more concerning these laws and people's attraction and work with the Enneagram and the Laws as described in *Beelzebub's Tales* seems not to have to do with an ever- growing quantity of knowledge but with an acquisition of a simplified principle that ties and unifies together their experience with themselves and their need for transformation and simultaneously gives that effort a universal, unified context, which is a human impulse, to be unified with the whole. And as our knowledge of what the whole is in a picture such as this grows, our mythologies and somehow our way of finding a place in that has to grow also. I am not sure it would be reflection of vanity to seek to develop that understanding if it could be something simple like three terms in an algebraic formula, for example. If you know how to manipulate the three terms you can solve a million problems. So it is not that I want to solve every problem it is that I want to know the fundamental processes that would allow me to do that.

Len Brown: I have been reading Joseph Campbell's Power of Myth recently and what he says is that the old myths of Creation have served their purpose and they are not useful any more. He is talking about The Seven Days of Creation in The Bible and other myths of creation that are occur all over the world in different cultures and against which we put what I have called here the 'Gurdjieff story of creation'. Campbell says that we need a new mythology and it occurred to me, Harry, that you were saying that this material, that is on the internet and that I gave you all a picture of is something that you are teaching in your class right now. And maybe this is leading towards a completely different mythology of creation that it is going to be essential to have if we are to have any direction or point towards which we are going as human beings.

Questioner 12: You mention the cosmic background radiation earlier in support of the current theory, Big Bang Theory. Cosmologists have gone to great deal of trouble to see how this radiation varies according to which way you are looking in the sky and it supposedly been found to be non-varying, in other words, in whichever direction you are looking in this energy is always the same.

Len Brown: Universal, yes.

Questioner 12: To a very high degree and although the cosmic background radiation is given, supposedly, temperature of about four degrees Kelvin, the variation within that is supposed to be incredibly small, maybe one hundredth of a degree in any direction, which indicates to me a Universal energy field, and this is given as evidence of the Big Bang. To me there is another possibility and that is that Gurdjieff talks about the Universal Active Element so to me there is a possibility that.

Len Brown: Is that Etherkrilno?

Questioner 12: Not only Etherokrilno but also Okidanokh, so do you suppose or do you suggest that there may be another way of looking at this other than the Big Bang Theory with this in mind?

Len Brown: I hadn't come to any conclusions myself.

Questioner 4: I am sorry because I have one little thing that goes back to what you (Sy) said and the creation of the Universe. You see I have a problem, one big problem that I cannot even begin to understand. And this is the problem: When you go to the teaching of Vedanta, when you go to the teaching of Buddhism, when you go to the teaching of Taoism and then you go to the teaching of Gurdjieff, I can see immediately the difference, the distinctiveness of the teaching of Gurdjieff from any other teaching and this is it. Let us go Ramana Maharshi (d. 1950) the great Saint from India and whom you mentioned in your article. He is the representative of the pure Vedanta, 'I am the Self'. But what is the problem? The problem is when I am the Self - the World does not exist. And when the World exists - the Self does not exist. Either you go for the Self or you go for the World but in the teaching of Gurdjieff both exist! The Self exists and is real but the World also exists and it is very real. So what is it? I was four years in Buddhism, I had a teacher and everything, I could not understand. I do not know the answer.

Questioner 10: I will give you an answer that doesn't come from me but seems to make some sense. It actually comes from Madhava Ashish, some of whose papers we actually read here some years ago, and one of the things he told me, he said all of this kind of stuff, whether it is Gurdjieff's Hydrogens and his Worlds, or Blavatsky has this whole seven interpenetrating... He says that it is stuff to catch fish, in other words we are the fish and the ones that don't drop through the net. It brings us into these ideas. Ultimately it is just the Self as Ramana Maharshi said. He sent me to see once Nisargatta Dutta, who died in 1981, who he said, and I read his books extensively, is the purest, simplest statement of this whole thing. It is really just I AM and as far as the manifestation, which I think is what you are addressing, I don't know, have any answer to that. Ultimately it is the discovery of who we are.

Questioner 4: And then the World ceases to exist at that point. There is no more World because it contradicts the very teaching of Gurdjieff because...

Questioner 10: But you know that is so. If you are talking about the physical Universe, there is nothing permanent and in that sense there is nothing real, it all eventually dissolves in the exchange of energies, I mean just like our physical bodies dissolve.

Questioner 4: Yes but what was the fundamental question with which Gurdjieff started the whole thing? There was only one question in his mind. What is the purpose of organic life on Earth? If the Self is the only thing that exists there is no question about the purpose of organic life on Earth. That question is irrelevant. It has no meaning whatsoever. But that was the question in *Meetings With Remarkable Men*, he said it. That is my question. What is the purpose of organic life on Earth?

Len Brown: To save the Sun Absolute.

Questioner 10: Isn't this question really 'Who am I?' and 'What am I doing here?' Isn't that Gurdjieff's question? Not organic life on Earth that is a kind of subsidiary thing or part of this structure that he has built for us because some of us are attracted to this. There is nothing wrong with this, we have an obligation to try and understand this.

Questioner 4: I am sorry I cannot say that because in The Sixth Descent Gurdjieff has Beelzebub coming to end wars.

Len Brown: No, to find out the cause of wars, not to end it.

Questioner 4: Yes, but think, why go through all this if only the Self exists? Why even read Beelzebub if the only thing that exists is the Self? It doesn't make any sense to go through all this First Descent, Second Descent if the only thing that exists is the Self? I cannot see it. I mean why even study the book?

His Endlessness and Mr. Gurdjieff - Questions and Answers

Questioner 10: Well what you are saying is that anyone not following Gurdjieff's particular methodology can't possibly come to the answer of 'Who am I?' and we know that is not correct. We know this is one method, a very valuable method in my opinion, for me and for you perhaps, but there are six billion people on this planet and I don't know how many are working on themselves but everybody is not working on themselves in the Gurdjieff way. Like you mentioned, Ramana Maharshi and you are talking about the Advaita Philosophy (non-dualism) and that is another way to Work.

Seminar 2 - Chapter 16 of Beelzebub's Tales to His Grandson

Facilitator: Nick Bryce

Facilitator: I would like to say that before the conference I read this chapter several times, and whilst in some, of my readings the chapter seemed clear and fairly direct in its clarity, since arriving at Bognor and reading it again it no longer is so clear to me. So I am looking forward to what others have to say about this chapter. Would someone like to begin?

Comment: What I have to say is not directly related to what has just been said. It's a subjective understanding, or my subjective understanding of a certain part of this chapter which I studied before coming to the conference. It is to do with how I understand the book. A&E also contains instruction which is relevant to my Work on myself. I try to observe myself. I try to observe myself at various moments in the day, which does not always or necessarily result in any kind of experience. I will try to explain my understanding as best I can by reading from the chapter: (quoting from *A&E*, page 124, paragraph 44). And I reflected on what this meant, "The gaze of His Endlessness" and sometimes, as a result in attempting to observe myself; I have an experience that something quite other and different notices my existence and, in simple terms, because I am really a simple person, "The gaze of His Endlessness" is always there. And by my efforts, seeking to be understood, to be known, to be recognized by something higher than myself; I can have an experience where a different kind of awareness is present to me and the flavour of that - I cannot describe that experience, only the flavour it leaves me with, which is that everything that I took to be myself is not myself - his faults, his ego, is John - and that by an effort to observe myself it becomes possible - the fleeting moment in which something in me partakes in "the gaze of His Endlessness." It reminds me of a saying - and I don't know where it comes from - "The "I" by which I see God is the "I" by which God sees me." And so I associate this part - this Egokoolnatsnarnian-sensation - as perhaps what happens in those moments that something of a much higher nature becomes available to me.

Comment: I would like to say what CT called the personal testimony and I hope to be able to take it a little further than that. I will describe something that has happened again and again, but I will describe the first time because it was the most intense. I was about 26/27 years old. I had already met G's Work and it was probably the first time I really remembered. One aspect of this remembrance I would like to describe was the feeling that it's me again. The world was like that when I was a child. It was so rich and so close, this experience. It was some minutes or seconds before that I felt like that, but it was probably 20 years that had passed and I remember asking myself - not in my mind but I really asking myself - "Who is this who has wasted, who has stolen all these years from me?" So it's like the boy from earth and Hassein living in the same physical

Seminar 2 - Chapter 16 of Beelzebub's Tales to His Grandson

body but either one or the other will make use of time, one wasting and the other living really. This feeling of suffering I am describing, of shock at the realization, is very similar to the one Wim described before, as what has been done cannot be undone. What am I to do from now on? So I think if Hassein is able to make use of this time it will be a long life. That is probably an answer to why Mr. G. could accomplish so many things in a lifetime - it was really a long lifetime.

Comment: I would just like to share a little note that I found by someone called Paul Anderson on time. I found it very severe but it may be true. "Time, the Merciless Heropass, is meted out for us all and it is so doled out that we have limited amounts, yet we act as if it were not so. Our attitude about time does not reflect any of its real meaning and real point. Time is a very important thing to understand in this Work and especially the idea that it is doled out and that it is connected with the law of Trogoautoegocrat and with the operation of the universe as we conceive it from our standpoint. Also, since time is meted out to us, and since there is a limit to it, and since we are in the Work, we must never, never miss the opportunity of taking advantage of what is before us at any moment because it may never come back again in that way. And you may never have the opportunity to experience it, and once having lost it you will not be able to get it back."

I thought I would like to share that. And the other thing is the question on thinking about time and reading the chapter. We all have these moments of presence as was spoken about earlier. Is it simply, when we have those moments, a more intense moment on the line of linear time, or is it a different experience of time?

Is there another time? That's the question.

These are moments where there is a feeling of timelessness. And I think that when G points out that as we are we don't understand what time is, he is challenging us to seek out other forms of experiences than the one we regard as experiences, which is not really what it seems. One very clear indication for me of the lack of presence is that when there is lack of presence there seems to be a lot of time, in one strange sense. For example, impatience. When I am impatient there is something that I don't accept. It's a form of identification with time and in all kinds of identification, that linear time is something that I am glued to or linked to. And it has been said that although Work must be done in time, there are points in time where you can have the feeling of leaving time. I think it is Nicoll who describes linear time. I don't want to give the impression that these moments that I try to say something about - it is impossible to speak about - are mainly connected with, at this point, where it moves upwards. To me it has become more and more possible only through deeper and deeper contact with my physical body. So it's nothing apart from a physical experience. It's as if two levels merge, come together.

Comment: I wanted to read two paragraphs concerning the phenomenon - the question being, what is the phenomenon? (reads from *A&E* p.123) I was just noticing at the end of the chapter, the last sentence of the chapter, "They have not an approximately correct representation even of those cosmic phenomena that proceed on their own planet around about them." He is describing how time can be measured, if you will, and at the end I am seeing that we cannot even have an approximate representation of that.

The question seems to be, what are the cosmic phenomena? Because the cosmic phenomena going on in this specific location in which time is being constated, are those cosmic phenomena that determine the way in which that time is experienced. What cosmic phenomena? What is he referring to here?

Comment: The real challenge in reading *A&E* is that each complete statement has seven aspects and three meanings. That doesn't come from me, by the way. It comes from Orage in the commentary on the *Tales*. And according to Orage, G himself told him that. Now let's look at time from the seven aspects. I have been able to work on four of them. The other three I don't have any idea what they are. But these four aspects are answered clearly in the book. They are: the subjectivity of time, the objectivity of time, the relativity of time, and the dimensionality of time. These are four aspects. I don't know what the other three are. Now, we saw the other, and K read it, about the subjectivity of time. Time flows of itself and by itself and we have no organ to measure the flow of time. That's the subjectivity of time. But let's look at the objectivity of time. The way I see it and experience it in my sitting meditation in the morning is that time acquires a sense of objectivity when it is related to my inner presence. That is to say, somebody brought the example of impatience and the opposite which is calm. When I am full of associations in the morning when I sit, time seems to drag on forever, like those beings who are hypochondriac. Two minutes of sitting seems like an hour. On the other hand, when I happen to have a good sitting I can sit for one hour, forty minutes, or twenty minutes, and it seems like I wasn't there. It feels like one minute. And this brings me the question, because when I was working for my Ph.D. I took a course on Einstein's theory of relativity and the professor said something that I understood when I read *A&E*. We were working on the equations when he said that somebody had asked Einstein, "Could you give me a very simple definition of relativity?" and Einstein said, "Yes, it is very simple. You sit for two minutes on a very hot stove and it feels like one hour. You spend one hour with your beautiful girl friend and it feels like one minute." But you see, when I read *A&E*, G knew more about time than Einstein, because the example Einstein gave is not relativity, it is objectivity. It is the objectivity of time that Einstein is talking about, not relativity. That time acquires a sense of objectivity which depends on my inner presence as is what J says about the beings experience the sacred impulse. Now, what is the relativity of time? Let's look at that. The relativity of time has to do with the question K asked. The relativity of time is when time is measured in terms of cosmic phenomena that are taking place where time is being measured. What are those cosmic phenomena you ask? The most simple for us, that we can see every day, is the rotation of the earth around the sun. In fact, when a person says, I am 25 years old, he/she is wrong. The way to say it is I am 25 revolutions of the earth around the sun. The saying, "I am 25 years old" has no meaning whatsoever. How can you measure 25 years? There is no way because we don't have the organ. But we can measure 25 revolutions around the sun. I remember I went for an interview for a job many years ago, and the lady who interviewed me asked "How old are you?" answered I am 50 revolutions of the earth around the sun. I didn't get the job incidentally. But now let's get back to the other because there are different scales. What about the beings in a drop of water? What are cosmic phenomena for them? It is different. A cosmic phenomenon for the beings in the drop of water is probably how long it takes for water to dissolve. That is relativity. What about the beings on the planet Karatas? They have a different measure of time because there it is not the revolution around the sun but it is how close the two suns Samos and Selos approach each other, and in that day Hassein was what? According to our standard of time he was 5000 years old. In fact, he was, because the time in Karatas and the time on earth is 384 years difference. So we can see the subjectivity; I cannot measure that. I can see the objectivity in my sitting meditation in the morning or during the day, and I can see the relativity in terms of the cosmic phenomena that are taking place around me and the drop of water, because it is the relativity of time. The dimensionality of time? We have read that there are three dimensions of time, the linear, the simultaneous and the 3rd dimension of time, the awareness of simultaneity. When I become aware of this simultaneity I am in the 3rd dimension of time.

Comment: It is written here "that beings arising on the planet Karatas sense the sacred 'Egokoolnatsnarinian' action for the definition of time 49 times more slowly than the same sacred individuals dwelling on the most Holy Sun Absolute," and should be the same way that we feel it on Earth. But if we can elevate our presence or consciousness into a higher world, we should feel it in another way. We should feel it quicker. And if we can elevate our presence into the Holy Planet Purgatory, because Our Endlessness appears there so often, then Our Endlessness can see us directly. That means we get to the objective definition of time, to the definition that the objective sign this is trying to give to time. And also I would like to say something about the definition of this 'Egokoolnatsnarnian' action. It doesn't matter what the rest means but the ego, in the beginning, gives it an element of subjectivity. So the way I sense it, it depends on which level my presence is at a particular moment. Or if I take it even further, the longer I can maintain my presence in the eyes of God, that's what defines my level of development of presence.

Comment: What are cosmic phenomena? It is possible to judge time only if one compares real cosmic phenomena that proceed in the same place and under the same conditions, when time is being constated and considered. There is another way of looking at cosmic phenomena. That everything that happens is a cosmic phenomenon because it's based on the laws of gravity, etc. So a cosmic phenomenon is something I perceive as a cosmic phenomenon. When seen from this point of view, it seems that there's a line drawn between what is objective reality and by what is being perceived as being something subjective.

Comment: (A quotation from Nicoll's *Living Time* was read.)

Comment: This is a thought concerning cosmic phenomena. One commonality seems to appear among several of the impressions I have shared. The pencil must move, and from that motion comes a perception of past, present and future. If here is no motion there is no time. If am seventy revolutions around the earth and that is my age, that is motion. It is the motion that I am raising as an issue to be discussed. That perhaps motion (or motions) is more fundamental because it is the motion that determines time.

Comment: We have come to accept that what is called time in modern science - or as Mr. G might say, "scientists of new formation" - is an objective thing. Mr. G causes us to look at what he is saying to us in *A&E* about looking at time from an objective point of view, from what he is telling us is objective, and not what we think is objective. For example, several mentions about the relevance of motion in measuring time, is that what we come to understand as time? The objective idea in science is that if two people perform the same experiment and come up with the same results, in different parts of the world, this is considered to be an objective result and therefore forms part of scientific doctrine. So if I measure the speed of a car in Australia and come up with a distance-time graph, and someone else measures the same speed in the same car in a different country and comes up with the same shape of graph, we can compare the graphs and we can say yes, this is the same; therefore this is objective; therefore it is true. But, in fact, what is being measured is not time, it is motion as has been said. Mr. G also says that we tend to divide things up like time, which we divide into seconds, minutes and hours, and he seems to go into some detail in pointing out what seems to be: that we are rather stupid in thinking we can divide time up. Because in this sense, time doesn't actually exist and what we are dividing up are bits of motion. So that in the text books you read seconds, minutes or hours; a list of universal constants might include mass, might include temperature, electric charge - it also might include time. But I would say we need to strike out the time in those textbooks because it doesn't exist there - and instead, if you have a division that we need to think of, I think, in terms of ticks on the clock, we could say - if we are counting seconds - these are not seconds really, these are just ticks on a clock. So it's not miles per hour, it's miles per number of ticks on a clock.

Comment: There was a paragraph read earlier in this conference - it's very short - "During this review Our Omnipotent Creator for the first time made it clear that the cause of this gradual diminishing of the volume of the Sun Absolute was merely the Heropass, that is, the flow of time itself." I have never understood this and I have all kinds of speculative ideas, but I noticed particularly that it is not talking about time; it's talking about the flow of time. I am not sure there is a difference, and if somebody could have some insight what we are talking about I would surely like to know it.

I am not sure that is much of an insight into it, but in reading what you just read myself, it occurred to me one day that time - and I have been asking myself since - that time is the ultimate negative force and that is something that, in my own day, I can see: my comments, "I wish I had more time." It is always the final thing in which I try and respond to, so it occurred to me when reading that part that's what Our Endlessness responded to.

Comment: We are going to have to expand that thought because not only is time the ultimate negative force, but isn't it also the ultimate enabling force? This is what has interested me for a long time. We think a lot about vibrations and vibrations are to do with the law of octaves. You can't have notes, music, vibrations, without time, can you? I don't think so. So even before, in the legends, the laws were changed. For anything to exist and be in vibrations, there had to be this property, time. And I find it of very great interest that for vibrations to exist time must exist. So it is the ultimate enabler. What is also interesting, I think, as a corollary to that, in a strange way, the

Seminar 2 - Chapter 16 of Beelzebub's Tales to His Grandson

Law of Seven is the law which requires time. But I have never been sure that the Law of Three isn't possible in simultaneity; it's like it's the law of absolute instant, so that the two laws combine linearity and simultaneity. And that's what makes pondering on this so lovely because, if one is fair, you can't think about it without coming back to this paradox of simultaneity and linearity. Now, can you think about it without entering that paradox?

Comment: When we look at the examples that have been given on the enneagram by people who have written about the enneagram, it seems that we can discern two types of examples. I will make this as clear as I can by referring to the examples given about light. Bennett gives an interesting experiment there, where this is light coming into a darkroom and this is deflected twice on a prism, and then there is the spectrum of light on a wall. And in the enneagram, the numbers represent the flow of time. In other words, first there is the light source, then light goes through a hole, then it hits the prism, then it is deflected, etc. etc., and he puts this on the enneagram. Now there are other kinds of putting light on the enneagram by its structure; in other words, 'Do' being the white light that contains everything, and then Red being whatever the sequence is red light, and orange, etc. etc. So this is like putting light on the enneagram in a static way, in a way that doesn't have time. It is always like that; its structure is like that. What I am trying to say is that there are two kinds of enneagrammatic descriptions, or two kinds of enneagramma always. This conflict is not so easily resolved in those illustrations because, indeed, there seem to be two families of illustrations: those of phenomena where time is still and somehow reveals the structure of the phenomena that are being perceived, and the other has the happening in time and moving these steps illustrated by the octave on the circumference of the circle.

Comment: Just one small comment in answer to that. I think that placing the colours of light on the enneagram is not an expression of non-time, because each light, each colour of light represents a different frequency, and it takes a certain amount of time for each cycle of each frequency to exist. Therefore each one of those has to occur later in sequence.

Comment: It would have been better to say that in each of these two enneagrams time appears differently, in a different way.

Comment: Going back to S's question on flow. Flow is a technical term and G said everything in the movements. We can have bound flow or free flow, and in the stop exercise this is an externally imposed bound flow. Self-remembering can be called an internal bound flow (in the section in *A&E*, the 'Bobbinkandelnosts." We can economize our experiences by producing bound flow. It has to do with the regulator.

To add to my confusion, a few paragraphs later than the one I read, Purgatory chapter says that "Endlessness solved the problem by creating the Megalocosmos" and I think that this was referred to earlier in this conference. That required the changing of the stopinders, because before that happened it would seem there was no time, and yet, he talks about there being a flow of time before the Megalocosmos was created. Is that possible? Is there something else? I don't understand it.

All & Everything Conference 2003

Comment: I have always had a tremendous respect for Ouspensky as a philosopher. I found that when he, as it were, sat at the feet of G and abandoned his own work, that was a great loss because he looked at time in the dimensional sense - moving on from Nicoll's *Living Time*. Ouspensky brought out a formulation of time as part of three further dimensions. We have three dimensions of space, and there has been a lot of talk about a 4th dimension. In fact, science talks, Einsteinian relativity talks of the 4th dimension as being space-time, but Ouspensky put it into the form of three further dimensions of time making a very nice, what we call a Cartesian result, and this was time - linear time - from back then until now, with the 2nd dimension of time not called recurrence but Hyparxis, or ableness to Be, and the 3rd dimension of time called eternity. With these three dimensions of time, it covers all the possibilities of dimensional time. When you have an object which is said to be three dimensions, it doesn't actually exist except as a picture in the mind. It has to have that 1st dimension of time present in order to make it have objective existence. We cannot sense these higher dimensions of time, but we can theorize about them, and it forms a very nice unity which doesn't exist if we don't look at the further dimensions of time as he explained them.

Comment: I want to address a side question about the flow of time. The way I see it from *A&E* is that there are only two things in the universe that are covalent: time and Our Endlessness. And if you pay attention to p.35 of *A&E*, there are only two beings that use capital letters: one is our "ALL COMMON FATHER ENDLESS CREATOR" always in capital letters, and the other is, "ALLCOMMON MASTER THE MERCILESS HEROPASS." They are the only two things that are capitalized, implying what? Implying that they are both independent. So the flow of time is totally independent of our Endlessness, which by the way is a Buddhist concept. So we can say that B took this from Buddhism, because in Buddhism there is no beginning and no end. This drove me crazy for some time. I had a pain in my head trying to understand how time has no beginning and it has no end. Every time I think about that I have a headache, because I cannot see that; it is beyond my seeing. But I know from Buddhism - I was for four years in a Buddhist centre - that in Buddhism time is nothing. The unit for measuring time in Buddhism is a Kalpas. One Kalpas is the time it takes for a monk sitting on top of Mount Everest trying to blow away all the snow on the mountain. That is one Kalpas. And the universe has existed for billions of Kalpasses.

Comment: A couple of comments that came up on mentioning the Heropass. This isn't my translation. Mr. Bennett spoke about it in connection with *A&E*. And the actual translation of Heropass is that holy one who is 'all' and the 'Hero' refers to 'Hero' and 'pass' to 'all,' hence the capitals for HEROPASS.

And the Heropass is that which emanating from the Absolute, it being the flow of time. There is also the flowback towards the Absolute which has to go against the flow of time. In the Hymn to His Endlessness, at the end, he speaks about "thou unique vanquisher of the merciless Heropass" which is the route of return back to the source again.

Comment: I have an idea that I would like to express to you. It seems to me that we do have a means of experiencing time, some sort of bodily function. It could be something molecular and it would have to do with speed; and I picture this, for myself as a wheel which is revolving in us.

Seminar 2 - Chapter 16 of Beelzebub's Tales to His Grandson

This wheel revolves at a certain speed, a speed which enables us to compare the time that something takes to happen with the time of things that we experience. The wheel turns in us and the speed with which it turns gives us a reference for comparing with what speed things occur in life. For instance, in the beings that live in that drop of water, the same wheel would be revolving at a much higher speed, so things happen very quickly which appears to them to be normal while to us they would appear to happen very quickly. And for the people who live on Karatas, the same wheel would revolve very slowly, so that what they experience to us seems to last a long time. That's how I think we experience time. That has made me think of a paragraph in a different chapter which I think is the most important paragraph of that chapter, and I would like to read it to you (p.388, 1st para.) This is just flowing with my own imagination but the reason for our experience of time would be the speed of revolution of this wheel. So if you were to be more objective perhaps, you could slow this wheel down and experience time in an entirely different manner.

Comment: I just want to say something from the quotation from Ashiata which you gave. You can look at that from another point of view and I think it one that G is referring to. It is the law of equalization of vibrations. What happened is that when we violate this law, as we are constantly doing, then we substitute quality for quantity, and that is happening more and more in our civilization. All we want is quantity, quantity of information, quantity of money, and we have quantity of people, six billion people on the earth. Now, with Ashiata everyone was working on himself because of the principle of Ashiata, and then because the quality was more than the quantity, the rate of birth and the rate of death diminished. So it had to do with time, but it had to do with the law of vibrations.

Comment: I would like to pick up on a couple of points you mentioned in the first half, one by S about the flow of time. If you consider for example flow as a rate of change, so that if you look at the speedometer on your car as you are travelling along at a constant speed, the needle seems to be indicating the same speed. It's not moving in fact; it's static. It's measuring the flow of the movement of the car on the road, even though the needle itself' isn't moving. In fact, if there is a change in the flow of the speed of the car, which becomes acceleration, you would notice a change in the needle. The needle would move up as the acceleration increased, or the needle would start to move down. So it's an indication to me perhaps that an organ measuring the flow of time may be a different thing than an organ that actually sensed time in itself. So it may be that time in itself may be one thing and the flow of that time may be a different thing.

The other point was about whether it is possible to think in terms of musical vibrations other than in terms of time. The problem here is that we are so accustomed again to the usual units of time which we have been brought up with. Again, the text books, you will see standard units and also derived units, so that some of the units like velocity, meters per second, or even hertz vibration per second, are all related to this what seemingly is now a false unit of time. And yet there are so many things in our life which have become accepted as having to do with time which actually have nothing to do with time but have to do with motion. Even vibrations per second is a relative measurement. You could say it is a relative thing to some other motion, so that if you have one vibration going at one rate and another going at another rate, then you would measure the one as opposed to the other, rather than something fundamental in itself. It would be merely comparative.

Comment: This isn't relating to anything, so I don't know if there was any comment to what you just said. I think that this may be a very strange question, but it really bothers me. When he talks about these little beings in the drop of water and he gives us a whole thing about how the universe came about and how all the suns, the tetartocosmoses, the moon, etc. Now he is telling us that in this drop of water there are these like three-brained beings that have moments of hypochondria, worrying about their lives. They are having three-brained experiences. Do you think bacteria can worry about runs of bad luck? Can a non-three-brained being have a thirst for self-perfection? It's just an odd thing he has brought in. When he does something like that, it almost seems literally everything he says is in some way true. Now all of a sudden we have this world within a world, within this little drop of water, having these experiences, and it just makes me wonder. Why did he use that example?

The second question I have is one of his big questions: the reason he initiated himself this time on the 5th descent to find out why does war happen. He wanted to find out for himself. At the end of the chapter on war he says, "If it is still possible to save the beings of the Earth, then time alone can do it." And a little further on he says, "...time alone, thanks either to the guidance of a certain Being with very high reason or to certain exceptional cosmic events." I wondered if anyone thought about that as well.

I have thought about that deeply over the years and was always wondering what was going to happen. Have we already had the very high being that G was talking about in *A&E*? Some people thought that this very high being had appeared from time to time. Mr. Bennett thought that. People from various religions have been expecting some very high being to appear. Then if this doesn't work Mr. G, or Beelzebub, gave Hassein a very, very strange look when he was talking about some cosmic events. I have often though about this cosmic event; was something going to happen? There have been all sorts of prophesies. Even right now, something was going to happen this March. A piece of a comet or asteroid was going to hit the earth. The last copy of Nexus, a magazine printed in Australia, hinted at this. G must have known something to put that in that book. There has been prophecy going back to before Jesus in the Old Testament. Whatever happens, be in your Iamness.

Comment: Whenever I fly and we're taking off and I look out of the window down on the city from the air and I see, and it always me impresses me, amazes me, how many people there are in the world, and how many people there are down in that space. I try to imagine that every one of those persons has a life, that they have their families and their concerns, their aims. But it also seems like the beings in their drop of water because there are just so many. What's the difference if the beings in the drop of water experience their time similarly to the way we experience ours or another experiences theirs. What matter? It's me and billions of people. This idea of living a one- or two-brained existence, I imagine much about. I certainly have runs of bad luck and other types of experiences like that. In terms of time along with a Being of very high reason - I'm not sure it needs to be conceived as a Being external to us. That it could be the result of whatever being we can acquire in the time that we have. Because I certainly don't recognize nearly enough that there is the inevitability of my death and I live with the disease of tomorrow because I don't think about a beginning as an end to that time. So I live like a two-brained being or as a one-brained being frequently just for what my needs are at the moment, with no future and frequently not even a past that I am conscious of.

Comment: I think in *Living Time*, this is where the story comes. It's been something that I remember now and then, the story Rodney Collin talks about, there is a helicopter in the sky and there is a car leaving from say, Bognor Regis and is going to London, and there is another individual who is leaving London and is coming to Bognor Regis. Somewhere they pass, but for the individual who is leaving Bognor Regis, moving towards London - and that's his future while Bognor Regis is now his past. The individual who is leaving London is leaving London in his past and Bognor Regis is his future. The moment that they pass each other on the road is each of their presents. But for the man or woman in the helicopter above them, his moment is in the now for each individual because there is not a past or a future as far as he is concerned for either of those individuals. It's all now. Obviously his past and future are relative. That's the end of the story. Often when I remember that story I am driving home from work, or I am leaving home and I am driving to my place of work. When I remember that story there is a change in my perception. How I experience that change is that I try to be present to my home and to my place of work and be there during that time, so that it is not past and future in the same way. What happens to me, what I experience, as a change in perception is that I find myself not thinking so much and I am more aware of my surroundings. I remember crossing over the bridge. I remember passing certain places. And when I am not aware of that my perception is usually caught up with whatever I'm thinking.

Comment: I wonder how often we represent the situation to ourselves as there being a single sense of time. But could it be that there are different senses of time, going on in us simultaneously? I ask that question from a quite practical standpoint, for those who are interested in the practical work of the science of being. We can't ignore the fact that the centres work at different speeds. At the same time we are told that if the centres are not related in a certain way there is no unity, and this has many consequences. So maybe we could just ponder for a moment - maybe we could see it as another - that there are these engines working in different tempos, which have to find a common resonance. Maybe we could represent that common resonance as yet another tempo, like beats or something. And the experience of what happens when those disparate tempos come into alignment. How then is time experienced? As if by the tempo of a super-centre or a super-state, or something quite different. And it seems to me to have a very practical bearing on the inner experience of change of state.

G said time is breath, which seems significant. People have talked about the Foolasnitamnian principle and the Itoklanoz principle and I have been trying to bring them together and trying to think what does this mean: that time is breath and what H was saying about thoughts being all over the place. It's with that kind of discussion with what C said. I am just trying to come to something with all of that. The usual condition in which I find myself is hallucination - two-centered hallucination. My thoughts are always running into the future or going over the past; feelings are all over the place. The only part of me which is always in the present moment is my body. The only time I'm in touch with that is when I am sensing or if I place my attention on my breathing. This tends to calm the thoughts, centre me in my body and bring me to the present moment, give me a chance of being three-centred for once. I say that because I think there is something significant in what G said about time is breath. We all talk about experience, and reality is what we attend to. The only thing we can do at any moment in time is use our attention, is to collect our attention from wherever it is scattered and do something intentional with it to change our condition. I would like to begin from there. I think this was connected to what N was saying about the second conscious shock, or, the second kind of being food, which is breath. If I pay attention to breathing, I am paying attention to that second being food. It is never automatic; it can only be done intentionally, and I wonder if there is anyone here who could say anything about that, or who could expand at all on what the breath means in terms of time, in terms of being more present and being more real. I sometimes experience that by attending to my breath. That brings me more into the condition in which I would like to be and I know is possible. I am sorry I am not very clear, but I feel these things are somehow connected.

Comment: That was very well said: this breath, presence and action. For instance, every day something is happening to us. So in order to be present, in order to sense ourselves, by sensing ourselves we become present of course. We must put half of our attention on what is happening and the other half of our attention we must put into our breath so that we can fill and sense and be present.

Comment: I agree with what has been said about the balance between the centres. But we must make available a sort of balance when there is a disequilibrium between the centres, a sense of attempting. When I sit here now my emotional centre tends to be nervous, but I will not give up. I cannot say that I am calm, but I will not give up. What I am trying to say is that I have this picture of presence only as the centres balanced in the form of calmness, something that we aim for. But there are moments when there is no calmness and these moments are very valuable. This moment is here with me now. I look at the others. They have the same tendency as my biological apparatus has when they get this microphone, and I can recognize their state through their facial muscles. If you look at my facial muscles you can recognize some of your own. But I will not give up. This is more my situation and it is a Work situation. Calmness, yes! But if it is not there I have to be able to work in the dark.

Comment: I want to say two things. First about the question T put about the beings in the drop of water. This is my take on what I think G was trying to illustrate. We have spoken about time being merciless, but we haven't considered the other aspect, that time is just. If it were only merciless we would be finished, but it is just. It means that time flows in the same sequence for all the beings in every cosmos. There is only one thing, with which the flow of time is compared in *A&E*, and that is the flow of divine love.

Seminar 2 - Chapter 16 of Beelzebub's Tales to His Grandson

Comment: I would like to read something from one of G's Paris meetings as published in William Patrick Patterson's book, *Voices in the Dark*, pages 58 to 60.

End of Session

Where Do We Go From Here?

Facilitator: Sy Ginsburg

Introduction: Sy Ginsburg, Facilitator:

(Transcribers' note: The cassette tape recordings of this session that I have been given to transcribe are in general quite clear when people were holding the microphone while speaking. There were instances, mostly, I think, having to do with people holding the microphone too far away from themselves or speaking without benefit of holding the microphone, where the tape was either muffled or inaudible. When people spoke without holding the microphone, it was often impossible to discern what was said. To the extent possible, I have attempted to discern what was said and to transcribe it as accurately as possible, but some of this discernment may have required the interpretation of unclear words. In other instances of total inaudibility, it was necessary to omit a phrase or sentence or two. In these instances I have attempted to preserve the gist of what was said from the portion that was audible. In other instances the inaudible statement is omitted entirely. Punctuation, such as determining the finality of sentences is mine as is the addition or omission of connecting words).

Facilitator: Good morning. Those of you have attended previous conferences will how what this session is about. For those of you who have not, some explanation is in order. We divide the overall session into two sessions. The first session, before morning coffee, is to open up the discussion of what the All and Everything Conference is all about. It is an opportunity for you to comment and criticize. Those of you who wish to do this will have an opportunity in a moment. In the second session, after the coffee, we need to deal with certain specific issues. For example, there is a planning committee of eight people this year who have organized this conference. The planning committee has changed from year to year over the past eight conferences.

At least two of the current committee have made it known that they are not able to participate in the planning of next year's conference indeed, there will be another conference. Changes to the planning committee are addressed in the second session. Then there are other questions.

Is there a sufficient wish to do this next year and then some details?

If so, where? It has been here at Bognor Regis every year but one.

If so, what dates? We can talk specifically to this because I have some information from the hotel as to what dates are available to hold it here. We can talk about this in the second session.

Where Do We Go From Here?

Of the two people who will not be able to serve on the planning committee for next year, one is Bert Sharp. Bert has done a lot of things that need getting done in order to hold a conference. So, we have to see if we can get these things done in his absence.

The other person is Pat Bennett. Even though we do not have organizational officers or a hierarchy, Pat has acted as treasurer. There are some ideas about this. For example, Conti Meehan has taken over these duties at this conference.

What I would like to do now in the first session is to turn this over to Harry Bennett of the planning committee, who will present a question that we can address. If you want your name to appear in the published Proceedings please state it before you speak. (The names of planning committee members making administrative and procedural statements will be included in the Proceedings).

Participant statement 2: In years past, it has been the tradition to go around the room and ask each person to share their impressions of the conference. This year we decided that we would at the outset break away from that. The floor is open so you can share any impressions of your experience that you would wish to share with everyone. But along with that we would also like to take the time to ask again a broader question of how do we understand the relationship of this thing that we call Work to the whole of life, to people outside of the Work, to the world, and do we see that this conference fits into our understanding of that in any way? Do we see this conference as fulfilling in any way, our understanding of what work for the Work is? And if there is benefit in this type of event or not? Are you willing to share your perspective on that?

Participant statement 3: I just want to say that when you were introducing the session, this thought came up. That we come here as mere mortals, as it were, and there is only so much that we can do. But God willing, something higher enters and which allows something real to take place and during my stay here I think that has taken place, and for that I am grateful. That is one of the great benefits and results and fruits of this type of gathering.

Participant statement 4: I second that.

Participant statement 5: I don't know whether it's too specific at this time or whether it counts as Work, but I would like to see more structure in the reading of the chapters in the afternoon sessions. I hesitate to put too definite a plan on it but, for example, I would like to see somebody who offers or is directed to make an in depth study of the chapter and present it as a lead-in to the chapter, the particular point of view of that person. Then others can respond to that. That's one possibility. I don't say that it is the way it should be. Or several people should be asked to present their own interpretation of the chapter.

Participant statement 6: In regard to the question that you raise, we discussed in a little get together of the planning committee immediately before the conference, this exact question. One of the suggestions, and perhaps since Harry made it first he might elaborate on it, was that rather than have a chapter orientation which we have had for the last several years, that it might be more interesting if we had certain kinds of key words or key concepts drawn from *Beelzebub's Tales*. Whether this is Okidanokh, whether it is Kundabuffer or whatever, it would be something that would span a number of chapters and would give at least the possibility of an organized kind of approach rather than something that is focused on one chapter. So that is one possibility.

Participant statement 7: Regarding what you said about key words and what you said about protecting the Work and conserving it in an electronic way, it would be very useful to have the Work in an electronic way because this allows real fast computer searches and gives you a total overview of the key word or the subject you are looking for.

Participant statement 8: It also was brought up that rather than have one person prepare something as a kind of an overview, that always kind of betrays a prejudice or a particular perspective. Several of us mentioned that maybe it is more appropriate to leave the effort wide open, so that when people come they don't have anything that has kind of focused them ahead of time. They just have a concept or a Work idea or whatever, and then however they put that together, that becomes shared in the group without any kind of precondition.

Participant statement 9: I feel that what I would like to see is a reading of the chapter, that we sit down and read it together. Obviously this creates problems when you get chapters which are very long, but maybe they could be split up or maybe even just read for a designated period of time on an allotted chapter which we select. I think something can happen with a group reading and even if people only read one sentence and pass the book to the next person, I think this would establish some kind of level which would add to the atmosphere, instead of just selecting a bit here and a bit there to study, I find it could move into more of a combined effort. Certainly for me, I don't know what happens in other groups but reading within the group is a very entrusted exercise.

Participant statement 10: I agree with that, but I also think that the advantage of this setting, is to do things that aren't done, at least I haven't seen them done, in other places. I've been looking personally for a long time, maybe not hard enough, for some help from, shall we say, older people who had been thinking about these things in more depth or with greater connection than I had, for a long time.

With regard to the structure, I thought that the chapter structure is an interesting one to use because in retrospect people seem sometimes to make references to the key concepts in other places in the book, anyway. I realize that key concept is a very useful one but I'm perhaps concerned that things would be missed going that way.

Participant statement 11: In *Beelzebub*, right at the beginning, it appears that in every new undertaking, in every epoch, it begins with, "In the name of the father and in the name of the son, etc.", and this was interpreted that any new project embarked upon in any new field of endeavor should have a structure, a pattern and a plan. Through this prism one could hold very high ideals, and within this very high framework if one remained true to this structure then the details would eventually work themselves out.

Participant statement 12: I think it is possible to integrate both ideas: the idea of a key concept and the idea of chapter structure, in one. I have one idea that I would like to propose but I think that it is in the second half that we do it, or can I do it now? The idea is this: What is the meaning of objective science? Now, in order to begin to understand, and I am not saying that I understand it, but I am interested in the question. In order to understand this, we have to begin by understanding one of the basic propositions or formulations of objective science. And it is this: Everything in the universe, without exception, is material. Now this formulation of objective science is in the chapter, "The Arch Absurd," which follows the chapter on the relativity of time, and is in relation to the Omnipresent Okidanokh. It is not possible to understand the meaning of objective science if we do not begin by understanding the Omnipresent Okidanokh, and that is followed by the second chapter on this, "The Arch Preposterous." So, those two chapters which are about Okidanokh at the same time answer the question of what is the meaning of objective science, and we know that in *Beelzebub*, Gurdjieff puts a lot of emphasis on objective science. He continually says, "according to objective science," and not only that, we can move to other chapters because objective science is also taken up in the chapter on the Fourth Descent about Belcultassi who really was the one who initiated objective science on earth.

Participant statement 13: I would just like to say that I deplore the decision of the leadership to change the format of this discussion, because in the past the very valuable starting point was how people feel about everything that has gone on, and this brings a particular perspective that we need. Even though sometimes it may be a little bit sentimental it still is a very important angle. It really is a kind of weighing of the value at different levels of oneself. Instead of this we have already been confused by the question of the third line of Work which takes one's mind into a particular direction. I think that what we just heard from Will exemplifies the problem. It is a very good statement of principles but it is, as it were, a stage or two removed from what I think we need to do which is to really consolidate our collective impressions and our needs. And I would really like to hear, in a sense, a testimony first of where we are at, and gradually from that evoke a kind of conceptual framework for seeing it. I just thought I would say this. These things are so subtle that if you are invited to think before you have felt, I think it is rather less satisfactory.

Facilitator: As I understand it, the question that Harry posed was a broadening question, and even though we seem to have gotten into detail about the seminars, I was really going to say something else which might be in the direction of what you are suggesting. That is, I have been thinking about what this conference is and why we should have it; indeed, we should have it at all. It has become clear to me that this is third line of Work, that is, working for the Work. I cannot presume to know how Mr. Gurdjieff felt about how his ideas should be put out although there are some indications in the literature. But it strikes me that we are doing something in this conference which is useful because I know of no other forum like this where people can get together. You might say that we all honor the same teaching from many perspectives, from group perspectives and from individual perspectives. So, it strikes me, even though every year I wonder if we should have another conference, that there is something lawful about this.

I also wonder if we should aim to make the conference bigger because that would make it even more inclusive. This might cause problems in the actual discussions. These are technical problems and can possibly be worked out. I am just throwing out these questions and ideas because that is how I understand the purpose of this session. You might be interested to know that, so far as I can count, there are fifty-one people here this year. Last year I believe that it was about thirty-three, and participation has been in the low thirties during most of the previous years. I have been thinking about why this has happened. I do not have an answer to this, but I can think of two possible reasons. One was the Forum of Those Who Knew Gurdjieff which may have attracted people, and another possible reason were the musical presentations that we had this year but did not have last year. I am just wondering if there is something else or in addition, if we have another conference, that somebody feels should be put out into the broader world. I do not want to say, in promotion of Mister Gurdjieff's teaching, but simply to make it more available in some way. This is not to propose a specific idea. It is just what I have been feeling in answer to Chris's comment.

Participant statement 15: The experiences that I have been able to take back from this conference have been valuable in the past, but during this conference something solidified for me that I have had an inkling of before. It is that there are many different lineages here, there are disagreements that take place, and yet there is this respect that we have for one another and one another's understandings that goes beyond what normally happens in life and that is a walking away from one another when we don't agree. Here, we come together, and we continue to do that. So, I have had a number of experiences during this conference where I consider that the value of that exchange comes because we are all working and the Work is working in each of us to the extent that we can actually encounter a more civil approach to one another and the differences that we have.

Participant statement 16: Following on from what you have just been saying is something that I have been thinking about over a long period of time and that is that you have been talking about coming together and yet having differences. In *All and Everything* there is the idea that Mister G. was looking forward towards the time when there would be something like a unification over the whole of the planet such as world government or something like that. I remember that John Bennett did once mention that, whether it was in his own heart or whether he was following along the lines of what he'd read in *Beelzebub*. Of course, he'd also met Mister Gurdjieff. So, we have the U.S.A. that has been there for a long time and then we have got the E.U. starting, just a few countries getting together. Whilst this was happening, I just couldn't believe it when I saw the U.K. all wanting to split up like the Scots wanting to have their own parliament and also the Welsh. When are the people in Cornwall going to do the same thing? What's going on? This is not going to tie in with what G. wants and what Mister B. seemed to be thinking. Yet if you think of it, look at this E.U. now. In the last year it is growing like "topsy." Then there is all this fiction about Mister Bush and Tony Blair getting together and the French not wanting to know, as if there was a new Europe coming as compared to the old Europe and so on. So, here this organization that started off eight years ago or so, is quite something. It is like a nexus of people from all over the globe, interested in these ideas of Gurdjieff which are extremely powerful. I think it is absolutely wonderful that we have this and I hope it goes on.

Participant statement 17: As you realized yesterday, I am not born to be a speaker. But of course I can ask questions about any questions you may like or any solutions you may look for. First, I must say that about the third line of the Work that you mention, it is to work for the Work. Now, work for the Work does not mean just coming here, the way I see it or the way I know it. Work for the Work means to come here and to see how we can bring forward Gurdjieff's Work. How we can broaden it, how we can make it bigger, and not just give lectures, though with lectures, of course, knowledge is always good. But knowledge must bring the understanding behind it, otherwise nothing happens. So, in order for something to happen, we must tackle it practically more than theoretically. In other words, what do we do? How do we make it bigger, how do we broaden it? So, getting together, like we are, sitting here all of us together and being together, not just putting a collar in our lives that we are here together and all is very well. I think that is what this conference is all about, to work for the Work, because all of us are involved in Gurdjieff's Work, and we are here. For me it is the first time. What to do in order to bring forth Gurdjieff's Work? Because Gurdjieff said that he wanted to build a better world. Now, what are we doing about it? That is what we must think about. I know there are groups that we have or you have, and we all try to do our best, etc., but it's fragmented. I think we should all get together, not just each one of us thinking of our own interest and our selfish themes, etc. It shouldn't be like that, because this Work is to change completely. We cannot remain the same. We must be different men, different persons, which is according to Gurdjieff's teaching. Therefore, the conclusion is that to work for the Work means we must get together and find out which ways we can bring it forward. We should work together for Gurdjieff's Work first and not for our own little pride. As I said at the beginning, I am not really born to be a speaker but I will answer any question you might like.

Participant statement 18: I perfectly agree with what George just said. Of course, my position in that is that this is exactly what we are doing. We are coming from our old traditions and our old cultural backgrounds, and we are trying to find exactly that. Fine, how to do it? So, also yes, I would have to say that I am ready to answer all questions. So, whoever wants to address a question to me, that is fine.

Participant statement 19: When Martin spoke, he was the first one to speak, he expressed his gratitude for the week. If I can speak for the Manchester people, I have been listening for their initial reactions to the week, and they have all said that the quality of the papers presented and the ambience they've experienced this has been such that they are going back to the northwest of the U.K. with the firm resolve that they will introduce into their lives and hope to introduce into the group something of this level of quality. I must say, that goes for me as well. All of us confess that we didn't come here with much preparation. We came here as members of the audience. But they leave today with the firm resolve that they are going to put more quality into their Work.

All & Everything Conference 2003

Participant statement 20: I would really love to hear from a lot of the people who are here that we haven't heard from yet. So, I would like to propose that we pass this microphone around and if you wish to share something, I am sure that we would all very much benefit from it.

Participant statement 21: Well, I have to thank you for making this conference. I think it is a wonderful effort toward trying to bring some unity into the mishmash that is, as Gurdjieff put it, "The fine fix that I leave you all in." So, I did think about this a lot last night and I have had to write down some things. Contempt for others in their beliefs and behavior is a negative emotion and that has to be transformed into compassion. It's been about various conflicts among the various lines of Work represented here, and at times I do see moments of contempt between these various groups. Sometimes, it seems to me, that this arises from a sense of superiority or elitism. In other cases I see it arising from fear and jealousy. It's almost like there is a little war going on between all these various factions and groups. Just like there's a war going on in our world right now. I think we should all maybe take another look at the chapter on Beelzebub's understanding and opinion of war. There has been some talk about the dissemination of these ideas in a degenerative sort of sense into the world being picked up by commercial enterprises and popular psychology, etc. Unfortunately, we have no control over that. I do laud the attempts by the Gurdjieff Heritage Society to preserve the information that is available in whatever means they can. But in making these efforts to preserve the letter of the Work, we can't lose sight of preserving also, the spirit of the Work. A school that produces no graduates will eventually have no real teachers. I think we need to concern ourselves with how we apply the Work to the transformation of our own beings, and I don't think we need to spend as much time worrying about how others should be using the Work. Let us not be too fanatical in persecuting the heretics in the name of our personal dogmas. As Gurdjieff said, "only he can be called a real man who can bear the unpleasant manifestations of others."

Facilitator: Since we are passing the microphone, what we did in previous years is to try to limit ourselves to relatively short times. I don't know how many people actually want to speak, but we want to get this done before morning coffee, so we can discuss more specific things afterward.

Participant statement 23: I agree with what you said and I wonder if one could narrow it down to a feeling that in a conference like this, it is suited to the more cerebral among us. And I wonder if there is anything that can be done to make some of the very interesting intellectual papers and discussions more relevant to one's personal Work. I don't how if this can be done but, for instance (I think I got this from Edgar): What does the concept of time have to do with me in my Work? Is there any way we can relate our discussion of the chapters at a more meaningful personal level? That is my question.

Participant statement 24: I would like to add to that only with regard to the sharing of what is for me an extraordinary aphorism and a summation perhaps of the teaching of Sri Nisargadatta Maharaj whom Seymour has met, whom we have both met in Bombay, India, famous particularly for a book called, I Am That. The aphorism, if one may so term it, is that "awareness is love in action." The force of that aphorism struck me half a dozen years ago. I have begun to see its enormous significance. For me, if Mister Gurdjieff's Work is an ocean, that is a drop of the same material.

Participant statement 25: I must say that the best thing for me here is still to meet people from all different parts of the world and with different points of view of the Work. I think that the more different we are, the better is this meeting. George told me yesterday something about internal considering and external considering. So, if there is a great difference we can create a stronger third force within us and make some better relations and better approach the Gurdjieff Work to the truth, because each one of us sees the truth and the Work from one particular point of view. So, I learn a lot from everyone else here.

Participant statement 26: This is my fourth year here, and my perspective is that every year it changes. I get something different from it every year. Even though it is very intellectual, I usually get some little titbit here and there. I really would like to see it come down a little bit sometime and not be so intellectual. Maybe just one little lecture here and there in the midst of it for us common people who are not so bright as the rest of you all. But I think what I really do get from it is the people I meet. Every year there is somebody new and somebody different and somebody just so special. So, I think that this is such a great opportunity to look at the Gurdjieff Work in all its aspects, because sometimes in your group wherever it may be, you can get very stuck and not realize what is really out there and how many lives Gurdjieff has touched.

Participant statement 27: I am still thinking about what the gentlemen said about contempt. I have been reflecting since then if things that I have said have given rise to that impression, but not in the sense of trying to justify or excuse myself if that's the case. Having been here at all of these conferences, I note that there have always been very frank exchanges of opinion, but the overwhelming direction that this conference goes is in the direction of reconciliation and joining together. It has achieved more joining together among people, more relationships, but I think that it has created schisms. I accept what you say, and I will consider that and thank you for saying so. It is quite right to bring these impressions to us because maybe some of us who have come here year after year get used to saying things, making a comment about this or that in a rather glib way. So, I appreciate that. Another thing that I would like to say is that the quality of the people who come here always impresses me. Some people who have come here this year like the people from northern England, the people from Greece; that always really impresses me and I feel that this conference has to exist so that these people can speak together and be together, and find a way together. I think we have to allow for human nature, and it takes time to find the way to go forward.

Participant statement 28: I just wanted to say that my suggestion wasn't theoretical. There is a senior's facility in Vancouver, and generally the person who gets to present at it has his or her chief preoccupation, whereas the others don't necessarily have that and they can bring more of a broader view. It comes out very interesting and it works very well.

Participant statement 29: My Work easily gets stuck up. I find that in this instance I come together with other people, and this personally makes sense because we come from different backgrounds, different nationalities. It always surprises me that it happens so like a miracle, that when people gather in the name of the Work, Work is there. So, I would like to thank all of you and each one of you from the deepest of my heart as I feel it now.

Participant statement 30: For me it is the first time here, and I can't understand the language very well. So, I tried something else. I tried to feel people when they talk, and it became something like a miracle. I could understand you, what you say, without knowing the words. So, there is something behind the words. When we come here in the name of the Work, it comes like this, like a miracle. I'd like to thank you all to be here.

Participant statement 31: With *Beelzebub's Tales* and *All and Everything* as the focus, the overt focus of this conference, I assumed the third line of Work. Coming here to the degree that my inner economy is disturbed, there is the possibility for something new to enter. That's one of the things that has been valuable here for me, the second year, and to a certain extent in reading the Proceedings from the previous years. It seems that from my point of view, all of those of us who are drawn here are working on themselves., and that creates an atmosphere that even when there is disagreement it is not an unhealthy thing but it is the beginning of a new thing. How that is going to be new for each of as, for me that's up to me to find a way. Something may not make sense to me in my head, but if I am attentive here with however I may come at the moment, something of that enters and opens me up to another possibility. I have found the experience different from last year and equally enriching in its own way. I think it is due to the participation of all of us in as many different forms as we are here in body.

Participant statement 32: I want to especially thank John S. for what he just said before. It sums up my point of view of what's going on, and coming to this over the years becoming closer. Thanks, John.

Participant statement 33: This is just to say that I think it is difficult to get a balance in a seminar of this nature which is quite scientific. I was in a group in the seventies that didn't have discussions or reading. The regime was strictly physical, working on that kind of thing. There is a difference in the ambience. It is very difficult to get a balance.

Participant statement 34: When I get home from this conference I always say, "I am not going back there again." I don't know why I say that. I have come to this conference seven times, and each time, I ask myself, why the hell do I come here? I think there is a notion in me that Gurdjieff taught many different things to many different people, and we don't have a common language in that respect. We don't have a real common language when we actually discuss a Work effort. This is also a puzzlement to me, and a frustration why that should be, and it is true. But I keep coming back, I am still attracted, I am still very interested in meeting people from other groups and exchanging ideas. I'd like more music perhaps, or something that can balance it off emotionally, something like that. It think it is very encouraging that people come from Greece, from the north of England, from America, and I think it's pretty unique, even though, yes, what this gentleman said down here, that may be true. I don't like Toddy's left shoe here, but we have to get over that and there is a lot of friction. When I first came into groups, people treated me like shit. That's true, but you can't be that overly sensitive. It's just too bad and that's the way it is. But we keep coming back for more and that's part of the teaching, because that's fiction and there is no creation without friction wherever it comes from, and we all benefit from it. I hope the meetings continue and I hope that I can still come and still feel a need to come.

Participant statement 35: Larry F. had to leave and he gave me his impressions which I told him I would read for him. The morning sitting was very helpful, all the presentations were great, conversely, both seminars on the *Tales* were disjointed, feeling for me, dead, partly my fault. About one-half the time I felt painfully ill at ease with myself in this largely new and brainy crowd which has pushed me to see parts of myself more clearly. The other half of the time was tremendously fascinating, the variety of different people with their different backgrounds, different accents and individuality. A unique collection of Work folks un-homogenized by the single set of shoulds and shouldn'ts that a fixed group can have. It was an enriching time for me. Thank you, Larry F.

Participant statement 36: I just have two comments. One is on a personal note. What I found most valuable is that this conference was vivified for me because of the preparation. Because I knew which chapters we were working on, our little group in Salt Lake worked on the chapters before. We worked and worked on them, and eventually I realized that it didn't matter if we got to the conference, because it just opened up a world of questions which is now even bigger. So, that preparation made a complete difference. The second thing is what George brought up about the third line of Work and what you said about fiction being a potential for creation. For me the most fruitful result of the friction that is inevitable between human beings, and the question is quite alive in me right now, is: what is my responsibility regarding the third line of Work? I agree with you that it is not just for us personally. So, that question is alive and may it thrive.

Participant statement 37: I share the experience with Ana and John S., and my friend here. The thing is that what I found here personally, my experience, is this thing of meeting people from all parts of the world and with totally different views from me. Yesterday, I learned three things from George that I did not even suspect existed. Now, before coming here I only knew Toddy because we were at a conference in Portland. But in Portland, Toddy and I exchanged and then I exchanged with Bonny, and now I know that I have to exchange with at least fifteen other people. That is a problem, and we were talking about that last night. The Internet experience is very scary. I don't like it. I really don't like it. I am really scared of it. What is important for us is, yes, let's keep the Internet connection, but we have to meet. We have to find each other. We have to see each others face. We have to feel the warmth of the other person, otherwise this Work is not going to continue. For me, this is my new group. This is my new group because I lost my other group. It is finished, no more, so this is my new group.

Participant statement 38: I can only say that I find the conference invaluable to me. I'm very much on my own. It's a lifeline to me and it gives me an impetus that is very powerful and which lasts throughout the year.

Participant statement 39: I have been here for the first time so I have nothing to compare it to the other conferences from before. I came here to listen to the lectures which were given and to see what it was all about. My experience has been that even though it has been on a very intellectual level, I have had moments where I could grasp something. Those moments help me to get more interested in what I have grasped. So, I found this very important for me, to take something home with me. Also, with the people I have met here, there have been exchanges of ways of working, which have been very useful for me. I know that something will grow out of this.

Participant statement 40: I would also relate to those moments that are special, and I won't say anything more about them, except that they have a possibility to influence me if I can remember that there is joy available. What I am trying to say is that very often when I am touched inside, I become what you call "stern." I don't know if that is the right word, but I think it is "stiff." There is a lack of flexibility, and with the deep touch that I have had through this conference, without pointing out any particular thing, there is this clear tendency within me to be a little too serious. What Chris was referring to, to feel more, I think some of the material to be felt can be made more available, if I can remember that the Gurdjieff Work is really a joy. That sounds contradictory, but we need to remember joy, and I don't feel so alone about this because when I look at you, I see so much of myself.

Participant statement 41: I think there was a statement from the planning committee that this is not a Work meeting, in that people coming here are expected to have satisfied their Work needs. I don't see that this is the case. I think that most people see this as a Work event, and they take a lot from it. Anyway, it is a Work event in the way that they understand Work, and that's fine for me. I don't think more structure is really needed. I think maybe the opposite in that maybe we should make some more room for the unknown, for the, let's say, third force. I do enjoy the music and maybe I would enjoy some more moving things.

Participant statement 42: It's been a strange experience for me because not having been to a meeting like this before, I have nothing to compare it with. I can only say that really I am unfamiliar with Gurdjieff so I come here and I have understood a lot of what the language has been. It's been an exercise in attention for me because I have had to pay very close attention to what is being said, because it has been at a very intellectual level. This is just an observation, not a criticism. What it has done for me is that a lot of the Gurdjieff ideas have always kind of floated around my head, and what this has done for me is that it has been catalytic. By that I mean it is a kind of speeding up process, and it has brought it to life for me. For that, it has given me an impetus to go forward that I haven't had before. For that, it has been absolutely invaluable. I think for me it has been special. I haven't stayed in the hotel, and in retrospect I wish I had now. I wish I'd stayed here. I live locally so I have commuted, if you like. I think it has been special here, and

Where Do We Go From Here?

I have left here with a kind of a mood. There is a mood here which is very special. I am very thankful that I've come, and I hope we do have one next year.

Participant statement 43: I too hope we have one next year. I've come away with many wonderful experiences with all of you. One thing that I would like to add, that I hunger for at these meetings, is that as such a diverse group in the Work, that we ask ourselves as a group, what is our responsibility? So, that would not only mean to ourselves and the Work, but to this planet.

Participant statement 44: I would like to end, as being almost the last one, with a goal for hope, and faith and charity, because that is what this conference gives me. When you are working on your own during several years, and you meet somebody who confirms what you did from a totally different point of view, it should give you faith. It should give you faith in the Work of Gurdjieff Therefore, it is a proof to any selection of those who Work, that our differences are only words, not intentions.

Participant statement 45: I am feeling very grateful in this moment to all of you, and to Chris for reminding us, because it is so important for me to hear what everybody is feeling. This conference for the last eight years has been really a Work in progress, and having the privilege of being a part of the planning, we have had this opportunity where we make a lot of mistakes. We experiment and some things fail and some things succeed. We are always learning or hopefully learning how to Work better together, and I thank you for your comments in giving me an opportunity to see myself a little more clearly. I guess for me, that's a big part of what this is all about. I go away with so much food, so much the richer for seeing myself in a way that I don't see myself on a daily basis. Meeting so many new people, as Will says, I feel very much that this is my group, an ever expanding group. So, thank you. I hope we are together next year.

Participant statement 46: I resonate mostly with what Nick said, because each year for the last eight years there is this period of time where there is this reaction inside a part of me that says, "Do we really have to go through this all again? And that changes over time. What struck me from a number of impressions here, especially from folks who have been here over time, is that this is, for me now, my feeling about it is that this is such a marvellous example of the digestive process. Now, being a physician I look on digestion maybe a little bit differently than some of you do, because it is a very messy business. Digestion is not some ideal type of thing. Things really get kind of stirred up and mixed up, and the sorting process can lead in a lot of different directions that are not at all pleasant on the surface. But the end result is that I think what we are seeing, at least that's what I'm feeling, is that with many of us we are trying to share a little bit of what has gotten digested so that we leave all of this other stuff which is inevitable, lawful, necessary and we all complain about it. Yet that isn't what we really wish to share. So, every year there is this feeling of something so special, especially because I know that as soon as I go home one of my biggest battles will be that I tend to become quickly provincial. I go back into my own little world, and I'm in Maine and so forth and so on, and just to have the remembrance of the incredible variety of people and perspectives from different parts of the world. I fall into this trap of thinking that the Work is something in Maine. It may stretch to New York, but that's about it. This is such a great reality check, and such a positive endorsement of all that is real about Work. So, thank you again for the last eight years.

Participant statement 47: There is a word which I hate using. I have to wash my mouth out after I use it. It's "Work" and even worse, "The Work." So, I don't use it if I can help it, but I'll make an exception to that today. It's very interesting that this really isn't meant to be a Work gathering, but surreptitiously because of our interests and connections, it creeps in. I find this very satisfactory, because I think this is the right kind of balance. One shouldn't ape the Work by putting it on the pedestal. It should always be the subterranean backdrop to our way of being. To me, you can't have a Work event and a non Work event because all of life, if you're interested, is actually a forum for Work. It's not possible really to make a separation. So to me, the tzimmus is the fact that together we are interested in this process of understanding and transformation, but in the context of trying specifically to study the teaching, the ideas, what has been presented as material to Work with. And so, the thing I'm on the alert for is the general turn which I would express in the following words: "I know something about the Work, and I will close down your questions by telling you my knowledge." This to me is the great sin that all group leaders and would be knowing people, fall into. To me, the real exploration that I would very much like to see is, can we study the teaching from the standpoint of a wish to have this secret Work going on, and at the same time, sacrifice my desire to tell you, to make statements, rather than bringing questions to such an intensity that that very energy of battlement takes me to a more intense overall state? It happens as we meet, and I think that's what brings us together and makes us keep coming back.

(Intermission for Morning Coffee)

Facilitator: This second session has traditionally been to deal with the very specifics of where do we go from here. I just want to say by way of introduction, for those of you who are new, that there is no organization that runs this conference. It was started by a group of volunteers called a planning committee, and the makeup of that committee has changed somewhat over the years. People have gone on it, people have gone off of it. Some of us just got on the planning committee last year, some of us are a little long in the tooth.

So, here we are and the first basic question is: Shall we have another conference? I can divide that question into really three possibilities: another conference next year, another conference but at a later time than next year, or not have another conference. I believe that the simplest thing is to have a show of hands and this will pretty much determine for whoever is going to plan, if they are going to plan, if there is something to plan.

All who would like another conference next year, raise your hands.

(MOST HANDS ARE RAISED) It looks like a majority.

Would anybody not like to have another conference next year? (NO HANDS) It looks like we will have another conference next year.

Where Do We Go From Here?

The next question is: when? We have some information at least in regard to having a conference at this hotel and perhaps even in England. Incidentally, Easter next year is Sunday, April 11, 2004. This year it is Sunday, April 20th, which means it is nine days earlier. Our experience has been that if we have the conference before Easter, travel costs are lower, air fares are lower and the hotel is much happier with us because they are emptier. In fact, they were full this year as you know. Since we have voted to have another conference, the suggested dates since we try to have it about two weeks before Easter, and assuming it's the same length which is another question we can deal with, would be from Wednesday evening, March 24, to Sunday, March 28, 2004. Maybe I should just ask the question. Is that an acceptable date? All who feel or believe or know that is an acceptable date, would you raise your hands.

(MOST HANDS ARE RAISED)

Is there anybody who doesn't think it's an acceptable date? (NO HANDS) All right, then we will go for those dates. I did clear it with the hotel. That is, they are willing to informally block the rooms for us, and obviously they would like people to make reservations. But assuming we have it March 24 to March 28, are there any people who would like to have it at a different location, either at a different hotel in England or even in a different country? It has been here for seven out of eight years. In the year 2000, it was held in Portland, Maine.

Participant statement 49: Walter Driscoll would like to have it on Vancouver Island.

Facilitator: Anything is discussible. There is a caveat and that is that there needs to be some people to arrange it, wherever it's going to be. As a practical matter, we have two people who live in this area which has been very helpful. One is Bert Sharp who is done being involved in the planning for this. The other is Frank Brzeski who has not been at this conference for a while but he certainly has been very helpful to Bert and to the conference in general in dealing with the hotel, arranging for this equipment and this sort of logistical stuff. So, if anybody would like to propose another location, you need to take this into consideration.

Participant statement 51: I said that I would bring this up.

Facilitator: But you are not proposing it?

Participant statement 51: No.

Participant statement 53: The only point I would make is that when it was held in Portland, Maine, it seemed to significantly cut down on the international character of the conference. It collected many more Americans who have not come at any other time then when it was there at Portland. But a number of people who I was used to seeing here, with the added distance of having to come from wherever they were in Europe and also then having to go across the Atlantic and then to even add on top of that additional travel in the United States, seemed not to work. It just seems that the international character is part of the conference and it seems like it would want to be somewhere in the U.K or Ireland.

Facilitator: Any more discussion on the locale? (NO REPLIES) All in favor of having it here at the Royal Norfolk Hotel in Bognor Regis, March 24-28, 2004, raise your hands. (MOST HANDS ARE RAISED) So we have established that we are going to have another conference. We know the dates and we know where.

Now the next question really is: Who is going to do it? Let me give you just a little background. We have talked about Bert Sharp, and Bert says he is just not capable of doing it anymore. He has purposely stayed away yesterday, today and even Friday afternoon. So, we can't really depend upon Bert. Frank Brzeski has been very helpful. He is not here, but I have no reason to believe that he would not continue to help us. But that is not a known, so it is just something that we should be aware of.

Also, there are a number of other things that should or could be done to help the conference be better, all kinds of things like publicity, for example. On and off people have tied different freebees, getting little notices put in magazines, like that. Conti did a little of that this past year, informally. We have had eight people on the planning committee. As far as people being officially on, Bert won't be officially on. Pat Bennett won't be officially on. And what about you, Harry?

Participant statement 54: I will not.

Facilitator: Harry will not be officially on either, although Harry has volunteered to help with the website.

Now, what is going to happen, what we have done in previous years is that for those of us on the planning committee who want to continue, we usually meet in the pub after this meeting and talk about this thing generally. Is there anyone here who feels disposed to be on the planning committee and do some work to make it happen? Some of us old timers have some idea of different jobs that need to be done. Since we are actually losing three people who are on the committee right now, it is then down to five, possibly four. Incidentally, the planning is now done almost entirely by email. Decisions do have to be taken, for example, what the program will be. That's decided by the planning committee, along with whether we have seminars and what the nature of those are, putting out a "Call for Papers," a sort of traditional academic thing, and other similar matters. There has in the past been a newsletter sent out in July with what is called a "Call for Papers." These are all relatively little things, but important in order to have a conference of this kind. There are mailings involved, a couple of mailings each year. There is the website. There is whatever publicity we might want to do. There are the logistics on the ground. There are probably other things that we haven't thought about in terms of third line of Work that maybe could be done to enhance the conference. It is possible that personal contacts could be made with people who may not even know about this conference, but who are interested in Mister Gurdjieff's ideas. So, there are a number of things that are talked about during the year and, as I say, we mostly do it through email. I just wonder if there is anybody who is not on the planning committee who perhaps would like to help out?

(SOME HANDS ARE RAISED)

Participant statement 56: Keith asked me to help him with the review of papers. I am willing to do it. I would really love to do it. I cannot stay because my plane is leaving early. Another thing is that beginning next Saturday, I am giving every month, a lecture on Beelzebub, and then a discussion in New York. We already have fifteen people coming. So, I am going to give publicity to the conference.

Participant statement 57: I am very serious about this. If you get more than we have been this year, it changes its character. It changed this year from thirty, where it was very coherent and I thought that the energy was stronger simply because you have fewer members. If it gets very big, it won't be the same. I won't say it will be worse, but it won't be the same.

Facilitator: Marlena, you called this a work in progress. It really is because there have been a number of things experimented with over the years. Some things have been discovered not to be appropriate at all like an add-on Work period. We have done a number of things so we have some experience with it. Speaking as just one member of the planning committee, we try to figure out what is in the best interest of everyone.

(Inaudible comments)

We have had a number of relatively prominent people. I don't know if that word is appropriate in the Gurdjieff Work, but well known people anyhow over the years. There are some well known people who know about this conference and have chosen not to participate in it. Perhaps it's possible to get some of them here. Some of these people have done a lot of writing and may want to present papers. So, this is all part of what the planning committee needs to do.

Participant statement 58: Just one question. Are you thinking of limiting the number to a certain number? Is that what you are talking about because I am not sure what you mean?

Participant statement 59: As we say in England, "I couldn't possibly comment."

Participant statement 60: Do you think there is an optimum number?

Participant statement 61: An optimum number is somewhere between thirty and fifty, and its quality, not quantity that counts.

(Inaudible comments)

All & Everything Conference 2003

Facilitator: I would just like to make a comment about numbers to give you some information. Over the years of these past eight conferences, we have accumulated a mailing list, and we have also gotten a number of names where we have lost peoples' current addresses so we just haven't mailed to them. In some cases people have submitted names and we have sent them information about the conference but there was no response, and we have dropped those names. In other cases, for example, authors and publishers, we have kept them on the mailing list because we felt that it was important that they should know about the conference. This year, we mailed out a little over three hundred invitations. Theoretically, if all would show up, it would change the conference entirely. The first conference ran a little over fifty, like this. The second one, I believe, was around forty, and the ones in between were in the low thirties. All of a sudden, this year, it's back in the fifties.

(Some inaudible comments about websites)

There's that. There is also another website that had conference information, called the Gurdjieff Internet Guide, Reijo Elsner's. That's the kind of free information we can put out, at least to make it known. These are the kinds of things we obviously cannot decide here. So, whoever is going to be involved in arranging the next conference, these are the kinds of decisions that need to be taken. There was another person who raised their hand and volunteered for the planning committee. Was that you, Rob?

Participant statement 63: That was me, yes.

Facilitator: So, you are going to volunteer for the planning committee. That will be a great help because Rob lives fifteen minutes away. Incidentally, Will mentioned the reading panel. That's important. Bert also did that with Keith until this year so that would be great. There is a kind of implicit obligation if you are on the planning committee, to attend the conference. Now, that hasn't always been possible, but it should be mentioned. I don't have anything else administrative to bring up. We seem to have made the preliminary decisions. Maybe we can have a few minutes of silence to end the conference, but would anybody like to say anything else that we haven't covered?

(Inaudible comments about the email address list)

I will mention one other thing by way of experience. One of the things we've tried for two different years, maybe three, and I think Keith did this. We took the email addresses of people who have been here and then we collected a list of three or four proposed topics. Then we put them out there to the list to see if any people wanted to have a discussion on any of them by email, during the course of the year. This was through email, not on the web. This year, for example, it didn't take off. The previous year it did, and it's a way to keep continuity among the people here and even have a discussion on some topic we all don't agree about, and that's probably a very long list. Again, this would be for someone or some ones on the planning committee to undertake to organize this. These are all things that happen because people make them happen.

Participant statement 65: I would just like to remind people about the tapes that are here for the people who gave presentations so that they can transcribe them for the Proceedings.

Facilitator: Good point, and for those of you who don't know, although most of you know it, the Proceedings of the conference are published. Marlena, as one of the planning committee has volunteered for several years to put the Proceedings together. Are you going to do it again, put the Proceedings together?

Participant statement 67: Yes.

Facilitator: To make it easier for Marlena, the way we have done it is that everyone who has given a presentation or been involved in facilitating a seminar, gets the tape not only of the paper they presented, but also the questions, answers and discussion that follows. Then it is their responsibility to transcribe what's on the tape so that it is in digital form and get it to Marlena. That makes it a lot easier to put these Proceedings together than in the early years where we copied the typed papers. We have been fortunate to have two mail order booksellers who carry the back years of the Proceedings and they continue to sell them, By The Way Books, and Abintra the Bookseller. I know this from By The Way Books who tell me that they sell them one and two at a time, printing up copies of back years as needed. So, these Proceedings have made a permanent record and, I think, a contribution to the literature of the Work.

Participant statement 69: Several people, when we had the remarks around the room, were mentioning that they found a great benefit from the conference, but felt that it had gotten to a degree, very highbrow, very technical in some respects, and wondered if there could be some thought as to what might be feasible to make it not so technical.

Facilitator: I noticed the same thing when we were going around the room. Several people said that. So, this is something again, for those who are planning the conference, to take into consideration. Of course, the papers that are submitted, depending on where they come from, determine the level of complexity of the presentation.

Participant statement 71: I would just like to suggest that the planning committee consider in the guidelines for papers, a request for personal references or application to personal Work. That's very helpful to me when people give examples of the theoretical side and then say that this is what you have to do here.

Facilitator: In the call for papers that we put out with the Newsletter in July, it talks about two kinds of papers, and this idea originally was created by Sophia Wellbeloved. One class of papers are academic papers which need to conform to academic standards, and the other class we call personal view papers which are this class you are describing. Anyone who is disposed to put something together has done it, and perhaps it could be suggested that they put in personal examples.
(Inaudible comments)

Facilitator: One other thing comes to mind. The hotel has said that everybody waits until the last minute to make their reservations. We don't even know the price for next year. That has to be negotiated, and they have raised it up a bit over the years, but not too badly. In any event, we will certainly have that information and be able to disseminate it either by email or by the Newsletter in July. If you are planning to come, if you could make your reservations earlier, it is helpful to them and they are happier. They are glad to refund deposits if necessary.

Participant statement 74: The other advantage to all of us is that if you make your reservation earlier, this will allow the hotel to block out more rooms for us.

(Inaudible comments)

Facilitator: We did have at least one person staying at a place called the Homestead. It's a B&B right down Aldwich Road about half a mile from here. It's £20 per night. So, some people could save some money if they wish.

If there is nothing else, please now let us sit quietly for a few moments to end this conference: The International Humanities Conference: All and Everything, 2003.

End of Session

Appendix 1 - Obituary of Nicolas Tereshchenko

Obituary of Nicolas Tereshchenko by his friend, John Scullion

Dear Friends,

In paying respect to Nicolas whose passing sobers rather than saddens me, I wish too say a few words about the impressions Nicolas made upon me while he was alive in the same world.

Like all true individuals Nick exacted at least a reaction from me and early impressions were of an opinionated and argumentative man who clearly had an axe to grind. That first reaction was of course just that, a subjective reaction to someone differently experienced and older, and although I did not recognise it at first, challenging to my picture of myself. Nicolas was combative, emphatic and challenging.

Nicolas and Russell Smith at the early All and Everything Conferences put me in front of a problem of comprehension I am still unable to resolve for myself after many years trying and realising my lack of adequacy to the task. How to understand the working of the enneagram. I have a fundamental problem I am mathematically a virtual illiterate and the choice between embracing either presentation is beyond my powers. However it has been stimulating to try to comprehend the vision of each. I discovered in time that Nicolas spoke most to the world and the Work as I am able to understand it.

Leaving purely mental perplexities behind, I had the privilege of being a guest of Pat and Harry Bennett at the time of the Portland Conference and Nicolas Tereshchenko and Nikolas Bryce (who clashed so profitably at A&E Conference) were also under the same roof. This is where my most memorable impressions of Nicolas come from. I remember one evening meal in particular when Nicolas spoke about the life of a White Russian Cavalryman and the codes of honour among cavalrymen and the bond of symbiotic relationship between the cavalryman and his horse. In that atmosphere it was possible to receive what was discussed on more than one level. I have never before heard such accounts of a different and vanished world and that is what struck me and remains with me as an impression. Nicolas had such a deep and rich experience of life that I could not help but know the smallness and narrowness of my own by comparison. He was not boasting, neither was he seeking to impress but I was and remain impressed by him.

Nick was a rebel and a model of integrity. That is what I discovered about him. Beyond that sometimes prickly and even bombastic persona was a very unique and exemplary person. I would rather disagree with Nick than agree to a hundred lesser individuals. I could respect Nicolas whether on any occasion or on any point I was in agreement with him or not. That is the best tribute I have to offer.

May he rest in peace.

John Scullion
September 6, 2002

◆◆◆

Obituary of Nicolas Tereshchenko by his friend, Sy Ginsburg

(from the forward to: Nicolas Tereshchenko, *Mr. Gurdjieff's Hapax Legomena*)

Nicolas Tereshchenko (1916 - 2002) was a renaissance man. I came to know him in 1981 because of my own interest in Mr. Gurdjieff's teachings. On a cold March day of that year, while on a business trip to London, I made my way to Watkins Bookshop in Cecil Court. In those days I was buying and reading anything I could lay my hands on that had to do with the Gurdjieff teachings and, if possible, arranging to meet the authors. There on the counter of the bookshop were a pile of periodicals with the title: *The Hermetic Journal*. It happened to be issue No. 14, Winter, 1981. As I flipped through that issue one article caught my attention: "Man and Bliss Souls," by Nicolas Tereshchenko. It was an introductory article on Gurdjieff's teachings by a man who obviously knew a great deal, and I resolved to meet him. At that time Nick was living in Paris and was a member of Jeanne de Salzmann's senior group within the Institute Gurdjieff. He had, in fact, moved to Paris from Australia especially to be her pupil.

Over the years Nick and I became close friends. I often visited him in Paris and he regularly visited me in Florida. We seemed to have a natural camaraderie. As I came to know Nick better and better, I realized what a treasure he was, not only as a very good friend, but as one of the most knowledgeable people I have ever had the pleasure of knowing. Here was a native born Russian who was totally fluent not only in Russian, but in English, French, Italian, and the Slavic languages. And he could more than hold his own in many other tongues. He had become a British surgeon and this took him to live in half a dozen countries around the globe, eventually making his family home in Australia where, with his wife, he raised four children.

Nick's knowledge of many systems of esoteric study was without parallel. A glance at the list of the many articles and books he authored (see following) on Astrology, Golden Dawn, Hermeticism, Kabbalah, Numerology, Rosicrucianism, Tarot and other esoteric systems evidences this. But it was his knowledge of Gurdjieff's teachings and writings, especially the *All and Everything* trilogy, that was, in my view, unequalled.

Appendix 1 - Obituary of Nicolas Tereshchenko

The volume you are holding is Nicolas Tereshchenko's last gift to the Gurdjieff community in general and to students of *All and Everything* in particular. It is a specialized scholarly work and Nick wanted students of the teachings to have the benefit of his knowledge. A final illness prevented him from publishing this work, and he asked me if I could see to its publication. This is not a document for the mass market, and I wish to thank By The Way Books for making its distribution possible to the benefit of the Gurdjieff community.

Many in the Gurdjieff community who came to know Nicolas Tereshchenko knew just how feisty he was, especially when it came to asserting aspects of Mr. Gurdjieff's teachings. Many, including myself, often disagreed with him. Most of the time, however, he was proven to be correct. More important than any of this was Nick's level of being. He was a wonderful friend, a true scholar and a very good human being.

Seymour B. (Sy) Ginsburg
January 2003

Appendix 2 - Writings by Nicolas Tereshchenko

Writings in English

Man's Quest for Consciousness, in the Sydney (N.S.W. Australia) Cosmos: The Living Paper, Vol 1, No 5, November 1973.
Practical Steps Towards Higher Consciousness, in Cosmos, Vol 1, No 7, January 1974.
The Tarot: The System & Philosophy Beyond the Symbolism of Western Occultism, in Cosmos, Vol 1, No 10, April 1974.
Practical Steps Towards Higher Consciousness, in Frontiers Of Consciousness: A Cosmos Anthology*, Melbourne, 1975 (Out of Print).
Gurdjieff and the Mastery of Life, in Cosmos, Vol 4, No 3, October 1976.
The Teaching of Gurdjieff, in Cosmos, Vol 5, No 8, March 1978.
Controlling Your Mind, in Healthy Living, November 1981 (London).
Man and His Souls, in The Hermetic Journal, (Edinburgh), No 14, Winter 1981.
The Teachings of Gurdjieff, in The Hermetic Journal, No 18, Winter 1982.
Danger! Sound at Work, in Healthy Living, March 1983.
A Look At Fourth Way Work, Hermetic Research Series, Edinburgh, 1983 (Out of Print).
The Cosmos Tarot, Askin Publishers Ltd., London, 1983 (Out of Print).
Meditation and Health, in Healthy Living, October 1984.
Israel Regardie and the Golden Dawn, in Aries, No 4, Paris 1985.
Mankind and the Stars, in Healthy Living, September 1985.
Sound and Numbers, in The Lamp of Thoth, Vol 2, No 5 (Leeds).
Application of Silence, in The Lamp of Thoth, Vol 3, No 6.
Creativity: the Curse of Our Time, in The Lamp of Thoth, Vol 4, No 4.
A New Look at an Old Anachronism, in The Hermetic Journal, (Annual Edition), Oxford, 1989.
Arcanum XXIII: The Drowned Sleeping Titan, in *New Thoughts On Tarot*, (Newcastle Publishing Co. Inc., Hollywood), 1989 (Out of Print).
Gurdjieff: A New Introduction To His Teaching In Five Lessons, (with Seymour B. Ginsburg), Privately Printed, 1994.
The Heptaparaparshinokh as Defined by Mister Gurdjieff in Beelzebub's Tales, in All & Everything 1996 Proceedings.
Suggested Numerological Structure of Beelzebub's Tales, in All & Everything 1996 Proceedings.
Introduction to SELF-Remembering, in All & Everything 1997 Proceedings.
Mister Gurdjieff's Hapaxlegomena, By The Way Books, Sacramento, 2003.

Appendix 2 - Writings by Nicolas Tereshchenko

Writings in French:

Le Tarot Pour Tous, in Astral, No 361-2, Janvier-Février 1982, Paris.
Le Tarot et les Centres d'Energie, in Astral, No 363-4, Mars-Avril 1982, Paris.
Le Tarot et l'Avenir, in Astral, No 365, Mai 1982, Paris.
Le Tarot à la Portée de Tous, in Astral, No 386-7-8, Février-Mars-Avril 1984, Paris.
La Réincarnation, in Astral, No 392-3, Août-Septembre 1984, Paris.
Monsieur Gurdjieff et Son Travail, in l'Autre Monde, No 82, Mai 1984, Paris.
Le Rôle du Rituel dans les Sociétés Secrètes, in l'Autre Monde, No 96 & 99, Juillet & Octobre 1985, Paris.
Les Trésors du Tarot: Accès aux Mystères du Cosmos, in Éditions Atlas/Guy Trédaniel, Paris, 1986.
Polyangles, Polygones et Polygrammes, in Le Monde Inconnu, Octobre 1991.
Gurdjieff et la Quatrieme Voie, in Éditions Guy Trédaniel, Paris, 1991.
Les Ancêtres Rosicruciens de l'Ordre Hermétique de la Golden Dawn, in Éditions Teletes, Paris, 1992.
Fragments de Gnose: Bases de l'Éotérisme, Éditions Guy Trédaniel, Paris, 1993.
Le Message de Gurdjieff, in Éditions Guy Trédaniel, Paris, 1995.
Au-delà de la Quatrième Voie, in Éditions Guy Trédaniel, Paris, 1996.

Appendix 3 - Obituary of Joy Lonsdale

Obituary of Joy Lonsdale by her daughter, Kerry Lonsdale

Joy Lonsdale was born in a country town in Queensland, Australia. She travelled extensively in that country before settling in Sydney, marrying, having a daughter, then working as a legal stenographer. She always had a great interest in antiquity and philosophy and a great appreciation of poetry and music.

During the 1980s, she travelled most extensively through Europe, the Middle East and America. She discovered the ideas of Gurdjieff at the end of that period. She joined a Gurdjieff group in Canberra and worked with them for several years while also investigating Hermeticism and Alchemy. In 1989, she came across the writings of English author, Roy Norvill, which set out his own exposition of the Hermetic Code. She became convinced that it was a key to the understanding of Gurdjieff's first Series, All & Everything, a book she was intrigued by and revered.

She subsequently spent eight years applying the Hermetic Code to that work which entailed exhaustive pondering of the text and continuous research and mental application. The work that emerged, *Gurdjieff and the Arch Preposterous - an Hermetic Descent into the Mind*, was published in 2001. It is an attempt to interpret the text of *All & Everything* with a focus on the six descents. Its emphasis is on the text as Gurdjieff's autobiography, which is one of the aspects clearly in it but rarely explored. She fulfilled most honourably and in full measure Gurdjieff's instruction to try and understand the sense and substance of his writings.

Joy left the Gurdjieff group toward the end of her life and became a dedicated member of the Rosicrucian Order in Australia, AMORC. Her book went on to sell out its first edition, which gave her much satisfaction as she considered it her life's work.

Joy was working on an Hermetic dictionary before her death in 2002.

Kerry Lonsdale, March 12, 2003

Appendix 4 - List of Attendees

Joseph Azize - Australia
Paul Bakker - Netherlands
Harry and Pat Bennett - USA
Bob & Jan Bows - UK
Len Brown - Canada
Martin Brown - UK
Nikolas Bryce - Canada
Frank Brzeski - UK
Ron Bullivant - UK
Keith & Marlena Buzzell - USA
Michel Bypost - Netherlands
Anne Clark - USA
Edgar Clark - UK
Tim Collins - UK
Wim van Dulleman - Netherlands
Richard Dunn - UK
Thansir Dzakopoolor - Greece
Stefanos Elmazis - Greece
Lany Forbes PO - USA
Ana Helena - Brazil
Sy Ginsburg - USA
Don Hartsock - USA
W. J. Jones - UK
George Kazos -Greece
Jacques Leurs - Belgium
Sean & Penin Mahoney - India
Christiane Macketanz - Germany
Ian & Stephanie MacFarlane - UK
Will Mesa - USA
Conti Canseco Meehan - USA
Robert Ormiston - UK
Dimitri Peretzi - Greece
Bonnie Phillips - USA
Astezi Popi - Greece
June Poulton - USA
Barbara Rosenthal - USA
John Scullion - UK

All & Everything Conference 2003

H. J. (Bert) Sharp - UK
Toddy Smyth - USA
Chris Thompson - UK
Prof. M. W. Thring - UK
Terje Tonne - Norway
Nikos Troullinos - Greece
Serge Urlike - Norway
Martin Walsh - UK
Sofia Wellbeloved - UK

Index

A

Abdil, 48
Abrustdonis, 134
Absolute, 42, 125, 133, 154
active, 4, 48, 63, 68, 72, 74, 75, 76, 81, 99, 145
Advaita, 147
affirming, 75, 127
Africa, 20
Aim, 18, 26, 30, 34, 35, 61, 85, 90, 93, 128, 158, 164
air, 19, 127, 134, 156, 173
Aisors, 99
Akhaldan, 114, 125, 128
Alchemy, 5, 184
alcohol, 90, 108
Salzmann, de, Jean; Michel, 14, 17, 27, 29, 59, 85, 86, 87, 91, 92, 100, 102, 180
Alexandropol, 57
allegorical, 5, 144
America, 11, 28, 33, 59, 84, 85, 169, 184
Anderson, Margaret, 149
Anulios, 52, 53
ape, 172
Arcanum, 182
Archangel, 144
archetype, 46
armagnac, 85, 90, 92, 102
Armenian, 107
ascending, 73, 74, 78
Ashiata Shiemash, 46, 137, 140, 144
Ashish, Sri Madhava, 13, 146
astral, 183
Astrology, 12, 55, 180
Astrolonomy, 135
Atlantis, 44, 49, 50, 52, 53, 55
Atomic, 143
Attention, 28, 47, 63, 78, 79, 80, 85, 86, 88, 102, 154, 158, 170, 180
Autoegocrat, 119, 121, 123, 132
awareness, 29, 95, 148, 151, 166
axis, 31, 116, 118

B

Babylon, 53
Beekman Taylor, Paul, 3, 4, 8, 12, 14, 95, 97
Beelzebub, 3, 5, 9, 11, 12, 19, 23, 40, 45, 46, 47, 48, 51, 52, 53, 54, 55, 58, 59, 64, 65, 68, 76, 78, 87, 89, 92, 94, 102, 123, 126, 127, 139, 140, 141, 144, 146, 148, 156, 162, 163, 164, 166, 168, 175, 182
Beelzebub's Tales
  The Tales, 40, 45, 49, 52, 53, 54, 55, 69, 71, 72, 74, 128, 139, 142, 144, 150, 169
Being, 16, 17, 18, 20, 21, 23, 24, 25, 29, 30, 32, 33, 34, 36, 37, 40, 41, 42, 43, 44, 46, 47, 49, 50, 53, 54, 57, 60, 68, 72, 73, 75, 76, 80, 81, 85, 89, 91, 94, 97, 98, 99, 100, 101, 102, 103, 104, 105, 117, 120, 121, 123, 125, 130, 131, 133, 134, 135, 136, 137, 140, 141, 142, 143, 144, 149, 150, 151, 152, 153, 154, 156, 157, 158, 165, 166, 169, 170, 171, 172, 173, 174, 179, 181
being-bodies, 76, 134
being-effort, 80
Belcultassi, 163
Bennett, John G., 10, 11, 13, 15, 27, 30, 40, 64, 66, 84, 85, 87, 91, 114, 119, 121, 125, 127, 153, 154, 156, 161, 164, 174, 179, 185

Big Bang, 135, 136, 140, 141, 145
Blavatsky, Helena P., 146
Bliss, 180
bone, 87
Brain, 24, 44, 86, 127
breath, 23, 24, 157, 158
breathe, 30, 85, 134
breathing, 85, 158
Brook, Peter, 29
brother, 12, 14
Buddhism, 145, 154
Buddhist, 154
Buzzell, Keith, 1, 2, 4, 9, 10, 13, 84, 87, 92, 114, 123, 124, 125, 126, 127, 128, 185

C

Campbell, Joseph, 137, 144
Canada, 13, 185
carbon, 100
carriage, 18
Castanios-Flores, John, 11, 14
center, 11, 13, 21, 43, 44, 69, 70, 73, 93, 95, 102, 115, 119, 123, 136, 140, 154, 157, 158
cherubim, 131
child, 44, 48, 65, 86, 92, 102, 148
children, 19, 53, 86, 89, 92, 102, 180
Christian, 4, 24, 53, 59, 82
Christianity, 34, 53
coat
    coated, 76
comet, 42, 52, 54, 156
Commission, 143
compassion, 91, 166
concentrate, 70, 71, 131, 132, 133
concentration, 70, 71, 131, 132, 133
Conscience, 16, 52, 80, 87, 91, 134
conscious, 18, 19, 34, 36, 68, 72, 76, 102, 106, 127, 157
Conscious Labor, 19, 127
consciousness, 14, 17, 18, 19, 24, 55, 80, 86, 96, 134, 143, 151, 182
constate

constated, 150, 151
contemplate, 65
Cornelius, George, 33
cosmic, 3, 9, 16, 18, 22, 54, 68, 69, 70, 71, 73, 74, 75, 76, 78, 79, 81, 82, 111, 119, 121, 126, 127, 131, 132, 133, 134, 137, 139, 141, 145, 149, 150, 151, 156
Cosmic Consciousness, 18
cosmology, 111
Creation, 36, 37, 52, 68, 73, 75, 81, 111, 114, 120, 126, 133, 134, 135, 140, 141, 143, 144, 145, 169
Creator, 84, 152
Creed, Lewis, 11, 14
crystallize
    crystallization, 76, 82
    crystallized, 44, 51, 126, 144

D

Daly, Tom, 57, 66, 95, 99, 100
daughter, 5, 12, 14, 86, 101, 102, 184
death, 11, 13, 15, 18, 25, 28, 32, 49, 54, 80, 85, 87, 90, 104, 155, 157, 184
deflections, 132, 133
Demiurge, 111
Denying, 75, 96, 127
descend, 120
descending, 73, 102
descent, 5, 48, 78, 156
Descent, 5, 46, 146, 163, 184
Deuterocosmos, 120
devil, 55, 62, 96
diatonic, 111
Dicker, The, 11, 14
die, 25, 45, 80, 91
digestion, 58, 127, 171
dimension, 115, 142, 143, 151, 154
disharmonized, 133
Disputekrialnian, 76
Djartklom, 127
dog, 23, 31, 85, 111, 141
Dramatic Universe, 114, 119

E

Earth, 16, 50, 52, 53, 54, 108, 109, 135, 136, 137, 139, 142, 146, 148, 150, 151, 155, 156, 163
Ego, 142, 148, 151
    egoism, 41, 54
    egoistic, 50
Egypt, 59, 62, 124
Egyptian, 22, 53
Einstein, 150
electricity, 19
electron, 69
element, 41, 43, 60, 61, 72, 119, 121, 145, 151
emanation, 71, 74, 126, 134
emotion, 44, 93, 95, 102
emotional, 31, 43, 44, 106, 158
Endlessness, 3, 9, 125, 130, 131, 132, 133, 139, 140, 143, 144, 148, 151, 152, 153, 154
England, 4, 44, 167, 169, 173, 175
Enneagram, 17, 76, 144, 153
entropy, 134
esoteric, 14, 18, 58, 102, 180
Essence, 5, 19, 22, 29, 30, 33, 35, 36, 90, 96, 140
Eternity, 25, 53, 154
Ether, 110
Etherokrilno, 71, 126, 131, 145
Etievan, Alfred, 13
Evil, 16
Evolution, 16, 33, 35, 72, 78, 82, 126
    evolutionary, 38, 73, 74, 76, 79, 81
Evolve, 73, 126
Exercise, 6, 15, 16, 18, 20, 21, 22, 23, 24, 28, 47, 49, 87, 98, 100, 106, 120, 142, 144, 162, 170
External Considering, 167

F

Faith, 17, 171
father, 44, 56, 57, 58, 89, 92, 117, 130, 162
Feeling, 6, 21, 22, 24, 44, 47, 57, 58, 85, 86, 88, 90, 92, 94, 144, 148, 149, 164, 166, 169, 171
Fire, 24, 53, 75
first being-food, 73, 75
    1st being-food, 127
first force, 74
flood, 53
Food, 58, 91, 104, 108, 127, 134, 158, 171
force, 19, 24, 35, 56, 60, 69, 72, 74, 80, 82, 96, 127, 135, 137, 152, 166
Formatory, 88, 143
Foundation, 8, 11, 13, 14, 81, 99, 100, 102
Fourth Way, 3, 9, 11, 12, 15, 16, 17, 20, 21, 25, 27, 28, 29, 59, 60, 61, 62, 66, 182
France, 8, 92, 108
friction, 76, 169

G

Geometry, 78, 114, 115, 124, 126
Germany, 185
Ginsburg, Seymour, 2, 5, 7, 10, 12, 13, 14, 144, 160, 180, 181, 182, 185
God, 19, 24, 34, 49, 53, 81, 82, 83, 89, 90, 91, 96, 110, 130, 137, 139, 144, 148, 151, 161
Good, 16, 64, 130, 160, 177
gravity, 16, 35, 44, 69, 70, 73, 132, 136, 151
Great Nature, 53, 81
Greece, 14, 37, 167, 168, 185, 186
Greek, 22, 43, 54, 107, 111
Groves, Dr. Philip, 3, 9, 15, 16, 20, 23, 25
Gurdjieff, G. I., 3, 4, 5, 6, 8, 9, 11, 12, 13, 14, 15, 16, 17, 18, 19, 21, 22, 23, 25, 26, 27, 28, 29, 30, 31, 32, 37, 38, 42, 48, 49, 50, 52, 53, 54, 55, 56, 57, 58, 59, 60, 61, 62, 63, 64, 65, 66, 67, 68, 84, 85, 86, 87, 88, 89, 90, 91, 92, 94, 95, 96, 98, 99, 100, 101, 102, 103, 104, 105, 106, 107, 108, 109, 110, 111, 112, 123, 125, 126, 130, 134, 135, 137, 139, 141, 142, 143, 144, 145, 146, 147, 163, 164, 165, 166, 167, 168,

170, 171, 174, 175, 176, 180, 181, 182, 183, 184
Mr. G., 100, 130, 149

H

harmonium, 100, 109
Harnel-Aoot, 68, 72, 133
Hartmann, Thomas and Olga de, 11, 13, 28, 57, 66, 99, 101, 112, 113
Hawking, Stephen, 88, 136
Heap, Jane, 85
heart, 15, 109, 140, 164, 168
heaven, 12, 14
Hebrew, 53, 123
Helkdonis, 134
Hell, 168
Heptaparaparshinokh, 68, 72, 132, 133, 182
Hermetic, 5, 180, 182, 184
Heropass, 9, 131, 132, 149, 152, 154
hierarchy, 30, 161
higher being-body, 76, 82
Hindu, 13
Holy Affirming, 74
Holy Denying, 74
Holy Reconciling, 74, 127
Hope, 17, 23, 27, 40, 53, 54, 60, 85, 86, 87, 91, 94, 101, 127, 143, 148, 165, 169, 171
Howarth, Dushka, 3, 4, 98, 101
Howarth, Jessmin, 100, 101
Hoyle, Fred, 135
Hubble, Edwin, 134, 135, 141, 142
hydrogen, 18, 25, 88, 142, 146
Hyparxis, 154
Hypnosis, 43, 48, 58
  hypnotised, 43
  hypnotism, 19, 43

I

I Am, 57, 65, 123, 166
Identification, 17, 149
Idiot, 90, 102
imagination, 47, 155
impressions, 9, 19, 121, 127, 151, 161, 163, 167, 169, 171, 179
In Search of the Miraculous, 11, 29, 59, 62, 63, 64, 66, 84, 86, 87, 88, 126, 127
  Fragments, 31, 60, 63, 64, 183
incarnation, 16
India, 28, 30, 59, 62, 145, 166, 185
Individual, 6, 15, 44, 54, 61, 72, 74, 76, 80, 128, 157, 164
initiation, 21
insight, 64, 102, 152
Institute, 8, 13, 60, 63, 180
Intellectual, 6, 60, 166, 167, 170
intention, 62, 72
Internal Considering, 167
Introvigne, Massimo, 11
Involution, 16, 33, 34, 35, 72, 78, 82
  involutionary, 35, 73, 75, 76
Iraniranumange, 69
Itoklanoz, 157

J

Jartklom, 127
Jesus, 156
Jew, 24
Jung, Carl G., 21, 137
Justice, 101

K

Kabala, 180
Karatas, 151, 155
Kesdjan, 68, 76, 82
King, C. Daly, 95
Kondoor, 52
Kundabuffer, 17, 41, 44, 46, 47, 51, 162

L

Lannes, Henriette, 87
laughter, 23, 47, 50, 89, 91, 107, 108, 144
Law, 3, 9, 16, 33, 35, 36, 68, 71, 75, 80, 82, 86, 114, 119, 121, 123, 125, 127, 131, 132,

133, 134, 135, 136, 139, 141, 143, 144, 151, 152
Law of Seven, 8, 68, 69, 71, 73, 74, 76, 78, 79, 82, 115, 119, 136, 153
Law of Three, 19, 68, 74, 75, 76, 78, 82, 115, 126, 136, 153
Law-conformable, 133
lawful, 36, 131, 164, 171
Life is Real, 11, 57, 58, 65
light, 23, 24, 35, 56, 66, 69, 134, 136, 137, 153
Littlehampton, 12, 14
Looisos, 144
Love, 17, 18, 41, 49, 54, 64, 80, 85, 158, 166, 175

M

machine, 86
magic, 81
Magician, 101
magnet
  magnetic, 24, 102
maintenance, 36, 68, 128, 133, 134, 143
Manchester, Sherman, 95
March, Louise, 64
Mars, 48, 50, 108, 183
material, 6, 11, 20, 25, 29, 54, 57, 58, 59, 68, 86, 87, 93, 99, 100, 136, 145, 163, 167, 170, 172
matter, 28, 30, 32, 34, 36, 44, 45, 46, 65, 75, 123, 135, 137, 142, 151, 156, 169, 173
Mdnel-In, 133
mechanical, 22, 29, 31, 37, 76
meditation, 13, 127, 143, 150, 182
Meetings with Remarkable Men, 22, 29, 30, 31, 56, 60, 65, 98, 146
Megalocosmos, 18, 125, 130, 131, 132, 133, 153
mentation, 130
metanoia, 25
Mexico, 12, 14
Microcosmos, 123
microwave, 136, 137

Milk, 102
mind, 5, 14, 24, 25, 33, 36, 42, 43, 62, 63, 75, 88, 90, 93, 115, 116, 119, 124, 145, 146, 148, 154, 163, 178, 182, 184
monk, 13, 154
Moon, 16, 52, 53, 135, 156
Moore, James, 11
Moral, 35
Moscow, 59
mother, 12, 14, 34, 44, 53, 88, 92, 95, 96, 100, 101, 102
Movements, 6, 8, 9, 11, 13, 18, 85, 86, 98, 99, 100
Moving, 6, 21, 31, 43, 44, 120, 125, 135, 153, 154, 155, 157, 170
Mullah Nassr Eddin, 22, 23
music, 4, 6, 8, 9, 21, 26, 38, 93, 94, 98, 99, 100, 111, 112, 113, 152, 168, 170, 184
mysticism, 16
myth, 52, 53, 54
mythology, 54, 139, 145

N

Nature, 2, 19, 21, 24, 25, 42, 53, 55, 65, 69, 73, 74, 75, 126, 140, 141, 148, 167, 168, 174
Negative emotion, 97, 166
nervous system, 24
neural, 137
Neurology, 20
Neutral, 74
  Neutralising, 18
  Neutralizing, 75, 76
New Age, 11, 27, 29, 30, 36
Nicoll, Maurice, 59, 149, 151, 154
nine, 35, 173
Nisargadatta, 166
nothing, 20, 23, 24, 29, 32, 33, 34, 37, 38, 39, 40, 45, 52, 54, 65, 73, 86, 88, 92, 96, 121, 127, 130, 131, 135, 139, 146, 149, 154, 155, 165, 170, 178
Nott, Stanley and Rosemary, 4, 8, 9, 16, 61, 84, 88, 89, 90, 92

Nyland, W, 11

O

Objective, 16, 17, 61, 78, 80, 81, 96, 132, 134, 151, 152, 154, 155, 163
Obligolnian, 68, 134
octave, 19, 45, 69, 70, 72, 73, 74, 102, 123, 134, 152, 153
octavic, 128
Okidanokh, 13, 126, 145, 162, 163
Oldham, Ronald and Muriel, 11, 14
Omnipresent, 13, 126, 163
one-brained, 123, 157
Orage, Alfred, 11, 12, 14, 89, 95, 101, 102, 150
organic, 21, 146
Ouspensky, P. D., 15, 21, 28, 29, 31, 56, 57, 59, 60, 61, 62, 63, 64, 65, 66, 67, 68, 84, 85, 86, 87, 88, 89, 90, 98, 100, 101, 102, 127, 141, 142, 154

P

Palmer, Helen, 32
Parable, 16, 91
paradise, 130
Paris, 12, 13, 14, 27, 40, 53, 60, 66, 84, 85, 86, 87, 90, 92, 95, 99, 100, 108, 110, 159, 180, 182, 183
Partkdolg-duty, 94
passive, 48, 54, 74, 75
patience, 96, 105
Pentland, John, 14, 27, 30, 33, 61, 62, 66, 86
Peretzi, Dimitri, 1, 9, 14, 26, 31, 32, 33, 34, 35, 36, 37, 38, 39, 185
Persian, 22
personality, 19, 26, 28, 33, 54, 90, 91, 137, 142, 143
Petersburg, 61, 142
Philadelphia, 13
photon, 69
physical, 24, 92, 106, 134, 135, 146, 148, 149, 168

physics, 88, 141
Piandjoehary, 73
pianola, 27, 28, 31
planet, 23, 24, 28, 46, 53, 54, 72, 134, 137, 141, 147, 149, 151, 164, 171
planetary, 24, 76, 82, 143
Plato, 49, 52, 54, 55, 59, 111
ponder, 26, 157
pondering, 16, 153, 184
Pope, 91
Popoff, Irmis, 13, 32, 36
Prayer, 99
presence, 29, 43, 44, 45, 75, 82, 92, 95, 102, 107, 108, 127, 130, 131, 133, 149, 150, 151, 158
Prieuré, 11, 12, 14, 95
Prime Source, 81, 143
prism, 153, 162
Protein, 128
psyche, 17, 40, 54, 55
psychological, 11, 14, 17, 22, 26
Psychological Commentaries, 59
psychology, 20, 59, 166
Purgatory, 18, 76, 114, 120, 127, 144, 151, 153
Putnam, Nick, 67, 95
Pythagoras, 33
Pythagorean, 33

Q

Quantum, 143
quark, 123

R

radiation, 17, 136, 140, 145
Ray of Creation, 121, 125, 142
Reason, 16, 18, 20, 24, 33, 38, 41, 42, 43, 44, 45, 46, 47, 48, 73, 79, 81, 92, 137, 139, 141, 143, 155, 156, 164, 174
Reciprocal, 44, 58, 109
Reconcile
    Reconciliation, 101, 167

Reconciling, 74, 75
Regardie, Israel, 182
Relativity, 38, 128, 142, 150, 154, 163
religion, 11, 18, 19, 88, 91, 101
Remember, 16, 33, 85, 88, 89, 91, 92, 95, 96, 99, 101, 108, 114, 123, 128, 142, 148, 150, 157, 164, 170, 179
    Remembering, 30, 84, 85, 94, 182
Remorse, 89
repetition, 80
resonance, 157
resonate, 171
Rosicrucian, 5, 184
Rumi, Jalaluddin, 21
Russia, 5, 27, 28, 57, 60, 62, 63, 104, 107, 109, 179, 180

S

Sacred, 26, 29, 52, 68, 71, 72, 73, 76, 78, 114, 115, 124, 126, 130, 131, 132, 133, 137, 143, 150, 151
Sacred Individual, 137, 144
sacrifice, 31, 35, 50, 172
Satan, 49
Science, 11, 14, 16, 52, 84, 87, 90, 132, 136, 141, 142, 152, 154, 157, 163
Scientific, 6, 21, 84, 134, 135, 140, 141, 142, 152, 168
second being-body, 68, 76
second being-food, 158
Second Conscious Shock, 158
second force, 74
seeing, 21, 45, 55, 93, 109, 121, 128, 139, 142, 150, 154, 163, 171, 173
Self, 9, 17, 18, 19, 25, 84, 85, 88, 144, 145, 146, 153
Self Observation, 17, 19, 25, 28, 30, 84
Self Remembering, 17, 19, 25, 28, 84, 85, 88, 153
sensation, 24, 85, 88, 148
senses, 18, 24, 109, 157
Sensing, 85, 158
seraphim, 131

seven, 69, 70, 72, 102, 113, 115, 132, 133, 146, 150, 168, 173
seventh, 70, 71, 73
Sex, 19
    sexual, 75, 88, 105
Sharp, H. J. (Bert), 1, 20, 25, 161, 173, 174
shock, 21, 27, 82, 89, 90, 149
sin, 79, 172
sister, 90
Sitting, 9, 102, 125, 150, 154, 165, 169
Sleep, 90, 105, 109
Smith, Russell A., 111, 179
solar plexus, 85, 127
son, 42, 56, 81, 88, 117, 121, 130, 162, 183
Sophia, 12, 42, 45, 46, 55, 177
Soul, 24, 35
sound, 56, 57, 134, 182
sounding, 112
Speeth, Kathleen Riordan, 3, 4, 59, 67, 102, 103
spinal column, 24
spine, 127
Spirit, 5, 22, 23, 25, 56, 58, 59, 82, 117, 166
    spiritual, 6, 16, 18, 22, 25, 26, 58, 88, 121
    spirituality, 63
St. Petersburg (also Petersburg), 63, 66
Staveley, A.L., 13, 27
Stjernvall, 3, 4, 104, 110
Stop Exercise, 153
Stopinder, 13, 68, 69, 70, 71, 72, 73, 75, 76, 79, 81, 82, 123, 132, 133, 140, 143
Struggle of the Magicians, 66, 101
subconscious, 22, 52
subjective, 69, 70, 71, 72, 75, 79, 80, 133, 134, 148, 151, 179
substance, 71, 74, 75, 76, 131, 184
Subud, 15
Suffer, 140
    Intentional Suffering, 19, 127
    suffered, 48
    suffering, 18, 91, 127, 140, 141, 149
Sufis, 20, 22

suggestibility, 40, 41, 42, 43, 44, 45, 46, 47, 48, 51, 52, 54, 58, 141
Sun, 16, 23, 24, 42, 53, 71, 74, 120, 126, 131, 132, 133, 134, 136, 139, 141, 146, 150, 151, 152
Sun Absolute, 16, 42, 53, 71, 74, 126, 131, 132, 133, 134, 139, 141, 146, 151, 152
Superego, 102
Supernova, 136
Symbol, 3, 9, 27, 32, 33, 36, 52, 88, 114, 118, 120, 121, 124, 125, 126, 127, 128
   symbolic, 114, 115, 119, 121, 123, 126, 135
   symbolism, 182
   symbology, 127

T

Tail, 139
Tarot, 180, 182, 183
telepathy, 17
Tereshchenko, Nicolas, 3, 5, 12, 14, 15, 19, 20, 22, 179, 180, 181, 182
Tetartocosmos, 156
The Fourth Way, 98
Theosophical, 13
Third Force, 17, 45, 68, 74, 82, 167, 170
Thompson, Chris, 186
Thoth, 182
three-brained, 44, 72, 75, 123, 137, 140, 156
Thring, M.W., Prof., 4, 8, 9, 43, 84, 87, 88, 89, 90, 91, 186
Timaeus, 49, 52, 55
time, 5, 6, 13, 16, 17, 20, 21, 23, 24, 27, 28, 29, 30, 33, 34, 35, 40, 42, 44, 45, 46, 47, 49, 53, 54, 55, 60, 61, 62, 64, 80, 84, 87, 89, 90, 91, 92, 93, 95, 96, 99, 104, 105, 106, 107, 108, 109, 114, 119, 121, 123, 128, 130, 131, 132, 136, 139, 140, 141, 142, 148, 149, 150, 151, 152, 153, 154, 155, 156, 157, 158, 161, 162, 163, 164, 165, 166, 167, 168, 169, 170, 171, 172, 173, 177, 179, 180, 181, 182
Toomer, Jean, 12, 14, 95

Tracol, Henri, 13, 87, 89
transform, 94
transformation, 11, 14, 25, 71, 72, 73, 120, 127, 144, 166, 172
transmutation, 16, 75
Transubstantiate
   Transubstantiate, 134
Triad, 114, 115, 116, 118, 119, 121
Triamazikamno, 68, 76, 78, 132
Triangle Editions, 5, 65
Trinity, 82
Trogoautoegocrat, 133, 149
two-brained, 123, 156

U

unconscious, 21, 54
understanding, 18, 29, 31, 37, 43, 44, 45, 47, 58, 60, 61, 69, 71, 78, 95, 96, 128, 130, 144, 148, 161, 163, 165, 166, 172, 184
universe, 19, 23, 25, 43, 53, 69, 71, 81, 87, 114, 121, 125, 126, 127, 131, 134, 135, 136, 137, 139, 140, 141, 142, 143, 145, 146, 149, 154, 156, 163
Urdekhplifata, 76
USA, 10, 185, 186

V

Vedanta, 144, 145
vibration, 45, 53, 69, 73, 85, 152, 155
vivifyingness, 72

W

Washington, 12
Water, 35, 75, 104, 135, 151, 155, 156, 158
Webb, James, 60, 61, 63, 67
Welch, William and Louise, 14
Wellbeloved, Sophia, 12, 55, 177, 186
Will, 1, 9, 13, 17, 19, 33, 46, 68, 81, 82, 114, 115, 120, 121, 123, 124, 125, 163, 171, 176, 185
Wine, 86
Wisdom, 20, 22, 24, 25

Index

Work, 3, 5, 6, 8, 9, 11, 13, 14, 16, 21, 22, 26, 27, 28, 29, 30, 31, 32, 33, 34, 36, 37, 38, 47, 49, 50, 58, 59, 66, 67, 68, 85, 86, 87, 89, 92, 93, 95, 99, 102, 103, 124, 126, 128, 140, 141, 147, 148, 149, 158, 161, 162, 163, 164, 165, 166, 167, 168, 169, 170, 171, 172, 174, 175, 177, 179, 182

world, 6, 8, 19, 20, 21, 24, 26, 29, 30, 31, 32, 36, 38, 42, 45, 48, 49, 57, 58, 62, 64, 68, 73, 81, 87, 90, 91, 102, 111, 114, 118, 119, 121, 123, 124, 125, 126, 127, 131, 134, 139, 141, 142, 143, 145, 146, 148, 151, 152, 156, 161, 164, 165, 166, 167, 169, 171, 179

Z

Zodiac
  Aries, 182
  Cancer, 53
  Capricorn, 53

www.ingramcontent.com/pod-product-compliance
Lightning Source LLC
Chambersburg PA
CBHW081919170426
43200CB00014B/2766